ARMS CONTROL

MYTH VERSUS REALITY

EDITED BY

RICHARD F. STAAR

HOOVER INSTITUTION PRESS
Stanford University, Stanford, California

The Hoover Institution on War, Revolution and Peace, founded at
Stanford University in 1919 by the late President Herbert Hoover, is
an interdisciplinary research center for advanced study on domestic
and international affairs in the twentieth century. The views
expressed in its publications are entirely those of the authors and do
not necessarily reflect the views of the staff, officers, or Board of
Overseers of the Hoover Institution.

Hoover Press Publication 304
Copyright 1984 by the Board of Trustees of the
Leland Stanford Junior University

First printing, 1984
Manufactured in the United States of America
88 87 86 85   9 8 7 6 5 4 3 2

Library of Congress Cataloging in Publication Data
Main entry under title:

Arms control.

Includes bibliographical references and index. 1. Atomic
weapons and disarmament—Congresses. 2. Arms
control—Congresses. I. Staar, Richard Felix, 1923–
JX1974.7.A675 1984   327.1'74   84-3797
ISBN 0-8179-8041-5

Design by P. Kelley Baker

CONTENTS

14
DINNER ADDRESSES

PREFACE

The United States announced arms control initiatives of major significance during 1981–1982, resulting in proposals that could have brought about cuts in nuclear as well as conventional weapons. President Reagan's "zero option" suggested elimination of all intermediate-range, land-based nuclear missiles; the United States proposed a one-third reduction in the number of intercontinental ballistic missiles; and NATO submitted a draft treaty that would have reduced ground troops to 700,000 on each side. Unfortunately, the Soviet Union refused to discuss any of them seriously.

In all three sets of ongoing negotiations, the bilateral Strategic Arms Reduction Talks (START) and intermediate-range nuclear forces (INF) negotiations as well as the multilateral Mutual and Balanced Force Reductions (MBFR) talks, the United States has had the same objectives since 1981. First, arms control should enhance security and reduce the risk of war. The process must result in substantial, militarily significant reductions and not upward limitations as in the past. Agreements must include equal ceilings for similar types of forces and effective verification measures. None of these objectives were acceptable to the East.

On 15 December 1983, in the Redoutensaal of the Hofburg Palace at Vienna, the Soviet and six other Warsaw Pact delegations attended the last scheduled formal meeting of the Mutual and Balanced Force Reductions (MBFR) talks. They departed without agreeing to resume these talks, after the holidays, with representatives from twelve NATO countries. Toward the end of the preceding month, the USSR also had broken off bilateral negotiations in Geneva with the United States on both intermediate-range (INF) and strategic (START) nuclear forces. This marked the end of all attempts to negotiate arms control agreements, at least for the near future.

These three steps represented the culmination of a sustained Soviet campaign to prevent NATO's deployment of ground-launched cruise missiles (GLCMs) and Pershing IIs, which had been agreed in December 1979 on the initiative of then West German chancellor Helmut Schmidt. Two years before this decision, the USSR had already begun to deploy its triple-warhead, mobile SS-20. It has continued increasing this force, despite negotiations to reduce and perhaps eventually abolish such weapons systems.

When the Soviets broke off the INF and START talks, they had more than 8,000 nuclear warheads targeted against Western Europe, some of them mounted on 360 of their SS-20 reloadable missile launchers. The Warsaw Pact disposes four million men under arms, compared with 2.6 million in NATO; some three and a half times as many tanks; double the number of tactical aircraft and helicopters; more than two and a half times the armored vehicles; and three times the number of artillery tubes.

The United States unilaterally withdrew some 1,000 theater nuclear warheads during 1980, and NATO was scheduled to begin removal of 1,400 more during 1984. In other words, a total of only 572 GLCMs and Pershing IIs will be replacing the 2,400 being taken out. By contrast, the USSR is deploying new SS-21, -22, and -23 short-range nuclear missiles in both East Germany and Czechoslovakia that will increase its stockpile.

In addition, Soviet bloc representatives had verbally attempted to intimidate key members of the West German parliament, foreign ministry, and media prior to the 21–22 November 1983 Bundestag debate on the new NATO missiles. Soviet ambassador V. S. Semenov issued a warning in the form of a three-page letter to Chancellor Helmut Kohl, which repeated the Soviet threats. Moscow sent identical communications to London, Brussels, Rome, and the Hague. All falsely depicted a Soviet proposal at the Geneva INF talks as having been offered by the U.S. negotiator.

During December 1983, the first nine Pershing IIs arrived in the Federal Republic of Germany. Sixteen cruise missiles were delivered to Italy at about the same time; sixteen others had been received in England in November. The remaining 99 Pershing IIs are not scheduled to be in place until the end of 1985 and the remaining 432 GLCMs until 1988.

Since the second round of deployments had been set for September 1984, there seemed to be no justifiable reason for the Soviet walkouts at Geneva and Vienna. Only one prime issue remained in the intermediate-range nuclear missile force talks—namely, actual deployment levels. Agreement had been reached to include nuclear-armed bombers in the negotiations; there was flexibility regarding worldwide ceilings on weapons systems; and British as well as French deterrents were to be taken up in another forum. All of these involved concessions to Soviet demands.

This last compromise had been suggested by the Soviet head of delegation in the INF forum. However, the Soviet foreign ministry denied he had done so and falsely attributed the proposal to the chief U.S. negotiator. This happened just before the talks were discontinued on 23 November 1983. Even the announcement the following day (attributed to Yuri Andropov) that the USSR had decided to deploy additional nuclear weapons "in ocean areas and seas" near the United States did not correspond to the truth since these deployments had been in preparation or under way for many months.

These negotiations and other matters pertaining to arms control were discussed at the Hoover Institution on the campus of Stanford University by about sixty experts from government, academia, and private research centers. Eleven papers were presented at this conference, and they elicited comments by discussants as well as by other participants. A selection from these appears in this book. If some of the prose sounds bland, it is in part due to the necessity of obtaining U.S. government clearance by certain of the participants to publish.

The volume opens with a survey of successes and failures in arms control. The authors suggest that the process itself may represent an exercise in futility since the United States has no leverage and that Washington educate the public with candor rather than rhetoric. The relationship between the nuclear balance and arms control has undergone a dramatic change during the past decade as the USSR spent three times more on defense than did the United States. Today the USSR is superior in virtually all indices of strategic nuclear capability in addition to command, control, and communications. Even if political relations between the two superpowers were improving, no equitable agreement could be reached when the balance of nuclear forces remains so markedly advantageous to one party.

This is also true of the conventional balance between the Warsaw Pact and NATO. An agreement could have been reached on Eastern terms; that is, by accepting the fiction that parity in manpower exists in Central Europe and that on-site inspection is unnecessary. A draft agreement, presented by the West in July 1982, listed seven verification and confidence-building measures. A year later, the East rejected the proposed treaty as a basis for agreement. More than a decade of talks did not lead to any compromise on the essentials.

Several conference participants argued persuasively that all of this must be explained to the electorates in both the United States and Western Europe. Public diplomacy should stress the nature and character of asymmetries between East and West, rather than their technical aspects. The purpose would be to concentrate on the fundamental political relationship between NATO and the Warsaw Treaty Organization. This contest of ideas should be channeled via nongovernmental organizations like the Conference on Security and Cooperation in Europe through its follow-up meetings, such as the one scheduled for November 1986 in Vienna.

Simultaneously, it is imperative to change Western military strategy from one based on deterrence to one of protective defense. The former, which dates back to the 1960s, has become known as mutual assured destruction and relies on the explicit threat of U.S. retaliation to preserve a balance of terror. Laser defense, creation of an electromagnetic pulse, and exploding small nuclear devices close to incoming missiles represent some of the possibilities that may be instrumental in changing U.S. military strategy. Other, more conventional devices, include the enhanced radiation warhead (the so-called neutron bomb), which would stop massive armored attacks and yet cause almost no civilian casualties.

In addition to providing for these future defensive systems, especially ones in space, the United States must continue modernizing its contemporary deterrent forces. Both of these programs will guarantee not only national security but also may lead to meaningful arms control agreements with the USSR. It is significant that most of the Soviet military buildup during the past decade took place after SALT I had been signed. That 1972 treaty allowed the USSR to increase its offensive nuclear power substantially.

The negotiating process itself is fraught with the danger of "mirror-imaging"—that is, assuming that the East shares Western objectives and values. Several conference participants warned that it would behoove U.S. officials to remember that their counterparts have no personal stake in a successful outcome of negotiations. Furthermore, Soviet diplomats operate under strict orders that preclude their own initiative. More frequently than not, the forum is used to address West European and American publics rather than their official government representatives. One must constantly be on guard against Soviet deception, which occurred most recently in the case of Poland in order to camouflage preparations for martial law in that country. With these caveats in mind, one should not expect the USSR to act other than it does, due to its "aptitude and apparatus for mendacity," as one of the speakers put it. Soviet allegations concerning Korean Air Lines flight 007 bear silent witness to this truth.

Finally, a few words about breaches of arms control obligations that were being discussed at year's end in the bilateral Standing Consultative Commission on the United States' request. These charges involve repeated Soviet testing of two new ballistic missiles, although only one is allowed by SALT II; encoding of radio signals during such test flights, also a violation of the same agreement; and a new radar complex in Siberia that, as an antiballistic missile (ABM) system, violates the 1979 ABM limitation treaty. One is left with the question: Why negotiate with an untrustworthy adversary who has never accepted international obligations in treaty form as binding?

* * *

I wish to express thanks to Mrs. Margit N. Grigory for her many hours of work as assistant conference coordinator; Mr. Brian Harvey, who carefully prepared the typescript and transcribed tapes; Mrs. Phyllis Cairns, publications manager for Hoover Institution Press; and last, but not least, book editor Mr. John Ziemer who made the conference proceedings readable.

Richard F. Staar
January 1984

CONTRIBUTORS

Samuel T. Cohen is a senior staff member of R&D Associates in Marina del Rey, California. After working on the Manhattan Project while in the U.S. Army, he joined the Rand Corporation as a nuclear weapons analyst in 1947. He has served as a consultant to the Los Alamos and Livermore laboratories, the U.S. Air Force, and the Office of the Secretary of Defense. Dr. Cohen's books include *Tactical Nuclear Weapons* (1978), *Echec a la Guerre* (1979), and *The Truth About the Neutron Bomb* (1983).

Joseph D. Douglass, Jr., is scientific adviser at IRT Corporation. Previously, he worked for System Planning Corporation, the Defense Advanced Research Projects Agency, and the Institute for Defense Analyses. Publications include *Soviet Strategy for Nuclear War* (1979, coauthored with Amoretta Hoeber) and *Soviet Military Strategy in Europe* (1980).

James L. George is assistant director for multilateral affairs at the Arms Control and Disarmament Agency. In 1983, he was acting director for three months. After serving as an officer in the U.S. Navy, he attended graduate school and worked as a professional staff member for national security affairs with first the Senate Committee and then the House Committee on Government Operations. Dr. George is editor of *Problems of Sea Power as We Approach the Twenty-First Century* (1978) and author of articles on naval and arms control matters.

William R. Graham served as an officer for three years at the U.S. Air Force Weapons Laboratory and then joined the Rand Corporation. In 1971, he left Rand to help found R&D Associates. Dr. Graham has served as consultant to the Office of the Secretary of Defense, the National Academy of Sciences, the U.S./U.K. Joint Working Group on Atomic Weapon Effects, the Defense Science Board, the USAF Scientific Advisory Board, and the Defense Nuclear Agency. He is currently chairman of the General Advisory Committee on Arms Control and Disarmament. He has been a contributing author to *NATO's Strategic Options: Arms Control and Defense* (1981) and to several other books on technical and strategic subjects.

Colin S. Gray has taught at the universities of Lancaster (U.K.), as well as York and British Columbia (Canada). After serving as assistant director of the International Institute for Strategic Studies in London, he joined the staff and then became director of national security studies at the Hudson Institute (1976–1981). Dr. Gray is now president of the National Institute for Public Policy in Fairfax, Virginia, and a member of the General Advisory Committee on Arms Control and Disarmament. His most recent book is *American Military Space Policy: Information Systems, Weapon Systems, and Arms Control* (1983).

William R. Harris is an international lawyer and member of the California and New York bars. He joined the Rand Corporation in 1972, where he has done research on treaty verification, measures to limit the spread of nuclear weapons, and the risks of accidental war. Mr. Harris has served since 1981 as an expert-consultant to the U.S. Arms Control and Disarmament Agency.

Werner Kaltefleiter is professor of political science and director of the institutes of political science and of security studies at the Christian-Albrechts-University in Kiel, Federal Republic of Germany. His most recent book, co-authored with Ulrike Schumacher, is *Conflicts, Options, Strategies in a Threatened World* (vol. 1, 1982; vol. 2, 1983).

Amrom H. Katz began working in reconnaissance intelligence in 1940 for the USAF Aerial Reconnaissance Laboratory, where he became chief physicist. He joined the senior staff at Rand in 1954. Appointed an assistant director of the U.S. Arms Control and Disarmament Agency, he served as head of the Verification and Analysis Bureau (1973–1976). Since then, Mr. Katz has been a consultant to, among others, the Department of State and the National Security Council. He has published extensively on the conceptual and technical features of arms control. As a member of the Committee on Security Through Arms Control at the National Planning Association, in 1956 he helped draft *1970 Without Arms Control* as well as *Strength-*

ening the Government for Arms Control, which proposed that an agency like ACDA be established. Mr. Katz is the author of *Verification and SALT* (1979).

John G. Keliher is defense legislative assistant to Congressman Dave Mc-Curdy of Oklahoma. A former U.S. Army colonel, he served as professor of military strategy and director of Soviet studies at the National Defense University (1981–1983). After three years on the U.S. Delegation to MBFR (1974–1977), he later became a member of the Defense Department's SALT Task Force. Dr. Keliher is author of *The Negotiations on Mutual and Balanced Force Reductions* (1980).

Robert E. Kiernan is a special assistant in the Bureau of Programs at the United States Information Agency. He did his graduate work at the Fletcher School of Law and Diplomacy, where he was editor-in-chief of the *Fletcher Forum.* Mr. Kiernan was also a national public policy fellow of the Institute for Contemporary Studies.

Charles M. Kupperman is presently executive director of President Reagan's General Advisory Committee on Arms Control and Disarmament. He has served as research associate and defense analyst with the Committee on the Present Danger. In addition, he has been a consultant to R&D Associates and has taught at the School of International Relations, University of Southern California. Dr. Kupperman has written articles on defense, SALT, and national security policy.

Charles Burton Marshall, a retired professor of international politics at the School of Advanced International Studies, the Johns Hopkins University, is a resident consultant to the System Planning Corporation of Arlington, Virginia. His books include *The Limits of Foreign Policy* (1954) and *The Exercise of Sovereignty: Papers on Foreign Policy* (1965).

Richard Pipes is Baird Professor of History at Harvard University, where he has also served as director of the Russian Research Center (1968–1973). He took leave-of-absence to become director of East European and Soviet Affairs at the National Security Council (1981–1982). Dr. Pipes is author of several books, the most recent being *U.S.-Soviet Relations in the Era of Détente* (1981).

Robin Ranger has been an associate professor of international relations with the Defense and Strategic Studies Program at the University of Southern

California since 1981. His most recent book is *Arms and Politics, 1958–78: Arms Control in a Changing Political Context* (1979). Dr. Ranger has held fellowships from NATO and the Department of National Defence in Canada. He has been a visiting fellow at the London School of Economics and the School of Advanced International Studies, the Johns Hopkins University.

Gough C. Reinhardt has been a physicist and weapons systems analyst at the Lawrence Livermore National Laboratory since 1969. Before retiring from the U.S. Army with rank of lieutenant colonel, he had been chief of the radiation physics division at the Defense Atomic Support Agency (1966–1969). Dr. Reinhardt is author of several articles on weapons systems defense.

Mark B. Schneider is special counsel on arms control in the Office of the Secretary of Defense/International Security Policy. He had been a defense analyst in the Office of International Security Affairs, Department of Energy (1974–1979). Subsequently he served on the professional staff of the U.S. Senate Select Committee on Intelligence (1979–1981) and as a member of the Policy Planning Staff of the Department of State (1981–1983). He is a member of the bar in the District of Columbia and in Maryland. He is author of numerous articles on arms control.

Harriet Fast Scott is a Washington-based lecturer and consultant on Soviet military affairs. She is a member of the General Advisory Committee on Arms Control and Disarmament as well as a senior research associate at the Advanced International Studies Institute. Her latest book, coauthored with William F. Scott, is *The Soviet Control Structure: Capabilities for Wartime Survival* (1983).

Richard F. Staar is a senior fellow at the Hoover Institution. He took leave-of-absence for public service to serve as U.S. ambassador to the Mutual and Balanced Force Reductions (MBFR) negotiations in Vienna, Austria (1981–1983). His training and background includes both academic and government work in Soviet and East European affairs. Dr. Staar is author of *Communist Regimes in Eastern Europe* (1982) and serves as editor-in-chief of the *Yearbook on International Communist Affairs*. Currently he is at work on a study of Soviet foreign policy. Dr. Staar serves as a consultant to the U.S. Arms Control and Disarmament Agency.

Edward Teller, a nuclear physicist, served until his retirement in 1975 as associate director of the Lawrence Livermore National Laboratory as well as professor of physics at the University of California. Since that time, he has been a senior research fellow at the Hoover Institution and a consultant to Lawrence Livermore. Dr. Teller's most recent book is entitled *The Pursuit of Simplicity* (1980).

W. Scott Thompson, on leave from the faculty at the Fletcher School of Law and Diplomacy, is associate director for programs at the United States Information Agency. A lecturer at the Georgetown University School of Foreign Service and the Johns Hopkins University School of Advanced International Studies, Dr. Thompson has written in the fields of national and international politics, the Third World, and U.S.-Soviet relations. Most recently, he edited *The Third World: Premises for U.S. Policy* (1983).

William R. Van Cleave is director of the Defense and Strategic Studies Program at the University of Southern California and a senior research fellow of the Hoover Institution. He served as a member of the first SALT Delegation and as special assistant in the Office of the Secretary of Defense (1969–1971). Professor Van Cleave became a member of the "B Team," charged with reviewing official national intelligence estimates on Soviet strategic programs and objectives (1976). He was senior defense adviser to Ronald Reagan and served as director of the Department of Defense transition team (1980). Author of numerous publications on strategy, arms control, and national defense issues, Dr. Van Cleave's recent books include *Tactical Nuclear Weapons: An Examination of the Issues* (1978) and *Strategic Options for the Early Eighties* (1979).

Nils H. Wessell is director of the Foreign Policy Research Institute as well as editor of *Orbis*. He serves as an assistant professor of political science on the graduate faculty at the New School for Social Research. Dr. Wessell did research for his doctoral dissertation at Moscow State University. He co-edited *The Soviet Threat* (1978, with Grayson Kirk).

ACRONYMS

ABC	atomic, biological, and chemical
ABM	anti-ballistic missile
ACDA	Arms Control and Disarmament Agency
BMD	ballistic missile defense
C^3	command, control, and communication
CSCE	Conference on Security and Cooperation in Europe
EMP	electromagnetic pulse
FA	frontal aviation
ICBM	intercontinental ballistic missile
INF	intermediate-range nuclear forces
IRBM	intermediate-range ballistic missile
MAD	mutual assured destruction
MIRV	multiple independently targetable re-entry vehicle
MBFR	Mutual and Balanced Force Reductions
MRBM	medium-range ballistic missile
NPIC	National Photographic Interpretation Center
NSDM	national security decision memorandum
NSC	National Security Council
NTM	national technical means

PD	presidential directive
SALT	Strategic Arms Limitation Treaty
SCC	Standing Consultative Commission
SLBM	sea-launched ballistic missile
SSBN	fleet ballistic missile submarine (nuclear powered)
START	Strategic Arms Reduction Talks
TEL	transporter, erector, launcher
USIA/S	United States Information Agency/Service
WTO	Warsaw Treaty Organization

ARMS
CONTROL

1

THE ARMS CONTROL RECORD: SUCCESSES AND FAILURES

William R. Van Cleave

In surveying the recent record of U.S. arms control experience, failures are easy to find; successes are far more elusive. The overall record, particularly since the beginning of SALT in 1969, has been disappointing. As Secretary of Defense Caspar Weinberger concluded, "A melancholy chapter in the troubled history of the last decade or two is that on arms control."[1]

This discussion focuses on the failure of arms control to achieve those objectives postulated by U.S. policymakers. A discussion of successes and failures does raise the question of standards or criteria for evaluation. Many use a simple test of success—the mere conclusion of formal arms control agreements, regardless of their content and consequences. Such a standard is clearly inadequate and misleading, as the debate over the flaws of SALT I and SALT II demonstrates.[2]

In October 1971, while SALT I was still being negotiated, I raised several questions at the Fifth International Arms Control Symposium regarding standards for success and failure:

> Should the SALT be evaluated by the way the strategic balance has changed during the talks? By the strategic balance accepted or established, explicitly or implicitly, in an agreement? Should we ask if the agreement demonstrably "curbs the arms race" or reduces defense expenditures? If it does neither, should we ask if it enhances stability and eases specific strategic problems? What if it does not; do we then optimistically regard it as a first step to an eventual agreement that will? If the agreement itself does little along these lines, does it restrict U.S. strategic options? If it does not, for example,

provide for the survivability of our retaliatory forces, does it require that we leave them vulnerable?[3]

There must be national security standards by which to assess the successes or failures of agreements. According to the U.S. Department of State, agreements should make a measurable contribution to national security. But can any recent arms control agreement be said to have made such a clear and significant contribution? Under that demanding standard, agreements that many regard as arms control successes—the Limited Test Ban Treaty, Non-proliferation Treaty (NPT), and SALT I Anti-Ballistic Missile (ABM) Treaty—seem more like failures.

The Limited Test Ban Treaty (1963) accomplished virtually nothing that its supporters had promised. It did not limit or control nuclear armaments. It did not advance the cause of either parity or strategic stability. It certainly did not protect the United States' nuclear superiority, as then Secretary of Defense Robert S. McNamara had argued it would. It did not usher in a golden age of arms agreements and cooperation between the United States and the Soviet Union, as many of its Senate supporters had predicted. About all it did is what Edward Teller had predicted during the treaty hearings. Teller said that this agreement would not limit arms, indeed had nothing to do with limiting arms; it would only limit knowledge—our knowledge. And that it has done. It has limited our knowledge of Soviet weapons development and design, and it has limited our knowledge of critical nuclear effects phenomena such as the electromagnetic pulse—knowledge that may be essential in designing survivable forces and communications and in making decisions on space weapons systems and on an ABM system. It has made no commensurate contribution to national security.

I do not know what the NPT (1968) has accomplished, and I doubt that anyone else does either. At the time, it was a voluntary undertaking not to acquire nuclear weapons by states uninterested in having them nor to transfer nuclear weapons by states having no intention of doing so. It is impossible to show that it has restricted the number of nuclear-armed states, although it may have helped seal off the option of a European nuclear force. Perhaps it has had some international political importance, but it is essentially irrelevant as arms control. The NPT supports the conclusion that where there is no *real* problem, arms control agreements can be "effective" but unnecessary; and where there is a real problem, they are necessary but likely to be ineffective. Arms control tends to work best when not needed.

Undoubtedly, the SALT I ABM Treaty (1972) has been a "success," if its purpose was to administer the coup de grace to Safeguard and to erase the U.S. advantage in ABM research, development, testing, and engineering. Certainly, many experts regard the agreement that way. On the other hand, the

major expectation for the ABM Treaty was that it would reduce requirements for offensive forces. With ABMs stringently limited, neither side
would have any incentive to increase its offensive capabilities significantly.
An ABM Treaty, then, would lead inexorably to offensive force limitations
and reductions. But what happened? The USSR proceeded to increase its
offensive force efforts, and Soviet offensive capabilities expanded beyond all
expectations.

What the ABM Treaty really did was to encourage Soviet development
of a counterforce threat to U.S. land-based deterrent forces. It deprived the
United States of a potential means for strengthening ICBM survivability, and
it continues to work against that option today. It also allowed the Soviets to
gain an edge in ABM technology, and they now have advanced to the potential for a rapidly deployable nationwide system.

If there is no unequivocally successful agreement, what of the value of
the arms control process itself? Some commentators, while professing concern over the details of agreements, still argue the importance of the process
itself and the utility of agreements in keeping it going. This was a major
argument for both SALT I and SALT II. Yet there is no denying that strategic
trends accompanying this process have been decidedly adverse to the United
States or that the USSR has become increasingly bellicose and threatening.
And when one considers the depressant effect of the SALT process on U.S.
strategic programs and on the U.S. ability to cope with the Soviet threat,
there is surely no evidence that the process has been beneficial to this country. It has not been worthwhile enough to cause us to accept bad agreements
and overlook Soviet misbehavior in order to preserve the process.

Nonetheless, faith in arms control negotiations remains strong. Without them, it is argued, there is no chance for arms control. If arms control
means only negotiated agreements, useful or harmful, that may be so, but
what about no arms control? We should remind ourselves that in the democratic states of the West there is *always* arms control, even without negotiated agreements. Arms are controlled and limited by the West's traditional
values, by its political and budgeting processes, and by the influence of the
media and of public opinion. Even though not required to do so by arms
control agreements, the United States has considerably reduced both the
number of its nuclear weapons and the megatonnage of its nuclear stockpile
since the late 1960s.[4] The Soviets have expanded both categories severalfold
during the period most governed by arms control negotiations.

It is quite difficult to produce an unambiguous example of arms control
success during the past twenty years. One may point to agreements on nuclear-free zones—outer space, Antarctica, Latin America—as minor examples (all further examples of the effectiveness of unnecessary agreements).
Perhaps the best illustrations of "success" are the few times the U.S. govern-

ment has been able to use arms negotiations to relieve some short-term political problem—for example, the Mutual and Balanced Force Reductions (MBFR) negotiations to defuse the Mansfield amendment calling for withdrawal of U.S. troops from Europe or flexibility on intermediate-range nuclear forces (INF) to ease public arms control pressures on West European governments beleaguered by Soviet propaganda. Or, perhaps, one might see the utility of arms control as giving the U.S. government an excuse for not doing something it does not wish to do, such as, perhaps, deploy Safeguard. This is essentially the view that Lieutenant General Brent Scowcroft (USAF, ret.) seemed to present at a Lawrence Livermore Laboratory arms control conference in 1981. To him, SALT I had been useful because the United States was not competing with the Soviet Union anyway. (He also took the extremely uncritical view "that any kind of an agreement that we have with the Soviet Union is going to be in our interest.") [5]

Everything considered, however, arms control has been a failure. Neither the national security of the United States nor strategic stability has been improved by arms control. To the contrary, the threats to both are far more grave today than before. Arms control policies and their ramifications do bear much of the responsibility for this situation.

I do not wish to examine the arms control record in terms of the details of negotiation and agreements. Rather, I want to address what I perceive to be the general failures and adverse influences of arms control.

ARMS CONTROL CONCEPTS AND POLICY

In 1972, I wrote that the "greatest failure so far associated with strategic arms limitations endeavors may be an intellectual one." I argued that we were expecting too much from arms control and were letting it dominate strategic planning: "We have attributed too much importance to concluding a strategic arms limitation agreement and have expected too much from it . . . Success or failure will rest more with factors extraneous to a strategic arms limitation agreement than with any agreement itself." [6]

To substantiate this intellectual failure, it might be useful to review the original concepts and objectives of modern arms control and the way they have not only influenced policy but been influenced by policy.

Modern arms control concepts emerged particularly with the development of the ICBM and the concurrent increase of concern about surprise attack. Arms control was basically a technical approach to arms interactions. It was, however, based on certain political-strategic premises. American theorists assumed that each side held a common interest in "stable" nuclear arms relationships that would reduce the risks of war by surprise or accident. Arms control would help ease the threat of surprise attack (strategic stability) or pre-emptive attack (crisis stability) by promoting more survivable deterrent forces on both sides. (Arms control made no political distinctions: a U.S. first-strike capability was to be avoided as much as a Soviet one.) Arms control further would reduce the likelihood of war by reducing incentives for an arms race.

The attractiveness of the notion was demonstrated by the flood of books and articles on arms control in the early 1960s, written or edited by, among others, Donald Brennan, Hedley Bull, Thomas Schelling and Morton Halperin, Ernest Lefever, Louis Henkin, Arthur Hadley, and Alexander Dallin, many of which were based on academic arms control conferences and workshops.[7]

These theorists of the early 1960s, generally, may have been naive in their political and strategic expectations, but they saw themselves as realists. They rejected the idea of disarmament in favor of more modest measures of technical arms control. As Donald Brennan put it, the goal of arms control was to "reduce the hazards of present armament policies by a factor greater than the amount of risk introduced by the control measures themselves."[8] These writers acknowledged that control measures did carry risks and emphasized the need for verification. Formal agreements, arms reductions, and cost savings were unnecessary. What mattered was "stability." All agreed that the one objective to which arms control should contribute, to be successful, was strategic and crisis stability.

This concept of arms control was based on the notion that there would be areas of overriding mutual interest in improving the survivability of nuclear arsenals and reducing the risks of war. This, in fact, remained the central article of faith in arms control. There would be arms cooperation between the superpowers despite their political differences. Arms control itself would be apolitical.

Some of the early writers did not downplay the political differences between the sides, although nearly all ignored the possibility that profound *strategic* differences would dash their hopes for arms control. Hedley Bull, for example, argued that arms control could begin without the resolution of political disputes. However, he said, "We cannot expect that a system of arms control will be brought into operation, nor that, if it is, it will persist, unless certain political conditions are fulfilled . . . The political conditions may allow a system of arms control, or they may not."[9] Many—just like later policymakers—believed that arms control would help improve political relations, that cooperation would expand from the technical-arms sector to the political sector. "If the habit of cooperation," wrote Donald Brennan, "can be established in the field of armament policy, it may well prove 'catching' in other areas . . . [and] facilitate the achievement of some political solutions, which in turn would facilitate further measures of armament cooperation; and so on." [10]

The most optimistic commentators in this regard tended to be the Sovietologists, who readily fell into the trap of mirror-imaging. For example, a book based on a conference in the spring of 1963 sponsored by the U.S. Arms Control and Disarmament Agency (ACDA) employed enough qualifiers to avoid flat predictions, but its thrust was clear. Soviet leaders were adapting to the realities of a developing society and the need for international stability, becoming oriented toward the *status quo* and a relaxation of tensions; economic shortcomings demanded relief from arms expenditures; and Moscow accepted inferiority in the nuclear balance with the United States. As the pundits concluded, "The general thrust over the recent years has been the intensification of pressures on the Soviet leadership for a breathing spell in the arms race. Indeed, the present offers a unique concatenation of such pressures." [11]

Eventually, this more optimistic, mirror-image view came to dominate the arms control community, both in academia and government. As it did, expectations grew and arms control assumed greater importance, especially in the wake of the Cuban missile crisis and with the development in the United States of strategic concepts of assured destruction and mutual assured destruction. [12] Concurrently, concern over a superpower action-reaction "arms race" seized both academics and senior government officials. Arms control, an arms race image, and strategic deterrent concepts became mutually reinforcing and greatly elevated the importance and role of arms control in U.S. thinking and policy.

Arms control success required both sides to abstain from developing the capability to threaten the other's deterrent, as well as to abstain from force programs—in kind or in size—that might force the other side to react by initiating counterprograms. Since the Soviets lacked such capabilities, it was obviously up to the United States to set the example. As Alain Enthoven and Wayne Smith summarized the logic,

> If deterrence is also the Soviets' objective (as the available evidence has consistently and strongly suggested), we would expect them to react in much the same way to any effort on our part to reduce the effectiveness of their deterrent (or assured-destruction) capability against us . . . Any attempt on our part to reduce damage to our society would put pressure on the Soviets to strive for an offsetting improvement in their assured-destruction forces, and vice versa . . . This "action-reaction" phenomenon is central to all strategic force planning issues as well as to any theory of an arms race. [13]

Preventing this arms race and establishing a stable mutual deterrent relationship became the chief aim of U.S. policy and arms control strategy. This required that the United States point the way by moderating its nuclear programs and objectives, allowing the USSR to "catch up" but instructing the Soviets in the "proper" type of strategic goals and capabilities.

This led the United States to—

1. reject nuclear superiority;

2. offer nuclear parity to the Soviets, in the belief that parity would satisfy them;

3. attribute a role to arms control beyond that originally envisaged;

4. bias strategic programs away from counterforce and damage limiting and toward assured destruction; and

5. impute U.S. views and goals to the Soviet Union, which resulted in a thorough misunderstanding of Soviet strategic objectives and a chronic underestimation of Soviet strategic programs.

Arms control, when combined with related strategic concepts, helped blind Americans to Soviet motivations and objectives. It also led many to disparage the fundamental political and ideological differences between the United States and the USSR. After all, if political differences were irrelevant to agreement on strategic stability, how important could they be?

This can only be regarded as a profound intellectual failure related directly to arms control, and it led to errors in U.S. intelligence estimates and projections throughout the 1960s and well into the 1970s. The U.S. government and its intelligence organizations perceived Soviet objectives in terms of Western concepts. They therefore persisted in interpreting Soviet strategic programs in that context and, *a priori*, resisted evidence that the Soviets had quite different views and more ambitious goals.

In the first half of the 1960s, the United States officially believed that the Soviet Union had no particular goals or strategy to guide its strategic programs, that it was willing to tolerate strategic vulnerability and inferiority indefinitely (and, in any case, could do nothing about it), and that it would not seek to match the United States or to neutralize its deterrent forces. When the first signs of a new generation of Soviet strategic forces appeared, this evaluation changed slightly. The view was that the Soviet buildup was guided by a desire to narrow the gap somewhat and by the concept of a retaliatory deterrent based on assured destruction; the buildup would be very limited, constrained by economics, technology, the fear of an arms race with the United States, and a desire for arms limitation.

By 1969, as that buildup, at least in ICBMs, reached that of the United States in numbers of known launchers, the view was that the Soviets were satisfied with the parity they had attained —in fact, their agreement to SALT was evidence of this—and that they shared U.S. views on a mutual deterrent, which they wished to codify in SALT.

Accordingly, the United States' initial expectations for SALT were fairly ambitious. Although specific limitations remained to be settled, U.S. officials spoke in the beginning of a SALT agreement freezing the existing strategic balance and thereby constraining future threats, preserving mutual deterrence, and assuring the survivability of deterrent forces. And, of course, the agreement would usher in a new era of negotiation and cooperation between the superpowers. The outcome of SALT I fell far short of these expectations and far short of the types of specific limitations envisaged in 1969 and 1970. Nonetheless, Washington loudly proclaimed its pleasure with the agreement. Its rationalizations of the inequitable agreement represented yet another failure associated with arms control.

Arms control continued to affect intelligence estimates. The official U.S. view at the conclusion of SALT I was that the Soviets were satisfied with the balance and would not try to upset it; that they were genuinely interested in arms control as the Americans saw it; and that Soviet leaders had such a vested interest in SALT that they would avoid any appearance of noncompliance, including programs that seemed incompatible with SALT.

As evidence contradicting these views mounted, skepticism grew. Some government officials recognized that the USSR held very different strategic objectives and continued in fact to develop ambitious capabilities in accordance with those objectives and that this greatly dampened the prospects for arms control. Even as late as the end of 1976, however, the unpalatable conclusions about Soviet goals, motivations, and accomplishments reached by the "B" Team (the committee of outside experts asked to assess CIA national intelligence estimates) met considerable resistance in the intelligence community.

The most fundamental failure of arms control during this period was Washington's inability to comprehend that the basic premises of its arms control and strategic logic were being negated by the very political and strategic factors that were not supposed to disturb arms control. The results included intellectual, intelligence, and policy failures. Meaningful arms control presupposed that both sides viewed stability in the same light, assigned it the same overriding priority, and would cooperate to achieve it. Political and strategic differences should not interfere with such cooperation. This was the original key to the rationale of arms control. The entire structure of this logic collapses, however, when one side does not follow the same logic and seeks to exploit the other side's interest in arms control and to seize and then maintain a military advantage. All of this, the Soviets have done.

The early U.S. intellectual framework for SALT correspondingly fell apart. Had the Soviets shared the U.S. vision and approach, meaningful and equitable agreements would have been possible. They did not, and agreement was not possible.

Yet the United States continued to believe that the USSR would agree, through arms limitations, to enhance the very survivability of U.S. deterrent forces, which in the meantime the Soviets were working so diligently to erode. The U.S. government continued to believe that the Soviet Union would voluntarily reduce, by agreeing to equality in a SALT agreement, the nuclear advantage it had acquired. Why the USSR would undercut in arms control what it so successfully had sought and achieved on its own was never answered, or even officially asked.

One could point to other areas of U.S. failure in arms control as well. Elsewhere I have written on negotiating and bureaucratic and technical failures and, hence, will not repeat myself here.[14] On negotiating with the Soviets, suffice it to say that the record tends to show the United States confronting malevolence with incompetence. Below, I discuss two major areas of failure: (1) reconciling arms control with strategic planning and (2) dealing with Soviet noncompliance.

ARMS CONTROL AND STRATEGIC PLANNING

It would seem axiomatic that arms control positions would follow the determination of strategic policy requirements and be based on them. Experience shows, however, that this seldom happens. Except for the original ascendancy of the mutual assured destruction concept, the U.S. approach to the SALT negotiations was never consistently based on official strategy, or even any coherent strategy. Rather, the formulation of arms control positions occurred separately from the formulation of strategy. To the extent that one overlapped and influenced the other, SALT influenced strategic policy and programs far more than the other way around. Even if a strategic rationale reflecting U.S. strategic objectives—for example, force survivability and stability—can be seen behind certain SALT positions at certain times, this rationale did not prevail over those positions designed to promote agreements. And seldom, if ever, did the U.S. approach to SALT make explicit assumptions about nuclear doctrine.

Ironically, U.S. strategic policy underwent a metamorphosis away from reliance on assured destruction. One of the fundamental reasons for this change involved the Soviet refusal to accept the preferred U.S. vision of strategic reality. It would not be incorrect to regard National Security Decision Memorandum 242 (NSDM-242) of 1974, and Presidential Directive 59 (PD-59) of 1980, as implicit recognition that the Soviet Union was following a doctrine and pursuing a capability based on strategic nuclear war-fighting. If the United States were to deter effectively or, failing that, successfully cope with a nuclear war, it would have to maintain a wider range of nuclear capabilities and options than previously planned.

It is a commentary on the separation of strategic doctrine and SALT preparations that the United States' SALT positions did not faithfully reflect the new doctrine and requirements, but continued to be formulated largely on the basis of older doctrinal assumptions. The same seems true of the more recent approach of the Reagan administration. Of course, by no means have U.S. strategic force programs been consistent with the requirements of NSDM-242 and PD-59. The disjunction between official policy and the capability to carry it out is growing. One of the causes of this has been SALT and expectations about arms control. While the United States moved toward a more realistic and more ambitious strategic doctrine, which logically demanded that it redress the imbalance between U.S. and Soviet capabilities, its strategic programs—in no small part due to the influence of SALT—fell far short of that requirement.

SALT at times even became a substitute for resolute strategic planning. Plans and programs vacillated between what was needed to fulfill strategic objectives and to cope with the Soviet threat and what was deemed consistent with achieving a SALT agreement—or, to put it another way, what was acceptable to the Soviets within the SALT framework. Hence, through SALT, the USSR found a way to intrude on U.S. strategic planning.

In 1971, before the SALT I agreement, I expressed concern that the proposed agreement would not so much facilitate strategic force modernization, as President Nixon and Dr. Kissinger apparently believed, as contribute to failure by the United States to fulfill its strategic objectives and requirements. SALT "might well result in a paralysis of strategic force programs well beyond the actual terms of the agreement." I also predicted that there would be, on the part of the United States, "a disproportionate conformity to the 'spirit' of the agreement," while the Soviets would disregard the spirit and possibly the letter of the agreement.[15]

This has been the case. Arms control in general, and SALT in particular, have constrained the willingness of the executive branch to pursue and Congress to support programs consistent with U.S. requirements in the face of the Soviet strategic force buildup. As Dr. Kissinger later remarked in Senate testimony on SALT II, "We will not draw the appropriate conclusion if we do not admit that SALT may have had a perverse effect on the willingness of some in the Congress, key opinion makers, and even Administration officials to face fully the relentless Soviet military buildup."[16]

SALT, in other words, has not only failed to achieve the original objectives of the United States in arms control, but it has actually contributed to a worsening of the situation. Arms control has not restrained Soviet strategic programs or counterforce objectives, but arms control has dampened U.S. responses to those programs and objectives.

COMPLIANCE

Another marked failure of arms control is in the area of verification and compliance. These issues have been central from the beginning. Today, they are even more important for three principal reasons:

1. Soviet behavior in circumventing and violating arms agreements;
2. A U.S. compliance policy that has become a shambles of incoherence and permissiveness;
3. The inappropriate means chosen in both SALT and INF for controlling arms—namely, launcher limits.

It is increasingly recognized that to limit actual destructive capacity, verification and compliance are both more important and more problematic.

There is no mystery why there have been so many compliance issues. The USSR has systematically been circumventing the arms agreements that have been negotiated. Compliance issues actually cover a range of activities that include both clear violations, quasi violations, and circumventions that may not, in strict legalistic terms, be violations.[17]

Generally, the USSR's arms control policy has been to avoid limitations that restrict its arms plans and programs. When otherwise desirable limitations (because of their effect on the United States) threaten to contain the Soviets' behavior, they have been careful to insist on wording that preserves the illusion of control while actually leaving them literally unconstrained and free to pursue their programs. The U.S. government has abetted this behavior by first accepting loopholes and ambiguous language in the agreements, then ignoring or downplaying them in the selling of the agreements to Congress and the public, and finally, adopting an overly literal and legalistic approach to compliance when the Soviets begin exploiting the loopholes.

Verification and compliance are matters not merely of technical capabilities or the legal interpretation of agreements but of the compliance *policy* adopted. It is a political question, central to arms control, of how far the United States is willing to go in permitting Soviet circumvention of agreements.

One has only to compare SALT I, as described at the time of ratification, with SALT I as interpreted over time after Soviet actions undercut the original interpretations. A loose U.S. compliance policy undoubtedly has contributed to the erosion of most of the content of the SALT I agreements. Washington's policy has been to allow the Soviets considerable elasticity in compliance. This must have persuaded the Soviets that they can get away with virtually anything, however deleterious to the original agreement, so long as there is the slightest legalistic doubt or technical ambiguity involved. Soviet representatives at the Standing Consultative Commission established to handle disputes arising from SALT I have had a very easy task. Americans have pliantly accepted their rationalizations; at times, the U.S. delegates have even provided them.

The U.S. government has always been—and given the nature of U.S. society and government may always be—reluctant to denounce circumventions or even violations publicly. Whether because Washington wants to avoid wrenching perturbations in U.S.-Soviet relations, or because, as a democratic government, it has a strong vested interest in the integrity (or appearance of integrity) of an agreement it negotiated and sold to Congress and the public, the U.S. government has been unwilling to make major political issues of Soviet transgressions of arms control agreements. Now another rationalization for tolerating Soviet misbehavior has arisen—the argument that the United States lacks effective responses or that it would lose more by strong responses. In other words, we have not found the answer to the question posed over twenty years ago by Fred Iklé: "After Detection—What?"[18] Iklé argued that the *preconditions* for arms control included not only the ability to detect a violation but also the assurance that the United States would be able to react effectively. World opinion, he pointed out, does not suffice; it is amorphous, short-lived, and ultimately harmless. In fact, unless reaction is sure and swift, public support will be lost.

Of course, there will be no world opinion in the first place if the U.S. government is unwilling to make a major issue of Soviet noncompliance because it regards ongoing negotiations as more valuable politically than Soviet faithfulness to agreements.

LESSONS

The proper starting point for arms control is with a clear appreciation of the great difference between U.S. and Soviet political, strategic, and arms control goals. Arms control, as experience shows, cannot be isolated from that context, however fervently earlier theorists believed it could be. The attempted isolation was actually a belief in the congruence of U.S. and Soviet views and goals. The lack of that congruence but continued belief in it resulted in arms control failure.

What other lessons might be derived from the record of arms control failure? Among others, I would suggest the following:

1. Arms control cannot be divorced from politics. It cannot be isolated from Soviet political objectives or from the fundamental political differences between the United States and the USSR or from domestic politics.

2. Arms control agreements will reflect the reality of the existing strategic balance and trends in it. If we are not happy with that situation, we will not be happy with agreements based on it. The strategic situation must be improved before there is much likelihood of satisfactory agreements.

3. The Soviet Union is not interested in arms control to help the United States solve its problems and does not view arms control in terms of stabilizing mutual deterrence. The Soviet approach to arms control and Soviet strategic objectives are not congruent with U.S. arms control goals.

4. Consequently, arms control will not resolve the United States' basic strategic problems. Only a U.S. program can do that. Expecting arms control to produce a stability that does not exist in U.S. programs, or in those of the USSR, is to expect too much.

5. As weak a means to the end of national security as arms control has been, there is still a tendency to regard it as an end in itself. That should be resisted. Arms control should be pursued only to the extent that it may make a meaningful contribution to national security, and its success or failure should be evaluated in those terms.

6. The United States' strategic doctrine and objectives have been established as official expressions of national security requirements and policy. Arms control positions should be in strict concurrence with those requirements and that policy.

7. The United States does not yet have the leverage necessary to interest the Soviet Union in arms control agreements that would be helpful in solving these problems. It may be several years before it does, and by then it may be too late for truly meaningful treaties. The only agreements possible in the near future are cosmetic ones or ones that will be unequal and disadvantageous to the United States. Given the risk of the latter, the United States needs a carefully thought out and tightly controlled "damage-limiting" approach to arms control.

8. Arms control can be harmful to U.S. national security, perhaps less in the direct impact of agreements than in their indirect impact—in the *perverse effect* that agreements or the pursuit of agreements or

the general chimera of arms control has on the U.S. ability to produce, support, and sustain necessary force programs and in the self-delusions that promises of arms control inevitably seem to spawn. The more emphasis U.S. leaders place on arms control, the more adverse this impact is likely to be. In addition, overemphasis on arms control can weaken U.S. foreign policy. It can, for example, expand U.S. tolerance of and weaken U.S. responses to Soviet misbehavior, whether it takes the form of noncompliance with agreements, armed aggression, or bestial attacks on commercial airliners.

9. Arms control enthusiasts and politicians have been too careless about the realities of arms control; they have overstated both the possible accomplishments of agreement and the consequences of nonagreement.

10. When both the media and national political leaders engage in this practice, they are following rather than educating, and they increase political pressures for arms control of any sort. National political leaders, in effect, reinforce the political pressures on themselves: pressures that lead them to extol arms control, accommodate to achieve agreements, and then pretend that bad arms control is good arms control. Those same pressures are then brought to oppose necessary defense programs and their proper funding.

THE REAGAN ADMINISTRATION AND ARMS CONTROL

In the 1980 election campaign, it seemed clear that President Carter and presidential candidate Reagan held very different views on arms control. The latter's public stand on arms control strongly implied that if he were elected, there would be fundamental changes in the U.S. approach: a new realism in dealing with arms control, both publicly and in policymaking, and much less reliance on arms control, both rhetorically and actually. The 1980 Republican Party platform was explicit: "The Republican approach to arms control has been markedly different from that of the Democratic Party." [19]

During the first year of the new administration, there was much evidence that changes were being made: no precipitous rush into arms control negotiations with the USSR; the selection of Eugene Rostow, an articulate realist and arms control critic, as ACDA director; and sobering public statements by senior officials of the administration, including the president himself, on the nature of the Soviet Union, its imperialist aims, and the prospects for arms control.

Indeed, during this period, the administration appeared to set forth new standards, principles, and guidelines for the U.S. approach to arms control that seemed to reflect the lessons cited above. On the basis of official statements, ten "arms control commandments" can be identified: [20]

1. There will be no agreements for the sake of agreement. Agreements must be militarily meaningful and must promote stability and U.S. security. Nor will the United States accept agreements merely to keep the "arms control process" in motion.

2. There will be no more unilateral arms limitations in the hope that the USSR will reciprocate. (As President Reagan said, "We have tried time and again to set an example by cutting our forces in the hope that the Soviets will do likewise. The result has always been that they keep building.")

3. The United States has relied too much on arms control at the expense of defense programs. This has been detrimental to national security and also to the success of arms control. (To quote President Reagan again, "Unless we demonstrate the will to rebuild our strength and restore the military balance, the Soviets . . . have little incentive to negotiate.")

4. The United States will avoid coupling force modernization programs with arms control; programs will be pursued on their own merit.

5. Americans must lower their expectations about arms control, not only because of their experiences but because major problems now transcend arms control solutions. In particular, they must recognize that there is no prospect for agreements that will help solve such basic security problems as the vulnerability of U.S. land-based deterrent forces, at least until the United States demonstrates the capacity to solve them itself.

6. Washington must educate the public and U.S. allies on these realities and seek to de-emphasize the role that arms control plays in relations with the Soviets and with U.S. allies.

7. The United States has based arms control on limiting the wrong things, such as "launchers," which do not really reflect destructive capacity. It will now emphasize reductions, but in destructive capacity and in the most destabilizing systems. Any such reductions must be both stabilizing and equal.

8. Agreements will be based on strict verification, which will not be restricted to national technical means (NTM). The United States cannot accomplish what it wishes by NTM alone and must insist on cooperative measures as well as a "radical improvement" in Soviet willingness to provide accurate, reliable, and verifiable data. (As Rostow put it, "The day when arms control negotiations are conducted on the basis of data supplied by the United States is over.")

9. The United States will insist on full and faithful compliance on the part of the USSR and will not cover up or disparage the importance of noncompliance.

10. Finally, and most significantly, the arms control process must be placed in the context of worldwide Soviet conduct. As Secretary Haig stated, "Pretending that there is no linkage promotes reverse linkage. It ends up by saying that in order to preserve arms control, we have to tolerate Soviet aggression. This Administration will never accept such an appalling conclusion."

In the absence of agreements, it may be premature to attempt to evaluate the administration's consistency with its own principles. However, what Eugene Rostow has recently called "arms control fever" (which, he says, "defies the visible lessons of experience"[21]) has again arisen in Congress and among a vocal part of the public. Arms control enthusiasts—or politicians who deem enthusiasm politically expedient—began to cry for arms control progress and insisted on wrapping weapons programs and defense appropriations in the smothering blanket of arms control.

Critics accused the Reagan administration of not being "serious" about arms control, of demanding too much of the Soviets, and of being "inflexible." It is ironic that the most vocal proponents of the need for arms control, as the difference between a safe and an unsafe world, are also those who are least demanding and most uncritical of arms control agreements. Success to them apparently consists solely in having an agreement. One variant of this is the cry for reductions, without much concern for the impact of those reductions on U.S. strategic objectives or on stability.

Richard Perle, assistant secretary of defense for international security policy, answered these charges very well in congressional testimony:

> But what does seriousness in arms control mean? Is it a sign of seriousness to make concessions to the Soviet desire to accumulate and preserve significant advantages in nuclear weapons? Is the ease with which we abandon our objectives and make "progress" toward an agreement —any agreement—a sign of seriousness? Is there any relationship between seriousness and the content of the agreements we seek to negotiate?[22]

The "fever" influenced the Reagan administration to begin adopting some of the rhetoric of the movement, to couch many of its own strategic policies and arms programs in terms of arms control, and to show a willingness to adjust its positions in the two major ongoing U.S.-Soviet arms negotiations. In part, at least, these actions had some short-term success: they did undercut some of the freeze momentum; they countered charges in the

United States and Europe that the Reagan administration was "anti–arms control"; and they succeeded in gaining congressional support for an insurvivably based MX.

However, these acts may also be leading the administration and the country in the direction of forgetting experience and repeating past mistakes. The same initiatives that show "flexibility" and accommodate (but never satisfy) arms control enthusiasts also perpetuate the fifteen-year-old process that has led the United States to its present perilous predicament.

White House rhetoric has once again advanced arms control into the main arena of importance in the public view. It has encouraged individual congressmen, Republican and Democrat alike, to vie with one another in proposing one arms control scheme after another—all of which "defy the visible lessons of experience," and most of which reflect careless strategic logic (including the "build-down" and "double build-down" proposals).

If the Reagan administration succumbs to this arms control pressure, it will ignore its own early principles and repeat past mistakes in an attempt to achieve limited, short-term gains. Perhaps its whole-hearted endorsement of the Scowcroft Commission report is an example of such a trend.

THE SCOWCROFT COMMISSION REPORT
AND ARMS CONTROL

The Reagan administration's desire to save the MX has led the White House to accept as policy what is in many important respects an illogical report by the President's Commission on Strategic Forces (known as the Scowcroft Commission, after its chairman).[23] In effect, this means the implicit adoption of lower standards for strategic force survivability and explicit emphasis on arms control as the centerpiece of U.S. national security policy.

The Reagan administration began with the sound position that there was essentially no prospect of solving through arms control such a basic security problem as the survivability of the land-based ICBM force until the United States had demonstrated its capacity to solve such problems itself. This capacity assuredly has not been demonstrated. Yet the Scowcroft Commission turned hopefully to arms control for enhancement of strategic stability and to a vulnerably based MX (which detracts from stability) as the means to arms control. It is certainly demonstrative of the persistence of arms control mythology that a commission established to make recommendations on strategic force modernization uses the term "arms control" some sixty times in its 26-page report.[24]

With a fine disregard for the past twenty years of experience, the commission cheerfully concluded that arms control might contribute much to accomplishing critical objectives: reducing the risk of war, channeling forces into stabilizing rather than destabilizing paths, and making arsenals less destructive and costly. According to the commission, arms control might do these things *if* the United States had the MX. With the MX, the commission averred, there was a likelihood of a "stabilizing and equitable agreement." Without the MX, however, it was "illusory" to believe the United States could obtain a "satisfactory agreement."

The commission thus formulated an arms control rationale to support the case for deploying a vulnerable MX. This is ironic to say the least, inasmuch as the principal U.S. aim in arms control has always been to improve the survivability of deterrent forces and to lessen Soviet incentives for a surprise or pre-emptive attack.

A flaw in the U.S. approach to arms control, the limiting of numbers of *things* (launchers, which to the United States meant missiles), helped create the MX in the first place. It also reduced ICBM survivability options. Now arms control is being used to gain deployment of the SALT-created MX—in a vulnerable mode.

The White House paid an exorbitant price for a limited immediate victory. It forgot the logic of the window of vulnerability, on which Reagan had campaigned and which has served as the principal argument and motivation for strategic force modernization. It allowed resolution of land-based force vulnerability to be deferred for at least a decade. (The Scowcroft Commission argued that even though that force is currently vulnerable to "only a portion" of Soviet ICBMs, the problem really is not all that important.)

The commission argued, among other things, that the ICBM problem had been "miscast" in recent years (an apparent rebuke to the Reagan presidential campaign) by focusing on survivability; that even a vulnerable force can make a major contribution to deterrence; that ICBM capability is as important as ICBM survivability; and that the ICBM force is really less vulnerable when not viewed in isolation because of the difficulties of a coordinated attack on bombers *and* ICBMs. One of the authors of the report, former secretary of defense Harold Brown, apparently forgot what was written in his last *Annual Report* to Congress concerning such an attack:

> It is equally important to acknowledge, however, that the coordination of a successful attack is not impossible, and that the 'rubbish heap of history' is filled with authorities who said something reckless could not or would not be done. Accordingly we must take the prospective vulnerability of our ICBM force with the utmost seriousness for planning purposes.[25]

The Scowcroft Commission report emphasized the great benefits of a small ICBM: potentially high survivability; adaptability to several basing modes; dispersal over a large number of individually unattractive, less lucrative, and less threatening targets. But then it deferred the small ICBM to the 1990s and recommended a silo-based MX, which contradicts all of the commission's own criteria for stability.

Even so, the White House allowed force modernization (in the guise of MX) to be linked to arms control, and it promised Congress arms control "flexibility"—read accommodation to the Soviets—in return for a vote in favor of MX. Arms control enthusiasts in Congress have apparently been handed a club to wield each time a vote arises on MX funding in the future.

Instead of educating the public on the grim realities of arms control with the USSR, the White House has contributed to the "arms control fever" that surely will limit its own future options. And because the arms control negotiating process is now so politically important, the White House has decided to treat the expanding evidence of Soviet noncompliance with existing agreements as unprovable and unworthy of bringing to public attention.

CONCLUSIONS

What are the prospects that this record of failures might be replaced by a more successful arms control policy? As Norman Podhoretz, editor of *Commentary*, put it in another context, "We have fewer illusions and more information." [26] Unfortunately, the legacy of past failures will be difficult to escape. For every factor that might contribute to a more successful policy, there is also a counterfactor. Fewer illusions about Soviet behavior and more information about the strategic imbalance may, perversely, fan arms control fever and make Americans even more uncritical about agreements (as it already has done to many Europeans).

President Reagan certainly entertains fewer illusions about the USSR and the prospects for arms control than other imaginable presidents. The ten arms control commandments implied a fundamental change in the U.S. approach. Following them rigorously could at least arrest failure and limit arms control damage, which is probably the most that can be expected. Yet recent statements and actions by the Reagan administration seem to violate some of its own commandments, particularly the overemphasis on arms control agreements and the United States' need for them.

Fifteen years of experience have provided abundant proof that the United States cannot expect the USSR to promote U.S. national security through arms control agreements. The Soviets will surrender no advantage, and the United States has not the leverage to force them to do so. Experience shows that the United States is more likely to be constrained than helped by the negotiating process. Yet even in the wake of incident upon incident of Soviet troublemaking and banditry, the U.S. president says that the arms control process is too important to jeopardize. This is exactly the reverse linkage that the Reagan administration pledged to avoid.

Arms control is now almost purely political. The strategic standards for evaluating it and the very meaning of the term itself have become obscured. Politically, arms control has become a normative, rather than a descriptive, term. Like disarmament, it apparently has become an end in itself, rather than a means to national security ends. Seemingly, standards for evaluating the success or failure of arms control have been reduced to at most three: (1) continuing negotiations; (2) reaching some agreement; and (3) reducing arms, however superficial the reduction or whatever its merit in terms of earlier arms control standards.

Perhaps the Reagan administration hopes to conduct two processes simultaneously: (1) the public process, playing the politics of arms control; and (2) an internal process, seeking to limit the damage of arms control. If arms control must be pursued but cannot reduce the threat, it must not be allowed to jeopardize U.S. options for coping with the threat. One can only hope that the Reagan administration will be more adept at this balancing act than its predecessors.

It seems far more preferable, however, for Washington to educate the public with arms control candor, rather than bowing to arms control fever as an unchangeable political reality. There is ample evidence that the public would respond to such national leadership. Polls have consistently shown that the public can distinguish between a general arms control ideal and a specific, bad arms control agreement. They show the public to be distrustful of the USSR and skeptical about Soviet adherence to arms control agreements.

Engaging in arms control rhetoric undoubtedly is safer politically than candor, but it runs the risk of trapping the United States in a process contrary to its security interests. Rhetoric can only strengthen forces that are uncritical of arms control, if not of the Soviet Union as well, forces that are antidefense, antimodernization, antinuclear. These same forces would interfere with—and, if strengthened, may prevent—necessary military programs.

At the same time, the Reagan administration has weakened its own case for what needs to be done. How is it possible to argue at the same time the virtues of reductions and the need for buildup or the importance of arms limitations and the need for major new strategic programs? Why should the president not tell the public that U.S. security does not depend on arms control agreements and that the types of agreements available are not desirable?

Despite what seems to be the cogency of arguments for candor rather than rhetoric, the Reagan administration for the most part seems to have rejected the former path and adopted the latter. To recast a pithy description of U.S. foreign policy by the late senator Henry Jackson, we have no arms control policy, and it is being mismanaged.

NOTES

1. U.S. Secretary of Defense, *Annual Report to Congress, Fiscal Year 1983* (Washington, D.C.: Government Printing Office, 8 February 1982), p. 19.

2. "Testimony of William R. Van Cleave," in U.S. Congress, Senate, Committee on Armed Services, *Military Implications of the Treaty on the Limitations of Anti-Ballistic Missile Systems and the Interim Agreement on Limitation of Strategic Offensive Arms* (Washington, D.C.: Government Printing Office, 1972); U.S. Congress, Senate, Committee on Government Operations, *International Negotiation* (Washington, D.C.: Government Printing Office, 1973), part 7; and "Statement and Testimony of William R. Van Cleave," in U.S. Congress, Senate, Committee on Armed Services, *Military Implications of the Treaty on the Limitation of Strategic Offensive Arms (SALT II Treaty)* (Washington, D.C.: Government Printing Office, 1979), part 3.

3. William R. Van Cleave, "Implications of the Success or Failure of SALT," in William Kintner and Robert Pfaltzgraff, eds., *SALT* (Pittsburgh, Penn.: University of Pittsburgh Press, 1972), p. 328.

4. Megatonnage was four times higher in 1960 and the number of weapons one-third larger in 1967 than in 1983 (U.S. Secretary of Defense, *Annual Report to Congress, Fiscal Year 1984* [Washington, D.C.: Government Printing Office, 1 February 1983]; and U.S. Assistant Secretary of Defense [Public Affairs], "The U.S. Nuclear Weapons Stockpile," *News Release* no. 424–83 [25 August 1983]).

5. Warren Heckrotte and George Smith, eds., *Arms Control in Transition* (Boulder, Colo.: Westview Press, 1983), pp. 7, 32.

6. Van Cleave, "Implications of the Success or Failure of SALT," p. 314.

7. Donald G. Brennan, ed., *Arms Control, Disarmament, and National Security* (New York: George Braziller, 1961); Hedley Bull, *The Control of the Arms Race* (London: Weidenfeld and Nicolson, 1961); Thomas Schelling and Morton Halperin, *Strategy and Arms Control* (New York: Twentieth Century Fund, 1961); Ernest W. Lefever, ed., *Arms and Arms Control* (New York: Praeger, 1962); Louis Henkin, ed., *Arms Control: Issues for the Public* (Englewood Cliffs, N.J.: Prentice-Hall, 1961); Arthur T. Hadley, *The Nation's Safety and Arms Control* (New York: Viking Press, 1961); Alexander Dallin et al., *The Soviet Union and Disarmament* (New York: Frederick A. Praeger, 1964), published for the School of International Affairs, Columbia University. For a discussion of these works, see Robin Ranger, *Arms and Politics, 1958–1978* (Toronto: Macmillan Co., 1979).

8. Brennan, *Arms Control, Disarmament, and National Security*, p. 36.

9. Bull, *The Control of the Arms Race*, pp. 9–10.

10. Brennan, *Arms Control, Disarmament, and National Security*, p. 41.

11. Dallin et al., *The Soviet Union and Disarmament*, p. 181.

12. The United States and the USSR, it is frequently said, reached different conclusions about nuclear superiority as a result of the Cuban missile crisis. Maybe and maybe not. Certainly, the United States reached different conclusions from those of the Soviets regarding superiority, crisis management, and the proper use of threats and rewards. However, the proposition that Soviet leaders recognized the importance of nuclear superiority only in October 1962 is debatable. That is likely yet another myth that emerged from the crisis.

13. Alain Enthoven and Wayne Smith, *How Much Is Enough?* (New York: Harper & Row, 1971), pp. 175–76.

14. See "Testimony of William R. Van Cleave," before the Senate Committee on Armed Services; U.S. Senate, Committee on Government Operations, *International Negotiation*; and my "Political and Negotiation Asymmetries," in R. L. Pfaltzgraff, ed., *Contrasting Approaches to Strategic Arms Control* (Boston: D. C. Heath & Co., 1974), pp. 9–29.

15. Van Cleave, "Implications of the Success or Failure of SALT," p. 118.

16. U.S. Congress, Senate, Committee on Foreign Relations, *The SALT II Treaty* (Washington, D.C.: Government Printing Office, 1979).

17. For a discussion of this with respect to SALT I, see my "SALT on the Eagle's Tail," *Strategic Review* 4, no. 2 (Spring 1976): 44–55.

18. Fred C. Iklé, "After Detection—What?" *Foreign Affairs* 39 (1960–61): 208–20.

19. Republican National Convention, *Republican Platform* (Detroit, Mich., 14 July 1980).

20. These are drawn from various remarks by President Reagan, Secretary of State Alexander Haig, and ACDA Director Eugene Rostow during 1981 and 1982. Presidential statements are mostly from press conferences, with some addresses to the nation (e.g., televised speech of 22 November 1982, text in the *New York Times* the next day); Haig's remarks are from speeches (e.g., "Arms Control for the 1980s: An American Policy," 14 July 1981, published in Department of State, *Current Policy*, no. 292); Rostow's comments appeared in numerous speeches (available from the ACDA Public Affairs Office). In addition, see Secretary of Defense Weinberger's *Annual Reports* to Congress during those two years.

21. Eugene Rostow, "Arms Control Fever," *National Review* 35 (1983): 992–99.

22. Testimony before U.S. Congress, Committee on Armed Services, Subcommittee on Procurement and Military Nuclear Systems, Special Panel on Arms Control and Disarmament (12 July 1983), available from the Office of Assistant Secretary of Defense for International Security Policy.

23. The official title is *Report of the President's Commission on Strategic Forces* (Washington, D.C.: Government Printing Office, April 1983). The report is available from the commission's office, Room 3E129, The Pentagon, Washington, D.C.

24. I thank Dr. Gough C. Reinhardt of Lawrence Livermore Laboratory for pointing this out to me.

25. U.S. Department of Defense, *Annual Report, Fiscal Year 1980* (Washington, D.C.: Government Printing Office, 25 January 1979), p. 81.

26. Norman Podhoretz, "Appeasement by Any Other Name," *Commentary* 76, no. 1 (July 1983): 34.

2

THE STRATEGIC IMPLICATIONS OF THE NUCLEAR BALANCE AND ARMS CONTROL

Colin S. Gray

The United States requires nuclear forces capable of providing a convincing expression for its strategy. The design of those forces is, or should be, dictated by U.S. foreign policy commitments, by the U.S. theory of deterrence, by the strategy that reflects that theory, and by the characteristics of the Soviet (and other) target base. Naturally, the postural requirements that drive U.S. nuclear force acquisition must also be influenced by military considerations—by assessment of the damage that might be wrought through enemy initiatives and responses—and by judgments of the roles of nuclear-armed forces in war, where combat would involve weapons systems of all kinds.

Arms control agreements have the effect of focusing attention on the strategically irrelevant question of whether a tolerably even balance of forces has been negotiated. Save with isolated reference to the arms control process, the United States has no interest in achieving a tolerably even balance of forces. American policymakers and strategic planners require nuclear capabilities appropriate to the support of day-to-day diplomacy, to the successful management of crises, and—if need be—to the prosecution of armed conflict to the point where U.S. political objectives are secured. The road tests of crisis diplomacy and war will offer no plaudits to policymakers who designed U.S. nuclear forces so that they could be accommodated, unambiguously, within the terms of arms control agreements that provided only for nominal equality of different kinds.

Considerations of the meaning and importance of the nuclear balance must reflect fundamental attitudes toward nuclear weapons, nuclear war, and nuclear strategy. Nuclear weapons, as an integral part of national security policy, can serve both deterrent and coercive ends. While recognizing that civilian policymakers and the general public will always view nuclear weapons as differing qualitatively from other weapons—no matter how narrow the distance between nuclear weapons on the low end of the energy-yield continuum and conventional weapons of high potency—defense planners have no responsible choice other than to design strategies and tactics for the militarily efficient application of nuclear firepower according to the policy guidance that they receive. The U.S. policy problem is not to grapple intelligently with an abstract, capricious, malevolent possibility of nuclear war. Rather it is to deter and, if need be, defeat a Soviet Union that is wedded to a thorough "war-fighting" approach to nuclear weapons.[1]

STRATEGY AND THE NUCLEAR BALANCE

The meaning of the nuclear balance can be assessed only in terms of its ability to permit the accomplishment of fairly specific strategic objectives by the two sides. Bereft of political context, assertions that the balance is in a state of essential equivalence or that it has tilted against the United States or whatever are not very informative. All too often, claims to rough parity, or indeed to other conditions of alleged balance or imbalance, are supported by reference to static indices of weapons inventories during peacetime. Scarcely more meaningful are some of the dynamic analyses conducted according to the rules of arsenal exchange models that treat the superpowers as though they were two missile teams striving for some technical victory in a mad strategic-nuclear Olympics. Strategic analysis shorn of political calculation, of the local color of strategic culture, and of the national preferences that each party brings to its war-planning and military execution is likely to provide little insight for the education, let alone guidance, of policymakers.

Whether one judges the state of and the evident trend in the nuclear balance to be satisfactory is a function of a preferred nuclear strategy (and hence of a preferred theory of deterrence); of an assessment of the competence of non-nuclear forces; and finally of a belief concerning the fungibility of different kinds of forces. For example, many people are attracted to the deceptively simple concept of "freezing" strategic nuclear forces in their current condition because they conceive of nuclear war as a bilateral orgy of city destruction—Armageddon in an afternoon—and they note, accurately enough, that the United States today has more than enough nuclear weapons to lay waste the urban centers of the Soviet Union many times over. If the hallmark of stable deterrence is the mutual ability of the superpowers to destroy and damage cities by way of second-strike retaliation, then it follows that adverse trends in many indices of strategic power are irrelevant.

For excellent reasons, the U.S. government, from the drafting of the earliest nuclear war plans in 1947–48 until the present day, has never considered the destruction of Soviet society *per se* to be the appropriate goal for strategy.[2] However, it is true that U.S. policymakers, by a process of mirror-imaging, have tended to regard Soviet society as the ultimate set of values that could be threatened. Even during the brief period of his enthusiasm for a city-withholding strategy (that is, the policy of not attacking Soviet cities unless the Soviets attacked U.S. cities), Secretary of Defense Robert S. McNamara cited the threat to Soviet cities as having roughly symmetrical deterrent value as the threat to U.S. cities.[3] More recently, in 1980, the same year that Presidential Directive 59 (PD-59)—a document that stressed a traditional war-fighting approach to the design of strategic nuclear forces—was signed and promulgated, Secretary of Defense Harold Brown stated that the United States needed "first of all, a survivable and enduring retaliatory capability to devastate the industry and cities of the Soviet Union."[4]

Given the patrimonial view of society taken by the tsars and later by Soviet leaders, it is less than fully self-evident that much deterrence mileage can be secured by threatening Soviet civilian assets. Proponents of "freezing now" typically believe the "overkill" thesis—that U.S. nuclear forces already are more than adequate to destroy Soviet society. Opponents of a freeze all too often fail to realize that they cannot convince skeptical citizens unless they can persuasively relate force modernization in general and individual weapons systems in particular to the ability to achieve explicit foreign policy goals.

The authors of the Scowcroft Commission report of April 1983 expressed the central tenet of current U.S. nuclear strategy with admirable directness: "The deterrent effect of our strategic forces is not something separate and apart from the ability of those forces to be used against the tools by which the Soviet leaders maintain their power. *Deterrence, on the contrary, requires military effectiveness.*"[5] (Emphasis added.)

The state of the strategic balance must be assessed, not for evidence of symmetry or asymmetry, but rather for its meaning in terms of the net freedom of action permitted each side and of the implications of that judgment for conflict outcomes at all levels. Since the late 1960s, it has always been understood in the U.S. government that the most burdensome, if not the principal (indeed originally, prior to 1952–53, the only), mission of the strategic forces was extended deterrence.[6] American nuclear forces have never been designed or intended solely to deter the use of nuclear weapons by others. Instead, they have been seen as economical and (decreasingly) effective substitutes for locally deployed or deployable non-nuclear stopping power. The foreign policy and security commitments of the United States have altered remarkably little since the early 1950s. What has changed dramatically is the scale of risk that extended deterrence implies for the U.S. homeland and, as a necessary consequence, the credibility of U.S. nuclear, and particularly central nuclear, intervention in a regional conflict.

As the military balance shifted steadily to the disadvantage of the United States and its allies between the mid-1960s and the early 1980s, strategy became more important than ever before in the East-West military relationship. Intelligence and imagination have been needed to offset the loss in relative military muscle.

A useful beginning was made with the "Nuclear Targeting Policy Review," conducted during 1977–1979, which led—somewhat belatedly—to PD-59 (signed on 25 July 1980).[7] The principal difficulties with PD-59 lay in the near-term absence of adequate military means to give plausible expression to its vision of a U.S. force posture able to engage and defeat Soviet forces and in its neglect of strategic defense.

When considering the meaning of the nuclear balance from the perspective of U.S. strategy, two fundamental questions must be asked. First, is the United States able to pose the kind and quantity of threats that Soviet leaders, *qua* Soviet leaders, should find dissuasive? Second, if prewar deterrence should fail, or fail to apply, does the nuclear balance (and related elements) permit the United States an operational strategy that a president would judge to be in the national interest to execute?

Military balances between great powers are road tested on an unpredictable timetable. Assessments, or even just crude perceptions, of the state of the military balance are an important factor in the decisions of states to fight and also in the determination of the character of risks that they run in foreign policy. However, occasions when the question "to fight or not to fight" assumes immediate importance typically are produced by political events. A favorable military balance does not, *ipso facto*, mean that a country enjoying such an advantage necessarily will seek to solve some of its more pressing external (or internal) security problems by military means. On the other hand, such a state of imbalance does mean that the advantaged country will make a more generous judgment of its freedom of political action than it might otherwise.

Contrary to the contemporary belief of some prominent European commentators, a condition of "useful advantage"[8] in military power on the part of the United States is a guarantee of peace, while a condition of either stalemate or a marked disadvantage vis-à-vis Soviet military power is a near guarantee of war. Some of the West European allies feel comfortable living in an era of essential military equivalence between the superpowers. They fear the consequences of a U.S. military advantage scarcely less than they do those of a Soviet advantage.[9]

It is important to appreciate the different, though related, functions of nuclear forces. When considering the political meaning of the dynamic strategic nuclear balance, the U.S. government should recognize that it places the following burdens on those forces:

1. To help support international order, day by day, in peacetime, provide an appropriate backing to diplomacy, and supply convincing expression of the United States' view of its role and duties in the world;

2. To deter a direct attack on the United States;

3. To provide "top cover" for pre-crisis maneuvering, for crisis management, and for military action at subcentral strategic levels of violence;

4. To help deter attacks on friends and allies of the United States; and

5. To produce, should deterrence fail, sufficient leverage during war itself to contain the conflict and permit, or enforce, war termination on favorable conditions.

The United States requires strategic forces that can fight and win. Because of the geographical asymmetry between the superpowers and given the interests most likely to be at immediate stake in a conflict, the principal burden of decision regarding nuclear escalation is likely to be borne by NATO and the United States. If the latter lacks a nuclear advantage that translates persuasively into what Herman Kahn called "escalation dominance" (perhaps "pre-eminence" would be a more appropriate term),[10] it is necessarily rather difficult for the United States to persuade itself, its allies, and its prospective enemies that it would take nuclear actions that would place its national survival at prompt or even delayed risk. Escalation dominance, or pre-eminence, means that one can take a war to a higher level of violence in reasonably confident expectation of enforcing an improved outcome.

At the least, NATO's non-nuclear defense should be robust enough to place the burden of decision for the initiation of nuclear action on Soviet shoulders. NATO, by seeking to strengthen conventional deterrence, would not unilaterally raise the nuclear threshold. After all, it takes at least two to decide that a war shall remain non-nuclear.[11] Furthermore, Soviet military doctrine and defense preparations envision use of nuclear weapons as a coherent part of a unified theory of war.

To recapitulate, the nuclear balance should concern us in terms of strategy. Does the current and predictable future state of that balance permit the

United States and its allies to defend their vital interests (that is, those worth fighting for)? All else is of secondary or even trivial significance.

WEIGHING THE NUCLEAR BALANCE

Trends in the nuclear balance and the reasons for those trends are as easy to identify as a precise assessment of net combat prowess at any point in time is difficult. The Soviets' principles for force development may be inferred with some confidence. A country with the military history of Russia/the USSR cannot accept the idea of achieving and sustaining rough parity, or stalemate, with its enemies. Soviet leaders know that international conflict can have fatal consequences for societies that are militarily underprepared, and they appear to believe that any and every margin of military advantage may be useful—and may indeed make the difference between victory and defeat.

Not only is it difficult to weigh the nuclear balance, it is also difficult to make political sense of the outcome of exercises in net assessment. Quantitative analysis needs to be translated into policy judgment: Will the Soviets be deterred? —Will the West be deterred? There are obvious problems concerning the range of analytic assumptions and algorithms common to the Soviet and U.S. defense communities. There are less obvious but no less troubling problems in the realm of possible differences in superpower "styles" in the conduct of war.[12] Even if one can demonstrate with fair plausibility that one side can win a "points victory" in one or more rounds of a counterforce campaign—meaning that it clearly has either larger residual forces, post-attack, than the other, and/or that it destroys or disables more enemy throw-weight than it expends itself—so what? Military events plainly would, and should, influence political choices. However, will they determine them in circumstances when the destructive potential of remaining military options are substantial?

Unlike what we believe is the Soviet approach to strategic analysis, the U.S. defense community is prone to a narrow assaying of net prowess in long-range nuclear combat, ignoring the outcome on the ground of theater campaigns and certainly neglecting the political, social, psychological, and economic elements of the struggle that Soviet analysts attempt to capture when calculating the correlation of forces. Granting this, it does not follow that an assessment of the nuclear balance should not or cannot be made. In pointing to deficiencies, even absurdities, in some dominant modes of analysis in the United States, it is easy to go too far. For example, there is some truth, but only some truth, in Richard Lebow's claim that "analysts can come

up with almost any outcome they want if they choose the appropriate doctrine, rules of engagement, or indices of operational performance."[13]

True enough, save for the fact that the U.S. defense community is by no
means wholly ignorant of Soviet (or U.S.) doctrine, probable rules of engagement, or likely ranges of performance of weapons and organizations.
The same author proceeds to argue that if

> American strategists are unable to agree among themselves about how to
> simulate a nuclear war, it is reasonable to suppose that whatever consensus
> the intelligence community eventually reaches will bear only a chance re-
> semblance to the conclusions of their Soviet counterparts who would ap-
> proach the problem with their own doctrinal assumptions and data bases.[14]

Lebow is right in stressing the importance for deterrence of what he calls
the "social truths about nuclear war," and he is also correct in noticing that
"American . . . strategists have based their calculations, as well as their doctrine, on technical phenomena." He is on extremely shaky, indeed dangerous, ground, however, when he asserts that "there is at best only a marginal association between military capability and national will."[15] As a
general rule, the willingness of a society to bear the social costs of different
levels of defense preparation in peacetime is taken as an important index of
political determination. An important reason why static indicators for comparison of military power play a significant role in perceptions of trends in
the Soviet-U.S. competition is that in peacetime those numbers are the only
available firm evidence of national will and implied prowess in the military
realm.

The Soviets cannot, or at least should not, know in detail how the U.S.
government calculates force exchanges, how the latter would choose to fight
its forces, or how its military net assessment impacts on political decisions.
However, the basis in fact, as opposed to judgment, for Soviet perceptions—
whatever those perceptions may be—is the observable physical features of
the United States' strategic preparations. It is true that the United States cannot design a posture and a doctrine that would meet any and all needs of
deterrence and defense, should deterrence fail. On the other hand, this does
not mean that the United States is unable to design a strategic posture that
would make Soviet perceptions, calculations, and decisions benign by Western definition.

Lebow, together with many other academic students of strategic policy,
points persuasively to errors, lacunae, and difficulties in the assessment of
nuclear forces. But he then makes explicit and implicit policy recommendations or comments that are manifestly inferior to contemporary official
practice. Aficionados of this phenomenon can do no better than examine

Laurence Freedman's magisterial study of the evolution of nuclear strategy. In his judgment,

> the position we have reached is one where stability depends on something that is more the antithesis of strategy than its apotheosis—on threats that things will get out of hand, that we might act irrationally, that possibly through inadvertence we could set in motion a process that in its development and conclusion would be beyond human control and comprehension.[16]

As a caveat, this has much to recommend it, but as implicit policy advice it is both irresponsible and absurd. It fails entirely to address the Soviet approach to deterrence and the conduct of war. The United States cannot *plan* to behave irrationally or to lose control of events, although officials need no reminder that both may happen. Also, the Soviet style in defense preparation mandates the most serious, indeed the boldest, endeavor to seize and hold the initiative and physically prevent the United States and its allies from denying victory to Soviet arms. Political and military leaders in Moscow are not known for a willingness to rely on intra-war deterrence—they have long rejected the United States' notion that war can be waged in a limited fashion, controlled by the tactical needs of a signaling and bargaining process.

Those who advise that national will and courage are more important to stable deterrence than the balance of forces make a useful point. However, defense planners cannot program national will as they do forces; they cannot mandate national courage— particularly when the U.S. homeland is totally unprotected and courage could be terminally fatal. Finally, they cannot guarantee that even if Soviet leaders are impressed by U.S. (and NATO–European?) national will, they will be deterred. It is true that the balance of nuclear forces cannot predictably be related to particular policy decisions, taken by particular people, in unique circumstances, at unique points in time. However, it is the duty of U.S. policymakers to design the U.S. end of the nuclear balance so that whatever influence sober contemplation of the probable military-political operational meaning of that balance has on Soviet policy deliberation is an influence for caution and restraint.

Robert Gates was correct when he claimed that "we have trivialized the most profound contest in history into metaphysical debates about kill probabilities, throwweight, fractionation, fratricide and survivable C³." On the other hand, he was scarcely less correct in granting that "numbers are important."[17] American policymakers cannot with confidence manipulate the ways in which Soviet policymakers assess the uncertainties that necessarily attend arms conflict, any more than they can reliably direct Soviet perceptions of U.S. national will. However, the United States certainly can and should influence the scale and scope of risks, and hence of uncertainties, that the USSR must assess—albeit in a distinctively Soviet fashion. A primary source of that influence must be a force posture that can engage Soviet forces, deny victory to Soviet arms, and hold out a plausible prospect of enforcing the limitation of damage to Western values to a level leaders in Moscow should expect Western countries to see as an advantage in offering unqualified resistance.

TRENDS IN THE NUCLEAR BALANCE

As a consequence of outspending the United States on strategic forces by a factor of three throughout the 1970s and on the basis of a legacy from the 1960s of great program momentum across the board of military power, the Soviet Union has effected a cumulatively dramatic change in the state of the nuclear balance. That judgment can be offered with high confidence, regardless of the difficulties already alluded to regarding a precise assessment of the state of the balance. Commentators may dispute to what degree perceptions of nuclear advantage and disadvantage influence political behavior. But there is no dispute of substance over the trend in the balance or over the thesis that whatever net advantage may flow from perception of the balance or from the actual employment of nuclear forces accrues today to the USSR.

In the mid-1960s, the U.S. government believed that it enjoyed and would long continue to enjoy a meaningful measure of strategic-nuclear advantage over the Soviet Union. In order to contain the military budget, and as a theory of arms race stability, Robert S. McNamara retreated rapidly from his brief declaratory flirtation with a war-fighting approach to deterrence.[18] Nonetheless, the arms control theorizing of the 1960s—and the architecture of NATO's defense doctrine of flexible response—rested on the confident belief that the United States could and would maintain a healthy advantage in the nuclear competition.

By the end of the 1960s, the strength and steadiness of the Soviet determination to provide a convincing and survivable strategic nuclear counterdeterrent was beyond argument. However, the backdrop to the SALT I negotiations of 1969–1972 remained the continued official U.S. confidence that the United States was blessed with an important, if not commanding, technological lead in the competition and, moreover, would not permit any perceptually or operationally significant disadvantageous asymmetries to develop and mature.

The background to the package of 1972 SALT agreements contained not only physical manifestations of unambiguous U.S. technological superiority (reflected in MIRVed ICBMs and SLBMs, in quieter submarines, in a manned bomber force believed with high confidence to be capable of penetrating Soviet air defenses, in ballistic missile defense technology) but also the distinctively American belief that the Soviet Union would settle, indeed would have no choice but to settle, for some approximation of strategic parity. American theorists believed that the USSR either would be deterred from making a serious bid for strategic nuclear advantage by the enduring structural superiority of the United States as a competitor in military high technology or—if such a bid were made—that the United States would have little difficulty in defeating it. Perhaps the illusion was rife in 1972 that the SALT I agreements and the anticipated SALT II agreement would inhibit the right of the Soviet Union to pursue important paths that might lead to military advantage.

Overall, since 1972, the United States has permitted itself to slip from a condition of demonstrated technological superiority and rough, general strategic equivalence—a condition that looks attractive in comparison with the condition of the early 1980s, but was strategically incompatible with U.S. extended-deterrence duties—to a condition where the United States is inferior in virtually all indices of strategic nuclear capability. Informed opinion today ranges from those who claim that the USSR's strategic-nuclear advantage is of interest only to an astrategic analyst-accountant, because that nominal advantage is insufficient to accord Soviet policymakers any meaningful degree of freedom for political or military action (in other words, the United States, temporarily—perhaps—is in a condition that may be termed one of "tolerable inferiority"), to those who believe that the United States faces a "window of vulnerability," a "window of [Soviet] opportunity," or, in Blair Stewart's chilling phrase, a "window of coercion." [19]

Courtesy of technology transfer from the West, of the massive Soviet allocation of resources, of gaps and ambiguities in treaty language (aided and abetted by U.S. pusillanimity on the sanctions-for-noncompliance front), and of a stable Soviet strategic doctrine that equated the ability to prevail in war with stability and success in deterrence, the Soviet Union has achieved a transformation of the strategic balance to its advantage.

What the USSR has achieved is the construction of a "counterdeterrent plus." That is to say, it has built a strategic-nuclear force structure that denies the United States that freedom of nuclear-use initiative that is absolutely fundamental to the integrity of NATO's concept of flexible response (or controlled escalation if you prefer), or indeed of any of the extended-deterrent missions in the United States' global security commitments. In short, the Soviet Union, with its transformation of the nuclear balance, has placed the United States in a position where any nuclear war that the United States might begin in defense of distant allies and friends would be a war that it could not conclude on favorable terms. To be perfectly blunt, the

United States would lose. Whether the Soviet Union would lose, in Soviet terms, is a matter for dispute. The "plus" in the term "counterdeterrence plus" refers to the distinct possibility that the Soviet nuclear modernization program and buildup may serve not only to prevent U.S. nuclear intervention in any theater conflict but, in addition, to open the door to plausible nuclear threats by the USSR calculated to deny the West even *conventional* defense options.[20]

One cannot overstress that the Soviet Union's effort to field capable, modern strategic nuclear weapons has been part of a comprehensive endeavor to enhance its prospects for political success through intimidation and, if need be, through force of arms. The Soviet challenge extends from bribery, disinformation, and worse by intelligence agents through the heavy artillery of the ICBM force to a domestic structure of state authority that has been provided with the means of survival in the event of a general nuclear conflict.

While the United States has spent the better part of a decade debating whether and how to field a successor to the Minuteman III that could place hardened Soviet targets at prompt risk, the Soviet Union proceeded to deploy a fourth generation of MIRVed ICBMs (in no fewer than ten variants), which, as accuracy improved in the late 1970s, came to pose a near total threat to the U.S. ICBM force.[21] The story of the steady effort to modernize applies equally to the Soviet SLBM force. Since SALT I was signed in 1972, the USSR has deployed no fewer than ten new SLBM variants, and the missiles on its Delta I, II, III and Typhoon-class strategic nuclear submarines can strike targets in the United States from Soviet coastal waters. (We should not forget that technical comparisons between U.S. and Soviet sea-based strategic forces are essentially meaningless since those forces would not engage each other.)

The Soviet Union has neglected no area of strategic offense and defense. The USSR now has over 200 Tu-22M Backfire bombers, approximately half of which are allocated to the air force and the other half to the navy for protection of the sea coasts. If equipped with the long-range, air-launched cruise missile now under development, Backfire would pose a very credible intercontinental threat. In addition to the multirole Backfire, the Soviet Union may pose a qualitatively new air-breathing threat late in the 1980s if work on the new Tu-160 Backfire long-range bomber proceeds from development to series production.

The Soviet approach to defense of the homeland is comprehensive in nature. Soviet rejection of the "strategic deadlock" thesis is illustrated, redundantly, by its acquisition of major offensive counterforce capabilities— for attrition of the threat at source; of a vast inventory of all-altitude air defenses that increasingly merge technically with ballistic missile defense (BMD) competence; of the radar and command infrastructure for dedicated, large-scale BMD deployment (should international arms control circumstances change); by investment in hardened and dispersed facilities to ensure continuity in the political and military command structure; and by civil defense/war-survival preparation intended to guarantee that the essential assets for national recovery would survive.

Probably the single most important adverse trend in the nuclear balance relates not to forces but rather to the prospects of each side for sustaining command stability.[22] American theorists and officials have spoken, it seems endlessly, about stability—the Soviet Union has practiced it. For good reasons, President Reagan's strategic modernization program gives first priority to command, control, and communications (C³). The technical community generally agrees that the Soviet Union has a highly survivable command and control system and the United States does not. This, not implausibly, could well prove to be a war-winning/war-losing asymmetry.

Soviet improvements in theater and battlefield nuclear capability since the early 1970s have the same characteristics and generic strategic implications as their improvements in central strategic systems. Older weapons have been replaced or supplemented by new systems with greater accuracy, better survivability, and improved readiness, while gaps in capability have been filled in accordance with the evolution of military doctrine.[23]

The three-MIRVed SS-20 IRBM has attracted the most public political attention in the West and has been the focus of U.S. assault in the intermediate-range nuclear forces (INF) negotiations. However, that highly accurate, mobile (with reloadable launchers) weapon is only one element in a whole new family of Soviet surface-to-surface missiles.[24] In the tactical area, the SS-21 (replacing the FROG-7), the SS-23 (replacing the SCUD), and the SS-22 (replacing the SS-12/Scaleboard), have ranges, respectively, of 120, 500, and 900 kilometers. No less impressive have been the changes in Soviet frontal aviation (FA). Since the early 1970s, FA has evolved rapidly from being a distinctly short-range force, heavily committed to air defense duties, to a force capable of effecting nuclear strikes at low altitude throughout the European theater. The key development was procurement for FA of the Fencer, a deep-penetration, ground-attack aircraft.

The final gap in the spectrum of Soviet nuclear capability was filled in 1978, with the commencement of deployment of a family of nuclear-capable, self-propelled artillery weapons. Today, the Soviet Union has self-propelled, nuclear-capable artillery of 152-, 203-, and 240-millimeter calibers. These nuclear-capable weapons, representing a new departure for Soviet forces, have been mandated by the direction taken by the evolution of

Soviet ground-forces doctrine—with its emphasis on deep penetration and hence the need for rapid-response (nuclear) fire support of a kind different from that appropriate to the set-piece situation of a classic breakthrough operation of attrition.

CONCLUSIONS: THE NUCLEAR BALANCE AND ARMS CONTROL

The structure of the Soviet-U.S. political rivalry and the nature of the arms control process virtually guarantee that any agreement will address the least significant aspects of the forces to be regulated. It is a political fact of life that although countries can tolerate unfavorable asymmetries in forces, they tend to be unable to tolerate unfavorable legislated asymmetries. Nominal parity in nuclear forces typically must function to the disadvantage of the Western alliance. This is because the USSR has a proclivity for pressing around and beyond the bounds of competitive behavior that an agreement permits—or is interpreted by Western officials as permitting—while its U.S. adversary-partner is unwilling to walk away from the arms control process when the Soviets violate agreements. Nominal parity also works to the U.S. disadvantage because the architecture of U.S. strategy, reflecting the needs of extended-deterrence duties, requires maintenance of some useful advantage in nuclear prowess for escalation pre-eminence and control.

Both historical experience and common sense tell us that progress in arms control cannot be achieved when either East-West political relations are bad and deteriorating or when the balance of forces deployed is markedly advantageous to one party. Both conditions apply today.

But even if the Soviets and Americans agreed that the nuclear balance was in a state of tolerable equality, political considerations would dominate arms control negotiations. Nonetheless, while granting that the political context for negotiations will dominate the negotiating process, there is no escaping the residual truth that unless the United States corrects the adverse trend in the nuclear balance, there will be no basis for agreements in the INF negotiations or the Strategic Arms Limitations Talks that a U.S. president should accept.

NOTES

1. Useful commentaries include Joseph D. Douglass, Jr., and Amoretta M. Hoeber, *Soviet Strategy for Nuclear War* (Stanford: Hoover Institution Press, 1979);

Robert Bathurst, "Two Languages of War," in Derek Leebaert, ed., *Soviet Military Thinking* (London: Allen & Unwin, 1981), chap. 2; John Erickson, "The Soviet View of Deterrence: A General Survey," *Survival* 24, no. 6 (November/December 1982): 242–51; and Mark E. Miller, *Soviet Strategic Power and Doctrine: The Quest for Superiority* (Washington, D.C.: Advanced International Studies Institute, in association with the University of Miami, 1982).

2. On the evolution of U.S. nuclear war plans, see David Alan Rosenberg, "The Origins of Overkill: Nuclear Weapons and American Strategy, 1945–1960," *International Security* 7, no. 4 (Spring 1983): 3–71; and Desmond Ball, "Targeting for Strategic Deterrence," *Adelphi Papers*, no. 185 (Summer 1983).

3. Quoted in Albert Wohlstetter, "Bishops, Statesmen, and Other Strategists on the Bombing of Innocents," *Commentary* 75, no. 6 (June 1983): 24.

4. U.S. Secretary of Defense, *Department of Defense Annual Report, Fiscal Year 1981* (Washington, D.C.: Government Printing Office, 1980), p. 65.

5. *Report of the President's Commission on Strategic Forces* (Washington, D.C.: Government Printing Office, April 1983), p. 7.

6. See Edward N. Luttwak, "The Problems of Extending Deterrence," in "The Future of Strategic Deterrence," *Adelphi Papers*, no. 160 (Autumn 1980): part 1, pp. 31–37; and Anthony H. Cordesman, "Deterrence in the 1980s," *Adelphi Papers*, no. 175 (Summer 1982): part 1.

7. See Ball, "Targeting for Strategic Deterrence," pp. 21–22; and Thomas Powers, "Choosing a Strategy for World War III," *Atlantic Monthly*, November 1982, pp. 82–110.

8. The term is the one preferred by John Erickson to describe the Soviet perspective. See "The Soviet Military System: Doctrine, Technology, and 'Style,'" in J. Erickson and E. J. Feuchtwanger, eds., *Soviet Military Power and Performance* (Hamden, Conn.: Archon, 1979), p. 28.

9. For insight into European anxieties regarding U.S. policy, see Michael E. Howard: "Reassurance and Deterrence: Western Defense in the 1980s," *Foreign Affairs* 61 (1982–83): 309–24; and idem, "Weapons and Peace," *Atlantic Quarterly* 1, no. 1 (Spring 1983): 45–60. Perhaps the bluntest statement of the lack of European interest in a restoration of a major degree of U.S. military advantage over the Soviet Union is Hedley Bull, "European Self-Reliance and the Reform of NATO," in the same issue of *Atlantic Quarterly*, pp. 25–43.

10. Herman Kahn, *On Escalation: Metaphors and Scenarios* (New York: Praeger, 1965), p. 290.

11. See Joseph D. Douglass, Jr., and Amoretta M. Hoeber, *Conventional War and Escalation: The Soviet View* (New York: Crane, Russak, for the National Strategy Information Center, 1981).

12. See Nathan Leites, *Soviet Style in War* (New York: Crane, Russak, 1982); Peter H. Vigor, *Soviet Blitzkrieg Theory* (New York: St. Martin's Press, 1983); Bathurst, "Two Languages of War"; and Colin S. Gray, *Nuclear Strategy and National Style* (Cambridge, Mass.: Abt, 1984).

13. Richard Ned Lebow, "Misconceptions in American Strategic Assessment," *Political Science Quarterly* 97, no. 2 (Summer 1982): 193.

14. Ibid.

15. Ibid., pp. 196, 198.

16. Lawrence Freedman, *The Evolution of Nuclear Strategy* (London: Macmillan, 1981), p. 400.

17. Robert M. Gates, "The Soviet Threat," *Phalanx* 16, no. 2 (June 1983): 11.

18. See Henry S. Rowen, "The Evolution of Strategic Nuclear Doctrine," in Lawrence Martin, ed., *Strategic Thought in the Nuclear Age* (Baltimore, Md.: Johns Hopkins University Press, 1979), particularly pp. 146–51; Aaron L. Friedberg, "The Evolution of U.S. Strategic 'Doctrine,' 1945 to 1981," in Samuel P. Huntington, ed., *The Strategic Imperative: New Policies for American Security* (Cambridge, Mass.: Ballinger, 1982), pp. 67–75; and Ball, "Targeting for Strategic Deterrence," pp. 12–15.

19. Blair Stewart, "The Scowcroft Commission and the 'Window of Coercion,'" *Strategic Review* 11, no. 3 (Summer 1983): 21–27.

20. This thesis is advanced in Samuel P. Huntington, "The Renewal of Strategy," in *The Strategic Imperative*, pp. 33–34.

21. A good survey of Soviet military capabilities is U.S. Department of Defense, *Soviet Military Power* (Washington, D.C.: Government Printing Office, 1983). Useful details on the evolution of the nuclear balance may be gleaned from *The Military Balance*, an annual publication of the International Institute for Strategic Studies in London. Also of particular value are Cordesman, "Deterrence in the 1980s"; and John M. Collins, *U.S.-Soviet Military Balance: Concepts and Capabilities, 1960– 1980* (New York: McGraw-Hill, 1980), part III.

22. On command stability, see John D. Steinbruner: "National Security and the Concept of Strategic Stability," *Journal of Conflict Resolution* 22, no. 3 (September 1978): 411–28; idem, "Nuclear Decapitation," *Foreign Policy*, no. 45 (Winter 1981–82): 16–28; and Desmond Ball, "Can Nuclear War Be Controlled?" *Adelphi Papers*, no. 169 (Autumn 1981).

23. For a presentation and analysis of theater and battlefield nuclear weapons systems, see Donald R. Cotter, James H. Hansen, and Kirk McConnel, *The Nuclear Balance in Europe: Status, Trends, Implications*, Report 83–1 (Washington, D.C.: United States Strategic Institute, 1983).

24. The SS-20, with approximately 250 reloadable launchers currently deployed within range of NATO–European targets, is replacing the obsolescent SS-4 and SS-5. NATO's decision in December 1979 to deploy 572 ground-launched cruise missiles and Pershing IIs was a new departure in Western nuclear balancing. Since the early 1960s, NATO had not deployed IRBMs or MRBMs in the European theater to balance the large (600) Soviet force of SS-4 MRBMs and SS-5 IRBMs. NATO has always been nervous at appearing to endorse the idea of a "Eurostrategic" nuclear balance. Until 1983, the Soviet SS-4, SS-5, and SS-11 (and SLBM weapons on an uncertain scale) force targeted against NATO-Europe was "balanced" by a small

allocation of U.S. SSBN assets to Supreme Allied Command Europe, by British and French national "strategic" nuclear forces, by forward-based nuclear-capable aircraft, and by the general "weight" of the U.S. central nuclear systems. The arrival of perceived parity and then inferiority in the strategic nuclear balance during the mid-1970s, within the context of the SS-20, prompted NATO to reconsider its previous lack of interest in Eurostrategic missiles.

3

DISCUSSION

John G. Keliher

It is unfortunate that arms control negotiations have degenerated into the public propaganda forums we find today. Little if any progress has been made since the USSR invaded Afghanistan in late 1979. Given the current status of Soviet-American relations, there was little chance for improvement in this situation prior to or after deployment in December 1983 of the first Pershing IIs and cruise missiles. Both sides must share the blame. The USSR has shown an unwillingness to sacrifice its modernization program and has displayed a negative attitude toward verification enhancement. In its failure to ratify SALT II, the United States must accept a good part of the blame for the poor condition of the current arms control process. If that treaty had not been dropped by President Carter and then disavowed by the Reagan administration, the Soviets would already have begun to reduce the number of their strategic nuclear systems. Furthermore, because it had been planned to discuss cruise missiles and other theater nuclear weapons in the follow-on SALT III negotiations, the United States would not find itself in the contrived INF forum, which threatens to split NATO and forces the United States to play the Soviet game. Initiatives taken to modernize and strengthen the United States' force posture would not have precipitated negative reactions had it continued the SALT process.

Arms control has been well sold to the American public, some would argue oversold, but it is here to stay. To renounce arms control is political suicide. However, the United States seems unable to maintain the pendulum of arms control at the center position. In the 1970s, arms control was sold as inexpensive defense. Liberals saw it as a device to divert military funds to social programs. In the 1980s, the conservatives give the impression of trying to use it to disarm the Soviets "on the cheap." Arms control can accomplish neither objective. As distasteful as it may be, both negotiating parties must agree on arms control goals if progress is to be made. Neither side should expect to be able to reduce unilaterally those elements of the other side's force structure deemed essential for security. Indeed, this is a critical point largely unappreciated in the West. The Soviets will not agree to arms control provisions that require them to become dependent to any degree for their security on the restraint or good will of the United States. Unless the USSR becomes convinced that an arms control regime actually increases its security beyond what it can accomplish through unilateral military measures, we should not expect more from the USSR than a willingness to validate current force ratios and mixes while continuing its own modernization program and striving through propaganda to denigrate the West's efforts to improve its military posture.

Validation of current force ratios and mixes is not a goal to be disdained as a near-term measure. One of the few common goals the West and the Soviets share is avoidance of a nuclear war. Hence, there is a continuing need to establish parameters around the military competition by placing limits on certain categories of weapons systems, in order to create stability through predictability and transparency of major force components on each side. This is what arms control, as opposed to disarmament, really is all about: regulating and restraining the use of military force in peacetime for political objectives. With this in mind, let me offer some specific initiatives I believe should be taken.

First, it should finally be recognized, after more than a decade of attempts, that the Soviets will not significantly reduce their main source and symbol of superpower status, that is, the heavy missile threat to the United States. These missiles represent a threat that, I believe, has been largely encouraged and exaggerated to the extent that the West has virtually induced self-paralysis when it comes to ICBM modernization. Rather the West should focus on goals in START that limit weapons systems on both sides, while allowing a freedom within those limits for each side to achieve its desired force mix through modernization. This creates the climate for a reduction process to begin with systems considered expendable. Once begun, and as confidence increases, more significant systems could be reduced.

Second, now that the first installment of nine Pershing IIs and 32 cruise missiles has been deployed, the West should make every possible effort to move negotiations on these systems and the SS-20 into START. The West is playing the Soviets' game by continuing the INF forum. The SS-20 is a strategic system and should be covered by the START talks. Indeed, the West is also perpetuating the "grey area" problem (of whether a weapons system is intermediate range or strategic) rather than eliminating it.

Third, the MBFR negotiations should address the issue of ground-force nuclear weapons. The recent total modernization of the Soviet ground-force family of nuclear-capable missiles and the introduction of nuclear artillery in Eastern Europe have been largely ignored. These systems need to be *actively* captured in an arms control forum. Their threat, when combined with the Western allies' growing distaste for NATO short-range nuclear weapons and the increased desire to rely more on a conventional capability, make the current MBFR objective of reducing manpower (an objective largely unchanged since 1973) questionable as the best course for the enhancement of Western security.

In sum, the United States should not allow largely unattainable goals to frustrate the arms control process. It needs to structure arms control forces and objectives so that they complement Western security goals. Arms control is here to stay. The United States must do a better job in making it serve national security requirements, while effecting a reduction of the nuclear arsenal and the chances of war.

Charles M. Kupperman

The papers presented by Dr. Van Cleave and Dr. Gray demonstrate that despite more than a decade of strategic arms control, some very basic questions remain unanswered. Both note the enormous impact of arms control on national security policy and build a persuasive case that many expect too much of arms control. The pertinent questions today—given the adverse shift in the strategic balance—are the following: How to keep the role of arms control in national security policy in perspective? How to enhance the role of strategy in the arms control process? How to assure that public expectations of arms control are realistic? And, given the state of the balance and projected Soviet programs, what negotiating strategy will best serve U.S. national security interests? Developing answers to these questions at the national level is fundamental to pursuing a realistic arms control approach.

Finally, it would also be in the national security interests of the United States to view compliance with existing arms control agreements as a major indicator of how the Soviets approach arms control. Despite the enormous Soviet buildup, there still is a tendency for many in the U.S. arms control bureaucracy to assume that the Soviets have arms control objectives similar to those of Americans. Even though such an assumption is not supported by empirical evidence, the yearning to assume a mutuality of interests remains.

Compliance behavior is solid proof that the Soviets are pursuing fundamentally different objectives.

Gough C. Reinhardt

A sturdy supporter of arms control would take issue with Van Cleave's remarks on failure. He might liken the arms control community to a child learning to walk and speak of "learning experiences" and "constructive failures." Parenthetically, this is more kind than the analogy some would make: that of the goose, who wakes up in a new world every morning and repeats the failures of the day before.

Unfortunately there are costs associated with arms control. It has led the United States to delusion, to the false hope that the Soviets might bargain away the strategic capability they have produced with so much hard work over the years. The United States compromised on needed force structure because agreements existed or were in the process of being negotiated, and the very fact that such compromise would surely come about has caused defense planners to ask for less than prudent need would dictate. In place of hardheaded strategic planning, U.S. policymakers have learned to rely on the hopes of arms control. These all add up to an unacceptable price—the ceding of strategic superiority to the Soviet Union.

There are other, non-negligible costs that can be quantified more easily than the strategic ascendance of our malevolent foe. Not the least of these is the loss of talent that comes about when strategists and analysts of the caliber of those attending this conference devote themselves to arms control, rather than to more productive service to the Republic—and this is true despite the fact that most of us are here in a damage-limiting role. The cost, in dollars, of maintaining an arms control apparatus is not trivial, but it is probably the least of those I have addressed.

Even when we speak of stability, the before and after SALT comparison is disquieting. The vulnerability of U.S. strategic forces has made launch under attack a household phrase in this country today. What should we be willing to pay to avoid so bitter an alternative?

The constant pressure of the demand for arms control has swayed President Reagan. His early skeptical views of the process have apparently changed. He is now willing to abide by the terms of a treaty he once denounced as "fatally flawed." He is strong in his praise of the report of the President's Commission on Strategic Forces (the Scowcroft Commission). That report recommends that arms control, above all things, be recognized as a pillar of U.S. strategic policy. And thus, those who would appease the Soviet Union and find their last respectable refuge in arms control have swayed the very man who seemed to have recognized the Soviet threat so clearly.

Rather than continue to hammer away in this vein, let me make a suggestion that occurred to me as I listened to these excellent papers. Let us in the weeks ahead do two things. First, let us search diligently for an existence theorem for arms control: that is, a proof that arms control will increase the security of this nation. Or, conversely, we should seek a refutation of the argument that all future arms control efforts can only serve the Soviet Union. Second, let us ponder how to dismantle the arms control apparatus most painlessly and efficiently, in the event that the citizenry of the nation may just possibly demand that the apparatus be dismantled at some future date.

Thus, by searching for an existence theorem and at the same time studying the problems involved in dismantling the arms control apparatus, we will at least be in a position to speak knowledgeably about the latter if, as I suspect will be the case, we meet with no success in the former.

James L. George

My official position is that of assistant director for multilateral affairs at the U.S. Arms Control and Disarmament Agency. I am involved with all major arms control issues except START and INF. In other words, I am not an expert on those bilateral talks. More important, what follows are my personal views and should not be construed as representing any official position of the U.S. government. Let me now turn to the papers just presented.

As I understand it, both are optimistic about arms control. Professor Van Cleave's paper can be broken down into three main areas—on history, education, and arms control "fever," with comments about the Reagan administration.

First, on history. The entire history of arms control, which really comprises the record of multilateral, not bilateral, arms control, does not really lead one to an optimistic conclusion. Historians have cited an agreement in 456 B.C. between some Chinese warlords as the first arms control agreement. During the Middle Ages, there were attempts to outlaw the use of weapons such as the crossbow against Christians—not, however, against heathens—but no conclusive agreements were reached. Some writers cite the Rush-Bagot agreement of 1817 regarding the Great Lakes as a successful arms control agreement, which it was, but for as many sociological as for strategic reasons. In fact, the history of arms control in early or even mid-history is extremely sparse. Arms control represents a decidedly "modern" phenomenon.

Most commentators cite the 1899 and 1907 Hague conferences, initiated by the tsar of Russia, as the first true arms control forums. Their goals were admirable, and somewhat familiar. Nicholas II at the first of these conferences proposed both a quantitative and qualitative "freeze" on weapons, a renunciation of "first use," and a general commitment to disarmament, all of which sound familiar today. Some historians have noted that the tsar offered arms control measures because Russia was in a militarily weaker position than its European neighbors, a point that subsequent events were to prove all too true.

The interwar period witnessed many arms control forums. The most famous comprised the various naval arms control talks, which, at the time, were considered successful, but as we now know proved to be a dangerous illusion. The 1925 Geneva Conference did produce the Chemical Weapons Convention barring the use of these weapons. While some writers cite this agreement as preventing their use in World War II, most observers suggest that the reason Hitler did not use such weapons had more to do with U.S. military capacity and President Roosevelt's warning that the United States would not use such weapons "unless they are first used by our enemies."

Less familiar than the Geneva Convention is the League of Nations' World Disarmament Conference. This major event lasted from 1932 to 1935 but produced few results. Thus, despite the best and genuine efforts of the interwar generation, the world still found itself in another larger and more destructive conflict.

Since World War II, there have been approximately twenty arms control forums, in addition to the SALT, START, and INF talks. These vary from the 1958 Conference on Safeguards Against Surprise Attack through the 10-nation Disarmament Committee, which met briefly in 1960, to the more lasting 18-nation Committee on Disarmament (CCD) to the present 40-nation Committee on Disarmament. There also exist more regionally oriented conferences, such as the Mutual and Balanced Force Reductions (MBFR) talks, which have been meeting since 1973, and the new 35-member Conference on Disarmament in Europe (CDE), which will begin in 1984. All of these forums and talks, for various reasons, have failed to live up to their promise. Therefore, we should not be surprised at all by the problems faced in the SALT, START, and INF talks. Regrettably, there is little appreciation of this larger picture.

Just a few comments on Professor Van Cleave's reference to education and arms control fever. While I agree with his assessment, the education that is needed and the accompanying fever is not just domestic. I am not just talking about the "hot fall" of 1983, with its demonstrations against the Pershing II and cruise missile deployments in Europe. The issue is broader than that. In the various international forums, there is arms control fever, and the United States is finding itself increasingly isolated from ally and neutral alike. American positions are valid, but the communication and implementation of U.S. concerns are becoming an increasing problem that will require a massive education program.

Finally, I would like to comment briefly on the remarks made about the Reagan administration. This administration did not approach arms control with any illusions. Despite the tremendous pressure to do something immediately, the administration carefully reviewed the options before proceeding. Then, while negotiating, the administration started a major modernization program. It is building the B-1 bomber, the MX, Trident I, Pershing II, and ground-, sea-, and air-launched cruise missiles, and plans are ready for Trident II. This represents a most impressive modernization program, unlike any seen since the early 1960s. The Reagan administration, therefore, is under no illusions.

I have no basic disagreement with Dr. Gray's paper, but I wonder whether or not the debate might already be over. Rightly or wrongly, the United States is committed to both START and INF.

While the history of both START and INF, older talks such as SALT, and even the ones I mentioned previously, might make one pessimistic, I still think the search must go on. But, we must proceed in a realistic manner and not expect that an arms control agreement will solve all problems.

For example, the Treaty of Tlatelolco, which creates a nuclear-free zone in Latin America, is generally considered a successful agreement. However, it has not, nor will it be able to, solve the problems of Central America.

4

THE MBFR PROCESS AND ITS PROSPECTS

Richard F. Staar

The Mutual and Balanced Force Reductions (MBFR) negotiations commenced on 30 October 1973 between NATO and Warsaw Treaty Organization (WTO) representatives. Their agreed joint objective has been to reduce the level of opposing conventional ground and air forces in Central Europe.[1] The reduction area encompasses the area where most U.S. and Soviet troops are stationed—the territories of Belgium, the Netherlands, Luxembourg (Benelux), and the Federal Republic of Germany in the West; and Czechoslovakia, the German Democratic Republic, and Poland in the East. These negotiations almost by definition, therefore, represent a complicated undertaking. They involve the following members of two alliances:

From the West (12): the United States, Canada, West Germany, the United Kingdom, and the Benelux countries as direct participants with Denmark, Greece, Italy, Norway, and Turkey as indirect NATO participants.

From the East (7): the Soviet Union, Poland, East Germany, and Czechoslovakia as direct participants with Bulgaria, Hungary, and Romania as indirect WTO participants.

Probably for the first time in recorded history, representatives of opposing alliances have come to the negotiating table during peacetime to work on force reductions. As a result of the structure of these negotiations, there exists a direct and continuous participation in the MBFR by all members of the North Atlantic Alliance at Brussels. This is unlike the intermediate-range nuclear forces (INF) negotiations or the Strategic Arms Reduction Talks (START) in Geneva, which are essentially bilateral in nature, although they are carried out in full consultation with U.S. allies.

The focus in Vienna has been on the conventional factor in the East-West military equation. The goal is to establish a balance in conventional manpower forces between East and West in Central Europe at lower and equal levels. If accomplished, this (1) would serve in itself as a stabilizing factor by eliminating the large current disparity in favor of Warsaw Pact forces in Central Europe; (2) could lessen the possibility of sudden aggression, in the form of a surprise attack, by containing the use of these conventional forces; and (3) might, in turn, help ensure that a conflict will not become nuclear, since the latter most likely would evolve out of a conventional war.

The events of recent years, including the buildup of Soviet war-fighting capabilities in Europe, the Soviet invasion of Afghanistan, and developments in and around Poland, have underlined the need to improve NATO's conventional forces.[2] It has become axiomatic that arms control efforts cannot substitute for a strong Western defense. At the same time, however, Western leaders have reaffirmed their interest in seeking an agreement with the East that would contribute to increasing security through militarily significant and verifiable force reductions. Such a treaty should lead to stabilizing the political/military situation in Central Europe and, indeed, throughout all of Europe. It would also contribute to damping down the mounting spiral of defense expenditures.[3]

ALLIANCE MBFR GOALS IN CENTRAL EUROPE

Despite the protracted nature of the negotiations in Vienna, they have proved valuable (1) in encouraging an East-West dialogue on European security issues; (2) in bringing the positions of the two sides closer on issues and points of principle; and (3) in highlighting the size of the East's general purpose forces and the magnitude of Warsaw Pact ground force superiority, which remains the primary cause of instability in that area.

The object of these talks are the opposing ground troops, totaling approximately 2 million men, of the NATO alliance and the Warsaw Treaty Organization, which confront each other today along a north-south line, running from the Baltic Sea to the border of Austria. This represents the largest military confrontation of its kind in the world, certainly the largest in peacetime history and probably the most expensive peacetime force ever in terms of the magnitude of direct and indirect costs for manpower and combat equipment.

For the West, conventional forces backed by a credible nuclear deterrent have ensured alliance security since the early 1950s.[4] The burden has been heavy yet well worth the effort since it has preserved Western Europe's independence. As Thomas Jefferson once so wisely pointed out, "Eternal vigilance is the price of liberty."

At the same time, one of the primary goals of the Western alliance has been to alleviate the dangers inherent in the confrontation through negotiated mutual reductions of military forces in Central Europe to equal levels, together with a set of effective and interacting associated measures. Western proposals for the latter have been designed to ensure that an agreement will be respected and to provide each side with some assurance about the military activities of the other side. The Allies have long believed that such negotiations could contribute to stability, increase confidence, and reduce tensions in Europe. These have been the objectives since NATO foreign ministers, meeting at Reykjavik in June 1968, first invited the Warsaw Pact to participate in such negotiations.[5] They remain the Allies' goals today.

The primary Western objective has been elimination of the existing disparity between ground force personnel in Central Europe through establishment of parity, at lower levels of forces, and a ceiling on the ground force manpower of each side. This would require significant reductions by both sides.

For example, according to Western data, the Warsaw Pact armies in Central Europe have deployed 57 divisions totaling about 960,000 ground force personnel (including some 475,000 Soviet troops in that category). Direct NATO participants in MBFR have approximately 25 divisions in the reductions area, manned by about 790,000 ground force personnel (including some 200,000 U.S. troops in that category). "The numerical balance over the last 20 years has slowly but steadily moved in favour of the East."[6] The WTO disputes these figures, claiming to have only 800,000 general force troops in the area.

This substantial disparity in ground forces, with the Warsaw Treaty countries having over 170,000 more ground troops in Central Europe than does NATO,[7] represents a major destabilizing factor in the military equation. Its elimination could lessen the risk of armed conflict, including nuclear war, in Europe.

In addition to the problem of data, Western proposals have had to take into account the geographic fact that U.S. forces would be withdrawn more than 3,500 miles from Central Europe, whereas the Soviet Union would move its forces to the USSR, which is only 360 to 420 miles from the border between the Germanys. In addition, one-fourth of the Federal Republic's industrial production and almost one-third of its population are concentrated within sixty miles of this frontier.[8]

To meet these various requirements, NATO proposed only three weeks after commencement of the talks in 1973 that the two sides attempt to achieve parity in military manpower through reductions to a common ceiling at lower levels of forces. Specifically, the West suggested a common ceiling of about 700,000 ground forces, to be achieved in two successive phases. In the first phase, the USSR would withdraw one tank army consisting of five divisions, including 68,000 Soviet troops and 1,700 main battle tanks, in return for a U.S. withdrawal of 29,000 men. In the second phase, the ground forces of all direct participants would be reduced by the numbers required to reach the equal common collective ceilings on both sides.

NATO added to its basic proposal, on a onetime basis in December 1975, an offer to reduce certain U.S. nuclear armaments. It also agreed to include air force manpower in combined common collective ceilings of approximately 900,000 ground and air personnel on each side. In return for withdrawal of the Soviet tank army of five divisions, NATO would remove 54 aircraft (F-4s) capable of delivering nuclear ordnance, 36 Pershing I intermediate-range missiles, and 1,000 battlefield nuclear warheads.[9]

In yet another major effort to achieve agreement, the West in December 1979 proposed to simplify the negotiations by deferring some of the more contentious issues, including part of the overall data issue, and to focus instead on small, initial U.S. and Soviet reductions of 13,000 and 30,000 men, respectively. It also proposed a comprehensive set of associated measures.

The East has also made proposals. In the view of NATO, however, these only would have contractualized in the form of an international agreement the Warsaw Pact's numerical superiority in manpower and armaments. In other words, the Eastern proposals would not have led to the substantial reductions and attainment of common collective ceilings required to achieve parity in military manpower. The WTO has accepted the principle of common collective ceilings of 700,000 ground and 900,000 ground and air force manpower combined. However, it has made that acceptance contingent on Western agreement to Eastern data on its own forces in the reduction area—data that the West considers inaccurate and incomplete and whose use would make impossible the attainment of genuine parity.

THE NEW WESTERN MBFR APPROACH

From the beginning of 1981, one of the U.S. government's main preoccupations has been the unrelenting buildup of Soviet conventional as well as nuclear forces.[10] Soon after taking office, the Reagan administration began a thorough review of the United States' defense posture, including overall arms control policy, nuclear and conventional. The evaluation of the latter focused on MBFR.

After reviewing these issues, in particular the MBFR negotiations, President Reagan suggested a new approach to the NATO allies. Intensive consultations at Brussels resulted in a comprehensive Western proposal, announced by the president when he addressed the Bundestag on 9 June 1982. That initiative was given to the East in the form of a draft treaty one month later at Vienna.[11]

The approach reflected a NATO reassessment of the negotiations and, specifically, of the Western position. The alliance had concluded that the continuing and ever increasing importance of conventional arms control in Central Europe required that the MBFR talks be given new life. The Allies felt that the long-standing Western objective of parity at lower levels of East-West military manpower in Central Europe not only remained valid but should be pursued more urgently.

The proposal is fully consistent with President Reagan's call for substantial, militarily significant, and verifiable reductions to equal levels. It draws on nine years of negotiating experience in Vienna and takes into account the Eastern bloc's requirements.[12]

The draft treaty provides for one comprehensive agreement in which all direct participants on each side undertake a legally binding commitment to reach a combined common collective ceiling of approximately 900,000 ground and air force manpower, including a common collective ceiling of approximately 700,000 ground force manpower.

It proposes staged implementation of the reductions to these common collective ceilings. Each stage, however, must be fully verified. The Western package of associated (confidence-building and verification) measures, which had been offered in 1979, remains an integral part of the draft treaty. The first stage of reductions would, as in the West's 1979 proposals, be limited to U.S. and Soviet manpower reductions of 13,000 and 30,000, respectively.

Beginning manpower totals for both sides would be written into the agreement. Thus, the overall size of Eastern and Western reductions needed to reach the common collective ceiling would be established and specified in the treaty at the time of its signature.

The new approach differs in several respects from earlier efforts in the MBFR process. The major difference is that it would comprise a single agreement, instead of two separate ones. This effectively eliminates the so-called linkage issue from the negotiations since both sides would assume binding treaty commitments, affecting all participants, from the very moment of their signatures on the treaty, including all stages for implementation of reductions over the seven-year period envisaged by the NATO proposal.[13]

PROBLEMS AND PROSPECTS

With elimination of the linkage issue, there remain two major problems in the negotiations. These involve the questions of agreed data and associated measures. In order to resolve these two key issues, businesslike and constructive cooperation on the part of Eastern participants is needed.

The substantial difference between Eastern and Western figures on Warsaw Pact military manpower in the reduction area represents the central unresolved question in the Vienna talks.[14] The overall discrepancy amounts to about 170,000 men, not counting air forces. If the latter are included, the total comes to approximately 200,000 (see following table).

The data question, thus, is not simply a technical one. Without agreement on the size of the forces that are to be reduced and limited, a treaty would be unverifiable, unworkable, unenforceable, and, thus, politically unacceptable. NATO representatives have explained time and again that they cannot enter into any reduction and limitation agreement without first solving the data problem since data will form the basis for the Western requirement of establishing unambiguous objective standards of compliance with any treaty. Without prior agreed data, it would be impossible to ascertain precise residual manpower levels. Furthermore, there could be no clear understanding of what constitutes a violation.

Thus, the West has repeatedly called on the Warsaw Pact for a constructive discussion of the issue. The East has steadfastly insisted that its figures are correct and that any discrepancy results from errors in NATO estimates. It remains unwilling to discuss the matter.

The Eastern position on the issue of associated measures has created the second and only remaining major obstacle in the Vienna talks, even though the East agreed at the talks' inception in 1973 that such measures constituted an integral part of the subject matter for these negotiations.

In NATO's view, associated measures have the dual function of contributing to the verification of a reductions agreement and of enhancing confidence by offering assurances about the nonthreatening nature of the routine military activities conducted by both sides. For these reasons, the West, in its July 1982 draft treaty, included a carefully balanced package of measures designed to make a major and direct contribution to the agreed objectives of these negotiations.

The package consists of seven measures:

    1. Each side would notify the other in advance of out-of-garrison activity by one or more division-size formations. The sole exception is

DISPARITY BETWEEN FORCES OF EASTERN AND WESTERN
DIRECT PARTICIPANTS IN THE REDUCTION AREA
1 JANUARY 1981

	According to NATO Estimates		
	NATO estimate for WTO forces	Western figures for NATO forces	Disparity
Ground	960,000	790,000	170,000
Air	230,000	200,000	30,000
Total	1,190,000	990,000	200,000
	According to Warsaw Pact Data		
	Eastern figures for WTO forces	Western figures for NATO forces	Disparity
Ground	800,000	790,000	10,000
Air	180,000	200,000	−20,000
Total	980,000	990,000	−10,000

SOURCE: U.S. Delegation to MBFR talks in Vienna, Austria.

that alert activities need be announced only at the time when they begin.

2. The right to send observers to prenotified out-of-garrison activities would be guaranteed to both sides. The West has proposed that these two measures cover the territory of all European participants in the Vienna talks, not just the reduction area, and that they should include a considerable part of the western USSR.

3. Major military movements by ground forces of those direct participants whose home territory is outside the reduction area into the area of reductions would also be prenotified.

4. Each side would have the right to conduct an annual quota of inspections on the territory of the other side in the area of reductions.[15] Inspection teams would conduct their surveys from the ground or air, or both.

5. Permanent exit/entry points would be established to monitor military movements into and out of the area. Observers would be stationed at these points for the duration of the treaty, that is, for fifteen years.

6. Information would be exchanged on forces to be withdrawn,

and there would be continuing periodic exchanges of information on personnel strength and organization of forces in the reduction area.

　7.　Interference with national technical means of verification, meaning photography from reconnaissance satellites, would be prohibited.

In addition, the West indicated that participants should consider establishment of a consultative mechanism to oversee implementation of the provisions in the agreement. If the U.S.-Soviet Standing Consultative Commission, established in 1972 for monitoring adherence to SALT I, is a model, it would meet only twice a year. The USSR recently turned down a U.S. request for a special session.[16]

The East's views are close to those of the West on certain elements of the package. There is a basic disagreement, however, on some fundamental aspects of the West's associated measures proposal. These include (1) the geographic extension of the first two measures (that is, beyond the reduction area and into the European part of the USSR), which involve prenotification of out-of-garrison activities by one or more division-size units and the presence of observers at these prenotified activities; (2) the existence of exit/entry points for the duration of the treaty; and (3) on-site inspection.

The need for what are known as cooperative means of verification has been repeatedly emphasized to the Soviet Union at the highest levels. The late President Brezhnev indicated in an interview that "if confidence is reciprocally achieved, then also other forms of verification can be developed."[17] However, he thought that national technical means were sufficient. No concrete evidence of a change in the Soviet attitude on this question had occurred by the end of 1983.[18]

PROSPECTS

Notwithstanding present fundamental disagreements between the two sides on the key issues of data and associated measures, the Vienna forum has proved its value as an important and unique alliance-to-alliance negotiation on sensitive and complicated multilateral military security questions. These talks also are the only current ones dealing with possible arms control arrangements for conventional forces. Because of this, it is not unreasonable to expect that the negotiations will continue, drawing on the reservoir of experience already gained. Moreover, the East has accepted in principle some basic Western concepts and included them with certain variations in its own proposals.

First, in agreeing to the principle of parity, the East moved away from its original position of seeking equal reductions of 17 percent by the two sides. However, the importance of this move is diminished by the East's insistence that, according to its own data, rough parity in military manpower already exists in Central Europe.

Second, the WTO has agreed in principle to the concept of collectivity—a basic Western requirement—which in substance means that each alliance would determine independently the size of individual national components that make up its overall force levels under the ceiling. Thus, there would be no national subceilings specified for individual direct participants, apart from the United States and the Soviet Union. The East has qualified its acceptance with the demand that reduction allocations by NATO states be "approximately proportional" to the size of their forces in the reduction area and that no one direct participant can account for more than 50 percent of its alliance's forces in the reduction area. These conditions obviously would place constraints on full collectivity. For that reason, the West has rejected them.

Third, although the new draft treaty proposed by the East on 23 June 1983 gave no details concerning on-site inspection, it did list it among the associated measures. The document concentrates on monitoring final ceilings and not reductions. Several of its proposed associated measures are voluntary (perhaps even on-site inspection) rather than mandatory.[19]

Needless to say, the ultimate achievement of an agreement in Vienna depends heavily on the East. The Western draft treaty of July 1982 makes it clear that Warsaw Pact countries must reduce their forces significantly if the fundamental goal of parity is to be achieved. How have Eastern participants responded to that NATO initiative?

In brief, while the East at first acknowledged that the Western draft had been a "step in the right direction" because it solved the so-called linkage issue, its overall reaction has been negative. Warsaw Pact representatives have—

1. continued to praise the virtues of their own draft of 18 February 1982;[20]
2. argued that their "official" data on Eastern forces in the reduction area, submitted most recently in 1980, are sufficient for an agreement;
3. maintained that the Western package of associated measures is too extensive and too intrusive;
4. criticized the West for failing to address such issues as armaments reductions and separate air force ceilings.

On the basis of the East's reaction to the NATO draft treaty over almost a full year, there is little cause for optimism about the immediate future of the Vienna talks. In the end, Warsaw Pact representatives rejected the Western proposal as a basis for an agreement,[21] rather than agreeing that it could be accepted for negotiating purposes.

It should seem obvious that a verifiable agreement reducing and limiting the size of conventional forces in Central Europe would be to the security advantages of both sides. The East must recognize, just as the West does, that the massive military confrontation there is dangerous. Both East and West have a vital interest in lowering tensions and enhancing stability in that critical region of the world. After ten long years of negotiating in Vienna, one would think that the new Kremlin leaders might understand this. On the other hand, perhaps the talks have already deteriorated into a "most bizarre form of ritual."[22]

NOTES

1. Recent monographs about MBFR include William B. Prendergast, *Mutual and Balanced Force Reduction: Issues and Prospects* (Washington, D.C.: American Enterprise Institute, 1978); Jeffrey Record, *Force Reductions in Europe: Starting Over* (Cambridge, Mass.: Institute for Foreign Policy Analysis, 1980); and, the most comprehensive one to date, John G. Keliher, *The Negotiations on Mutual and Balanced Force Reductions: The Search for Arms Control in Central Europe* (New York: Pergamon Press, 1980).

2. General Bernard W. Rogers, USA [Supreme Allied Commander Europe], "The Atlantic Alliance: Prescriptions for a Difficult Decade," *Foreign Affairs* 60 (1981–82): 1145–156. See also American Academy of Arts and Sciences, *Strengthening Conventional Deterrence in Europe* (Cambridge, Mass.: European Security Study, 1983), especially pp. 33–35.

3. For amounts spent during the 1970s, see U.S. Arms Control and Disarmament Agency, *World Military Expenditures and Arms Transfers, 1971–1980*, Publication 115 (Washington, D.C., March 1983); foreword by Dr. James L. George, at that time acting director of the agency.

4. U.S. Department of State, *Security and Arms Control: The Search for a More Stable Peace* (Washington, D.C., June 1983); introduction by Secretary of State George P. Shultz.

5. In December 1967, the Harmel report on "The Future Tasks of the Alliance" already had expressed NATO readiness for dialogue and détente with the East (see "Report of the Council," *Texts of Final Communiqués, 1949–1974* [Brussels: NATO Information Service, n.d.], pp. 198–202).

6. International Institute for Strategic Studies, *The Military Balance, 1983–1984* (London, 1983), p. 137.

7. U.S. Department of State, "Arms Control: MBFR Talks," *Gist* (Washington, D.C.), March 1983, p. 2. According to the West German disarmament expert Jürgen Todenhöfer, since 1980 the USSR has increased its combat troops in the reduction area by 42,000 men. He describes the reported withdrawal of one Soviet division from East Germany in 1980 as a "gigantic diversion." (*Bild* [Hamburg], 3 September 1983.)

8. U.S. Delegation to MBFR, "Mutual and Balanced Force Reductions" (Vienna, Austria, June 1983), p. 3; mimeographed and unclassified report.

9. Department of State, *Security and Arms Control*, p. 40.

10. The overall disparity in weapons systems had increased from 1.5:1 (1965) to 4.4:1 (1980) (according to Phillip A. Karber, "Competition in Conventional Forces Deployed in Central Europe," in Uwe Nerlich, ed., *The Soviet Asset: Military Power in Competition over Europe* [Cambridge, Mass.: Ballinger, 1983], p. 81).

11. The NATO draft treaty is summarized in U.S. Congress, House of Representatives, Committee on Foreign Affairs, Subcommittee on International Security and Scientific Affairs, *East-West Troop Reductions in Europe: Is Agreement Possible?* (Washington, D.C., April 1983), appendix A, pp. 21–25. See also James L. George, "The New MBFR Treaty Proposal: An American Perspective," *NATO Review*, no. 5 (1982): 8–11.

12. See U.S. Delegation to MBFR, "Mutual and Balanced Force Reductions," pp. 7–8.

13. Reinhard Mutz, "Wende in Wien?" *Europa Archiv* 38, no. 10 (25 May 1983): 315–22. The "linkage" issue refers to Soviet concerns that an initial treaty dealing only with cuts in U.S. and Soviet forces might not be followed by reductions on the part of the other NATO allies.

14. The only achievement had been reallocation of some 20,000 to 30,000 Soviet troops from ground to air defense units (Lothar Ruehl, "MBFR: Lessons and Problems," *Adelphi Papers*, no. 176 [Summer 1982]: 29).

15. According to testimony in February 1983 before the Senate Foreign Relations Committee by Ambassador-designate Morton Abramowitz, the West will suggest a specific number of annual inspections.

16. *Washington Post*, 4 September 1983.

17. *Der Spiegel*, 2 November 1981, p. 58.

18. The East on 23 June 1983 submitted a draft agreement in Vienna. It offers the "opportunity to carry out on-the-spot checks, provided certain conditions are observed" (Interview with the head of the Soviet delegation to MBFR in *Volksstimme* [Vienna], 2 July 1983).

19. U.S. Delegation to MBFR, "Mutual and Balanced Force Reductions," p. 9.

20. This proposal is summarized in appendix A of U.S. Congress, *East-West Troop Reductions in Europe*, pp. 26–27. It offered nothing new, representing merely a compilation of known Eastern positions. See also "Warsaw Pact Proposes New Draft Treaty in Vienna Force Reduction Talks," *Policy Alert*, 25 February 1982, published by the Congressional Research Service at the Library of Congress.

21. See reply by Eastern spokesmen to question at the end-of-round press conference at the Vienna Hofburg (*Transcript*, 21 July 1983, pp. 22–23, prepared by the U.S. Delegation to MBFR).

22. Ken Scott, "MBFR—Western Initiatives Seek to End Deadlock," *NATO Review* 30, no. 4 (1982): 14–19, uses this play on words, albeit not in the same context.

5

STRUCTURAL PROBLEMS IN NEGOTIATIONS: A VIEW FROM EUROPE

Werner Kaltefleiter

Disarmament is a vision arising from the desire for peace, to be implemented by renouncing the use of military force in the settlement of conflicts. This vision has existed as long as war itself and has grown more intense as civilian casualties due to military action have risen. With the development of nuclear weapons and the subsequent fear of an apocalyptic destruction of entire societies and possibly human life itself, the drive for disarmament has increased, as have differences in priorities for arms control. The basic concept is simple: if potential adversaries possess no weapons, war becomes highly improbable. Disarmament thus represents an instrument for assuring peace. "Create peace without weapons" is the popular slogan.

DISARMAMENT AS SYMPTOMATIC THERAPY

In the political arena, disarmament is frequently confused with arms control. Originally disarmament meant the reduction or, in the extreme case, the total elimination of weapons or weapons systems. Arms control, however, is more comprehensive; it incorporates not only quantitative arms reductions but also elements of international law for the prevention of armed conflict. The U.S. concept of arms control goes even further. It is premised on a comprehensive limitation of weapons systems in recognition of mutual security interests.[1]

Actually, disarmament and arms control talks have never brought disarmament but only quantitative limits for particular weapons. These limits were tied to specific conditions, such as the verification of such agreements. These provisions belong more to the theoretical aspects of arms control. In this respect, both concepts belong to and reflect two different levels of thought. The political sphere speaks of disarmament; diplomatic circles more of arms control. As a result, West German chancellor Helmut Kohl proposed a slogan of his own: "Create peace with fewer arms."

The demands for disarmament and arms control arise from the assumption that the existing international conflict cannot be resolved and could lead to war. Disarmament is, therefore, therapy for symptoms:[2] if one does not believe in the possibility of resolving the conflict itself, one at least attempts to eliminate or limit the means by which it could be decided. This basic problem of all arms negotiations has two implications:

> 1. The negotiators mistrust one another. In contrast to private dealings where both parties proceed on the assumption that the other acts in good faith, arms control negotiators cannot do the same since there obviously is an insolvable conflict between them. This explains why the question of verification remains of such importance.
> 2. While parties in a civil law dispute can count on court action if one side breaches a contract, there is no analogous institution in the international arena. Just as the existence of such legal institutions creates an atmosphere of trust, their lack perpetuates mistrust. Deception can become a question of life or death for a state.[3]

The existence of conflict between arms reduction negotiators raises the question of identification or at least compatibility of their goals. An interesting parallel exists here. An often formulated thesis in the Western democratic societies is, to quote Immanuel Kant, that eternal peace is certain when all states become republics (or in the language of our times, democracies).[4] The hypothesis that democratic structures seem to represent the fundamental condition for peace, which remains the basic precondition for disarmament, is based on the idea that domestic decisionmaking processes will not lead to a consensus in favor of military action, whatever the nature of conflict, between two democracies. A "crusade" against a morally reprehensible adversary would be an exception. There are, of course, no contemporary examples of military action between fully developed democracies, but the basis in time for this observation is limited in comparison with the full span of human history.

The corresponding thought in Marxism-Leninism is the assumption that peace—that is, the absence of conflict that could lead to military intervention—as the prerequisite for total disarmament can be achieved only under socialism. Lenin said: "Disarmament is the ideal of socialism. There will be no wars in socialist society; consequently, disarmament will be achieved."[5] Obviously, this is based on a different concept of peace—one that sanctions the use of force against the populace of a socialist society. The battle against counterrevolutionaries in order to defend socialist achievements is an accepted component of the "socialist" family of nations. Dictatorship always means war against the people. Beyond these theoretical considerations, military conflicts between the Soviet Union and the People's Republic of China, the latter and Vietnam, and between Vietnam and Cambodia refute the thesis of peace among the communist-ruled family of nations. Dictatorships lack the domestic decisionmaking process in which a majority of the population, those affected by the consequences of war, have to support—at least by the rule of anticipated reactions—a commitment to military adventurism.

It follows that the chances of successful arms control or disarmament are necessarily influenced by the state of conflict in the world. One result of World War II is that international relations are now dominated by a systemic conflict between pluralistic democracies and communist dictatorships.[6] Systemic conflict means (1) that the political, social, and economic orders of each side are hermetically sealed against those of the other side; (2) that these systems are incompatible as a whole or in part; and (3) that at least one side is attempting to extend its order over the other. At the rhetorical level, the third condition holds true for both major sides in the present conflict: the United States and the Soviet Union. Historically, only the USSR has been successful in expanding its system since systemic conflict came to characterize the international system—that is, since the late 1940s. Beyond this, conflicts along the periphery—in the Third World—are forced into the dichotomy of this conflict as soon as they gain a certain momentum. The systemic conflict, therefore, dominates the international scene.

This situation, along with the existence of nuclear weapons, forms the framework for arms control and disarmament negotiations. Despite the numerous disarmament movements in the West generated by the existence of nuclear weapons, the existence of the systemic conflict increases the probability of military action as a means of solving the conflict. This creates further mistrust and explains the importance attached to verification. The arms control talks of the 1950s all broke down because of disagreements over verification.[7] The West believed that effective control could be secured only through on-site inspection, but the Soviet Union refused to comply on the grounds that it would be used for espionage. Arms control negotiations began to move only when national technical means of verification (which obviate the need for on-site inspection) had been developed. The first achievement of this new era was the Limited Test Ban Treaty of 1963. This agreement included elements that would characterize future ones.

EXPERIENCES WITH ARMS CONTROL NEGOTIATIONS

The Test Ban Treaty prohibited atmospheric tests but allowed underground tests. Verification was possible through national technical means and could also be done internationally. The official reason advanced for the agreement was the danger of atmospheric contamination. The essential motivation of the two signatories—the United States and the Soviet Union—was a mutual interest in preventing other countries from becoming nuclear powers. It seemed unlikely they could do so without atmospheric testing. Consequently neither the People's Republic of China nor France signed the treaty, and each continued to develop its own nuclear warheads. It was this mutual interest in nonproliferation that brought about the Test Ban Treaty so shortly after the Cuban missile crisis, which had adversely affected the relationship between the two superpowers. It may remain unknown to what extent this mutual interest or the mobilization of public opinion against the danger of contamination influenced the United States to sign the treaty. One can assume that the Soviet Union was interested in nonproliferation as a means of restraining potential adversaries and for propaganda purposes.

No less important a reason for Soviet interest was a certain asymmetry that characterized this treaty. Shortly before signing it, the Soviet Union had carried out a series of tests with extremely large nuclear warheads. This gave the USSR an obvious lead in such technology over the United States, which had specialized in miniaturization and development of small nuclear warheads. The ban on atmospheric but not underground testing prevented the United States from acquiring large-warhead technology, yet gave the Soviet Union the opportunity to pursue development of small warheads. This asymmetry has remained unimportant, as far as we can tell, since the essential technological developments have come in the area of miniaturization, which also made possible the development of the neutron bomb. More important is the fact that the ban on atmospheric testing denies the United States the opportunity to gain detailed information on the electromagnetic pulse (EMP), which the USSR may have acquired through testing before the treaty was signed.[8] Similar asymmetry has characterized later agreements.

To recapitulate, three elements in the Test Ban Treaty affected the form of subsequent treaties:

1. For the Soviet Union, there must exist solid interests (for example, in nonproliferation for reasons of power politics) because moral and humanitarian arguments (such as contamination of the atmosphere) are of rhetorical interest only.

2. The treaty must be verifiable without on-site inspection.

3. While seemingly equal and balanced, an agreement must contain an advantage for the USSR.

These features can also be found in the 1968 Non-proliferation Treaty. This treaty prohibits nuclear states from transferring nuclear weapons to non-nuclear states. The latter, in turn, commit themselves not to obtain access or control over such weapons. The reason given for the treaty was the assumption that the more states with such weapons, the larger the actual danger of a nuclear exchange. This corresponds with the superpowers' interest in nonproliferation. Such an hypothesis, however, is doubtful since the very existence of nuclear weapons remains a deterrent against any kind of military action.[9] This, of course, is valid only as long as executive powers are in the hands of responsible governments. These conditions have not always been applicable to the Third World in recent years.

This treaty solved the problem of verification in several ways. It left uncontrolled the commitment by nuclear powers not to transfer nuclear weapons technology because a certain amount of self-interest could be assumed. For all other states, the use of atomic energy for peaceful purposes had to be permitted. With the non-nuclear powers, the problem of controlling the use of radioactive materials was assumed by the International Atomic Energy Agency in Vienna and by Euratom for the European Community. This, of course, involves on-site inspection, but it does not apply to the Soviet Union.

This treaty also shows a definite asymmetry. Those affected by renunciation of nuclear weapons were almost exclusively allies of the United States or countries in the Third World that could more likely be found on the side of the United States—the nuclear threshold countries. The countries in these categories had achieved a level of technology sufficient to develop nuclear weapons. At that time, they included the Federal Republic of Germany, Canada, Australia, New Zealand, Switzerland, Sweden, Italy, Japan, Israel, South Africa, Brazil, and Argentina (other states later became nuclear threshold countries, but of these only India is known to have exploded a nuclear device). One could also count East Germany and Czechoslovakia among the threshold countries. The Soviet Union, however, did not need a nonproliferation treaty to prevent them from developing nuclear weapons. The treaty may have been useful to the USSR because it officially meant formal restrictions on both East and West.

This asymmetry appears most clearly in the case of the Federal Republic of Germany. In negotiating the 1954 German Treaty, Chancellor Konrad Adenauer renounced the use, manufacture, and possession of atomic, biological, and chemical (ABC) weapons. As U.S. secretary of state John Foster Dulles commented subsequently, it involved a *rebus sic stantibus* commitment in terms of international law.[10] In reality, this meant that the allies of the Federal Republic could release it from these commitments whenever they felt it necessary. With ratification of the Non-proliferation Treaty, this commitment to the allies also became one to the political adversary—the Soviet Union. Thus, the USSR won *de facto* the right to participate in one of the most central decisions of the Western alliance. Since then, a decision to arm a non-nuclear member of the alliance with nuclear weapons is no longer an internal decision, but presupposes abrogation of the treaty.

No less important for current practical politics and certainly just as problematic is the lack of any "European option"; that is, the treaty does not permit an entire alliance to equip itself with such weapons if one of its members happens to be a nuclear power. According to former U.S. Secretary of State Dean Rusk, there must be an active, comprehensive joint foreign and defense policy within the alliance before such a nuclear option could be considered.[11] This would mean that the alliance would have to become a confederation, if not a federal state, in order to justify such a nuclear option under the present treaty. This definitely moves beyond the realistic possibilities of European politics. Therefore, the Non-proliferation Treaty blocks the possibility of a new distribution of nuclear responsibility within the alliance whereby Europe would become an equally responsible and equally committed partner of the United States.

Strong political interests of the Soviet Union, firmly held beliefs in the West (for example, reduced probability of nuclear war), no verification conditions applicable to the USSR, and a significant advantage for the latter also characterize this treaty.

The next important conventions were the Interim Agreement on Limitation of Strategic Offensive Arms and the Anti-Ballistic Missile (ABM) Treaty, both of which were part of the 1972 SALT I package. Here again are these same three major elements, although the total is considerably more complex, especially since the Soviet definition of interests seems to have changed more than once during the negotiations. Essentially the USSR achieved numerical parity, if not superiority, in strategic nuclear weapons vis-à-vis the United States.

The Interim Agreement allowed the Soviet Union 2,347 and the United States only 1,710 strategic systems. The Soviet total included 1,607 land-based launchers (ICBMs or intercontinental ballistic missiles), of which up to 300 could be so-called heavy systems (ICBMs), and 740 missiles on submarines (SLBMs or sea-launched ballistic missiles). The number of SLBMs could be increased to 950, as long as the upper limit of 1,607 was not exceeded and SLBMs were not replaced by ICBMs. The United States could have 1,054 land-based systems and 656 (which could increase to 710) sea-based systems. There were no limitations on the number of strategic airplanes, maximum throw-weight, yield, or number of warheads. Further-more, each country was granted two defensive ABM systems, one of which was to be located around the capital. The Interim Agreement for the Limitation of Strategic Weapons ended five years later, in 1977; the ABM Treaty is of unlimited duration, although it may be abrogated after six months' notice if national security interests are at stake.

In the West, these agreements were justified with the argument that arms control measures in the era of détente had a stabilizing effect.[12] In addition, the United States hoped that concessions would make the Soviet Union willing to restrain North Vietnam, allowing for an honorable peace. This obviously was not attained. The declaration of principles in which the Soviet Union was recognized as an equal superpower had the same objective. Apart from this, the United States hoped that the agreement would help end the arms race and reduce military expenditures. Although some supposed that the USSR had corresponding interests,[13] they could not be detected. Further developments suggest that from the beginning the Soviets saw these talks as an instrument for changing the balance of power in their favor.

Verification was possible through national technical means, that is, by satellites. The number of launchers could be counted, which, at the time, equaled the number of missiles and warheads. Therefore, on-site inspections were unnecessary.

Again the imbalance of the agreement is of importance. It consisted, first of all, of the agreed numerical superiority for Soviet systems. This was conceded in view of the British and French systems, although there were only 162 of them, and because of the U.S. technological lead, chiefly in multiple independently targetable re-entry vehicle (MIRV) technology. The U.S. system also was more accurate. To the surprise of many Western observers, the Soviets quickly erased both advantages. In addition, the USSR already possessed a much higher throw-weight capability and could fire heavy missiles. This was to become a threat to the U.S. Minuteman land-based systems.[14]

The agreement also permitted an obvious asymmetry in technological options. At the time of SALT I, the United States had only small intercontinental missiles, with a highly developed accuracy almost at the limit of what was then technologically possible. The United States, however, did require heavier systems with higher throw-weight. Their development was not only costly, but was also hindered by the agreement, which allowed an enlargement of launchers only by 10 to 15 percent. The Soviets had to gain ground only in the area of accuracy, which was not difficult to accomplish and not hindered by the agreement. Therefore, SALT I gave the USSR an easy growth option, but created a problem for the United States.

Remarkable also is the asymmetry within the ABM Treaty, although at the time the system had not become fully effective due to technical difficulties. Protecting the capital, in the Soviet case, would not only protect Moscow but also an area in which some 300 land-based ICBMs are deployed. In the United States, the geographic coverage of such a system would include parts of the Atlantic Ocean. Apart from that, American public opinion would not agree to protecting the capital without protecting other major population centers. In 1974, a protocol added to the agreement reduced each side to one such system. Eventually, the United States dismantled its only ABM system (in North Dakota), while the Soviets reduced the number of launchers from 64 to 32 in the area around Moscow due to technical difficulties.[15] In 1982, they began to rebuild it to maximum strength.

Three technological changes of significance have taken place in regard to SALT II and later the intermediate-range nuclear forces (INF) negotiations and Strategic Arms Reduction Talks (START):

1. The installation of MIRVed missiles by both sides makes verification more difficult. The real threat depends not on the number of missiles but rather on the type of armaments, either a few large warheads or many small ones. This cannot be inspected through satellite photography. The SALT II agreement, which counted each missile as having the maximum number of warheads it had been tested with, solved the problem only in part. For example, the U.S. Minuteman III is counted as having seven warheads but carries only three. More important, for a first-strike capability, it is necessary to arm a missile with only a few warheads in order to knock out hardened silos. The Soviet SS-18 and SS-19 can accomplish this.[16]

2. With the development of a Soviet cold-launch capability, it has become impossible to verify the number of missiles by satellite because silos have gained a reload capacity and the number of launchers no longer coincides with the number of missiles.[17] Both this development and the installation of MIRVed missiles mean an end to effective satellite verification. This is the main reason why the U.S. Senate refused to ratify SALT II, not the Soviet invasion of Afghanistan.

3. By definition the SALT agreements concerned themselves exclusively with strategic—that is, intercontinental—systems. While SALT I was in effect, the Soviet Union developed and deployed a new system—the SS-20—which is based on the older SS-16, an ICBM that the USSR had renounced in SALT I. It is, for the moment, unimportant whether the Soviets had conceived of Eurostrategic missiles from the beginning or only after giving up the SS-16. The essential point is that the SS-20, with its range, mobility, and three warheads, is the optimal control weapon for the Eurasian landmass. There is no equivalent being planned or developed in the West. Second, the SS-20 constitutes

a reserve for the Soviet Union that was not counted in SALT. With relatively simple technology, the SS-20 could be converted into an SS-16 missile.

These technological advances and the new Soviet options were accompanied by the Carter administration's belief that progress in the field of arms control could be accomplished through unilateral renunciation.[18] The hope was for a favorable reaction from the Soviets to these signs of good will. Thus, production of the new strategic B-1 bomber and of the neutron bomb stopped. No equivalent response came from the Soviet side.

In 1979, two years after the end of the Interim Agreement, SALT II was signed. Provisions included limitation of the number of strategic systems to 2,400 for each side and the obligation to reduce these to 2,250 by the end of 1981. The limits for multiple warhead systems were 820 for land-based missiles and 1,200 for land- and sea-based systems combined. The number of bombers with cruise missiles as well as multiple land- and sea-based systems could not exceed 1,320 altogether. The so-called heavy missiles were to be frozen at their current level: 308 for the USSR and none for the United States. Multiple warheads were limited to the number tested, that is, 10 for land-based and 14 for sea-based systems. The freeze on heavy land-based missiles led the Soviet Union to develop further heavy sea-launched missiles (the SS-N-18) and to deploy them.

Apart from the unsolved verification problem, the asymmetry of SALT II is clear.[19] The USSR kept the SS-18, which has a first-strike capability against U.S. Minuteman land-based missiles; the United States had no equivalent. The Soviet Union could deploy the SS-19, which also has a hard-target kill capability, but it was not counted as a heavy missile. The new Soviet Backfire bomber was not mentioned in the treaty, although with mid-air refueling its strategic characteristics are obvious. Only a letter from Brezhnev promises that the plane will not be built in its intercontinental variant. Nor did the treaty consider Eurostrategic weapons (the SS-20s). Besides this, it limited U.S. technology in the form of the new cruise missile in several ways: a 600-kilometer range, air launch only, and a prohibition on sharing this new weapon with the NATO allies until the end of 1981.

Along with these central agreements, there remained several questions that either could not be reconciled or were of minor importance.[20] The most important among these are the Mutual and Balanced Force Reductions (MBFR) talks, started in 1973 at Vienna, to reduce the number of conventional land and air forces in Central Europe. The main problem involves reaching an agreement on the number of Soviet bloc forces in Eastern Europe. The Western estimate of Warsaw Pact soldiers is 170,000 higher than the Soviets'. In addition, the problem of verification arises again, not to mention the asymmetry that follows from the geographic proximity of the USSR, which would allow it to resupply the Warsaw Pact with soldiers easily. This means that an agreement can be reached only if the West concedes an advantage to the East.

NEGOTIATIONS BETWEEN OPEN AND CLOSED POLITICAL SYSTEMS

The political side effects of these agreements were just as important as the details of the individual treaties. The United States and its European allies considered the SALT agreements a success in curbing re-armament. Their military expenditures declined steadily during the 1970s, as did funds for research and development, especially in the area of missile defense systems. Critics, therefore, have reformulated the abbreviation SALT to read "Stop American Lead in Technology." This leaves open the question to what extent the USSR has circumvented the treaties directly and indirectly and in so doing undermined their unspecified formulations. This question touches many technical problems.[21]

Development proceeded differently in the Soviet Union. Military expenditures steadily increased, and the weapons arsenal was modernized. During these years of arms control talks, the USSR transformed itself from a traditional land power to a globally operating sea power. Finally, it developed considerable defense systems—for example, air defense—some of which are definitely effective against slow-moving cruise missiles and also may include some ABM capability. Extensive civil defense measures also change the relative effectiveness of any conceivable U.S. threat. The United States, on the other hand, neither developed an effective air defense nor took any civil defense measures.[22]

More important even than these military tendencies is the dynamic these arms control talks developed in the Western world. The talks led to a general reduction in the perception of the Soviet threat and a reduction, therefore, in the political will for defense.[23] Here is a fundamental problem of democratic systems: one cannot be in constant and multiple negotiations with a country that governments tell their publics represents a danger to their existence and, at the same time, shake the hands of its representatives and smile for television. When Henry Kissinger recommended in 1974 a network of links with the Soviet Union too expensive to be destroyed by either side,[24] he overlooked the dynamics of democracy. For example, even if the damage to the Soviets were far greater after a break in economic ties than it would be for a Western country, they probably could survive better domestically: a democratic system has a lower tolerance level, at least over the short term.

Arms control talks, as part of the diverse relations within the concept of détente, have proved a danger to Western security policies. They have not created more security but rather endangered it, since *de facto* they have brought about a change in the power potential in favor of the Soviet Union.

Such problems, resulting from the domestic dynamics of democratic systems, have increased through the asymmetry created by relations between open and closed systems. The USSR has many means for influencing public opinion in democracies, thereby placing democratic governments under more pressure. Closed systems are immune to such tactics. There is an almost endless chain of examples, from Hitler to Stalin and Andropov, showing how leaders of closed systems exploit this asymmetry to their advantage in negotiating with open systems.[25]

This dilemma is aggravated by the utilization of these talks by democratic governments to further their own domestic influence. This was obvious with Nixon in 1972 and Carter in 1979 with the SALT agreements. It should not come as a surprise under such conditions that treaties can only end with a certain advantage for the USSR. Beyond this, there are many examples of how such talks are used to help overcome domestic problems. Because in 1979 the West did not have the domestic strength for rearmament, it tied that process to offers for negotiation. Preliminaries to the unsuccessful MBFR talks commenced in 1971 to counter growing sentiment in the Senate for withdrawal of U.S. troops from Europe (the Mansfield amendment). The agreement to produce the MX was wrested from Congress in 1983 by Ronald Reagan with the promise to be "flexible" in arms control negotiations. Due to such domestic decisionmaking processes, disarmament talks are evaluated on the basis of whether results of any kind can be achieved instead of on the security needs of the United States and its allies. Disarmament negotiations then become perverted into an end in themselves and no longer serve national security purposes.

These experiences lead to the basic conclusion that arms control talks between open and closed societies, within the context of a systemic conflict, are incompatible with security requirements. Negotiations under these conditions are no longer a function of national security and represent a serious threat to such policies.

To escape this resulting dilemma, it seems that democracies can be liberated only through shock. The Soviet arms buildup has not been enough. In fact, it only increased the pressure for arms control negotiations. Despite the continuous buildup of SS-20 missiles—in addition to the SS-21, -22, and -23, which are of equal importance for the European theater but are not discussed in public—NATO reached the dual-track decision only in December 1979. This was the move to station 572 medium-range U.S. missiles (108 Pershing IIs and 464 ground-launched cruise missiles) after a period of four years, if negotiations proved unsuccessful. What *successful* meant was never defined. From the beginning, resistance to this decision (especially in the Federal Republic, Denmark, and Holland) showed just how far the erosion in the perception of the Soviet threat had extended.

The invasion of Afghanistan fundamentally changed the internal situation in the United States. The previous hostage crisis in Teheran and the critical discussion of SALT II obviously influenced events. Afghanistan, however, was a shock that changed domestic opinion, at least for the moment. Americans again saw the Soviet Union as a threat. Already under President Carter, a long-term rebuilding of the military was planned. The election of Ronald Reagan to the presidency in 1980 symbolized this change of opinion.[26]

In Europe, though, neither the events in Afghanistan nor those in Poland had such an effect. Europeans still believed in the priority of arms control and détente over defense buildup. This led to pressure on the Reagan administration and to differences of opinion in the alliance.[27]

The new U.S. administration had wanted to resume arms control negotiations only after redressing the balance of power. It assumed that the Soviets would not trade away existing systems for planned Western ones. Also, the continuing resistance in Europe to any rearmament, gave the USSR hope of stopping Western rearmament without any important concession on its part. This was also true for the planned reopening of the SALT negotiations. Here again, the new U.S. administration planned to re-establish the balance of power before expecting success in the negotiations.

Under pressure from the European allies, and especially to help the former Social Democratic–Free Democrat (SPD-FDP) coalition in Bonn with its problems with the peace movement and its SPD followers, the United States commenced the INF negotiations at Geneva in November 1981 and offered the "zero option" plan of destroying all intermediate-range systems.[28] The main reasoning behind this plan was the problem of verification. In light of the SS-20's mobility, its reload capability, and its multiple warheads, any other agreement would not be verifiable. Only on-site inspection, which was not acceptable to the Soviet Union, could solve the problem. We should not overlook, though, that the zero option would also have created disadvantages for the Western alliance. The Pershing II and cruise missiles are not conceived as a counter to the SS-20 since their range extends only up to 2,250 kilometers. They were thought of as a credible forward defense. The function of such systems would be to destroy communication centers, important transport intersections, and other military targets in case of a conflict and thus hinder the Warsaw Pact from resupplying its front from the second echelon, which is a precondition for successful forward defense.[29]

Although the Americans accepted the negotiating concept of the zero option under pressure from the Europeans, despite its disadvantages, they were soon accused of inflexibility. This came mostly from those who opposed any rearmament in the first place and now realized that the Soviets would not accept the zero option. Brezhnev's suggestion that the number of SS-20s be reduced to the number of British and French systems was greeted by some with enthusiasm despite the additional disadvantages. The British and French systems consist of second-strike missiles and cannot take on the function of an SS-20, a Pershing II, or a cruise missile. In any event, the Soviets already have systems beyond the SS-20 that fulfill duties similar to those of the British and French systems. Apart from these details, it is apparent that the public discussion was driven by emotional requirements for a denial of rearmament and not by clear security calculations.

Shortly thereafter, the START negotiations began. The United States proposed a reduction of strategic systems, assured verification, and a limitation on the actual threat, that is, the number and yield of warheads. The result of these negotiations cannot as yet be predicted. The verification problem, in view of new technology, is almost impossible to solve. In regard to the future, it is important to note that the original shock over Afghanistan is giving way to increased opposition to military spending, in part caused by budget deficits resulting from difficult economic conditions. The freeze movement, which wishes to maintain the present levels of arms—despite the Soviet advantage—is another indication of the declining perception of the Soviet threat. The episcopal letter of Catholic bishops in the United States, which questions the nuclear strategy of deterrence, is merely an additional indication of this same perception.

These developments illustrate a dilemma. If the international system consisted solely of democracies, then genuine disarmament would be possible. Under conditions of systemic conflict, however, real and considerable efforts are necessary for the defense of democracies. Under present conditions, Western democracies tend to see arms control talks as an instrument for lowering defense budgets. Thus, they develop all kinds of theories about the stabilizing effects of such negotiations. The situation is very different in the USSR. The concept of arms control is not part of its military strategy. In its political strategy, arms control is only a tactical variation on the concept of peaceful coexistence.[30] The Soviets see arms control negotiations as a means of developing a larger advantage in the balance of power and as an instrument of influence within the democracies. The process encourages hopes and expectations of successful results, thereby reducing the will for adequate defense efforts. The change in the "correlation of forces"—to use Soviet terminology—since the beginning of negotiations is frightening. Under conditions of systemic conflict, arms control negotiations between open and closed political systems lead to a partial or relative unilateral disarmament of the democracies.

The possibility that a different negotiating strategy could help the West achieve more positive results should not be excluded. The West, for example, could develop and deploy the necessary defensive systems, whose size and number would depend on the USSR's offensive weaponry. It could then come to an agreement on arms reduction only if the Soviets verifiably reduced their armaments. The responsibility for failure or success would be clearer. Considering the tendency of democracies to search constantly for new foreign policies, already described by Tocqueville,[31] the question remains whether such a strategy could be sustained for any length of time. Tocqueville has correctly pointed out that one of the important strengths of a democratic system—its innovative capacity—leads to constant changes in foreign policy as a function of the interplay between ruling and opposition parties. Experience tells us that such a new strategy would again lead to demands for more flexibility and more understanding of the needs of the Soviet Union.

NOTES

1. R. R. Bowie, "Basic Requirements of Arms Control," in Donald G. Brennan, ed., *Arms Control, Disarmament, and National Security* (New York: George Braziller, 1961), pp. 43–55; and Colin S. Gray and Donald G. Brennan, "Gemeinsame Interessen als Grundlage für Rüstungskontrolle?" in Uwe Nerlich, ed., *Sowjetische Macht und westliche Verhandlungspolitik im Wandel militärischer Kraftverhältnisse* (Baden-Baden: Nomos Verlag, 1982), pp. 511–40.

2. Ulrike Schumacher, *Rüstungskontrolle als Instrument sowjetischer Aussenpolitik in den Verhandlungen zur Begrenzung strategischer Waffen: Eine Fallstudie zu SALT I und II* (Ph.D. diss., University of Kiel, 1983), p. 224.

3. See Karl W. Deutsch, *The Analysis of International Relations* (Englewood Cliffs, N.J.: Prentice-Hall, 1968), p. 161.

4. Immanuel Kant, *Die Metaphysik der Sitten* (Wiesbaden: Suhrkamp, 1977), 8: 474.

5. V. I. Lenin, "O lozunge 'razoruzheniya,'" *Polnoe sobranie sochinenii*, vol. 30, *July 1916–February 1917* (Moscow: Gosudarstvennoe izdatel'stvo politicheskoi literatury, 1962), p. 152; and idem, "The 'Disarmament' Slogan," *Collected Works*, vol. 23, *August 1916–March 1917* (London: Lawrence & Wishart; Moscow: Progress Publishers, 1964), p. 95.

6. Werner Kaltefleiter, "The Systemic Conflict," in W. Kaltefleiter and Ulrike Schmacher, eds., *Conflicts, Options, Strategies in a Threatened World* (Papers pre-

sented at the International Summer Course on National Security, Kiel, West Germany, 1982), pp. 1–24.

7. Stefan T. Possony, "Reconnaissance in Time Perspective," in Frederick J. Ossenbeck and Patricia C. Kroeck, eds., *Open Space and Peace: A Symposium on Effects of Observation* (Stanford: Hoover Institution Press, 1964), p. 30.

8. The vulnerability of electrical and electronic systems to the EMP was recognized around 1960. This explains why the U.S. side was not fully aware of the impact of the test ban on the study of EMP. (Samuel Glasstone and Philip J. Dolan, eds. and comps., *The Effects of Nuclear Weapons*, 3rd ed., prepared by and published by the U.S. Departments of Defense and Energy [Washington, D.C.: Department of Defense, 1977], p. 514.)

9. Richard N. Rosecrance, "International Stability and Nuclear Diffusion," in R. N. Rosecrance, ed., *The Dispersion of Nuclear Weapons: Strategy and Politics* (New York: Columbia University Press, 1964), pp. 293–314.

10. Konrad Adenauer, *Erinnerungen, 1953–1955* (Stuttgart: Deutsche Verlags-Anstalt, 1966), p. 347.

11. "Report by Secretary of State Rusk to the President on the Non-Proliferation Treaty, July 2, 1968," in *Documents on Disarmament, 1968* (Washington, D.C.: U.S. Arms Control and Disarmament Agency, September 1969), p. 477.

12. Hedley Bull, "Die klassische Konzeption der Rüstungskontrolle: Ein Rückblick nach zwanzig Jahren," in Nerlich, *Sowjetische Macht und westliche Verhandlungspolitik.*

13. Gray and Brennan, "Gemeinsame Interessen," p. 515.

14. John M. Collins, *American and Soviet Military Trends Since the Cuban Missile Crisis* (Washington, D.C.: Center for Strategic and International Studies, 1978), pp. 88–96.

15. International Institute for Strategic Studies, *The Military Balance, 1983–1984* (London, 1983), p. 15; and Robert P. Berman and John C. Baker, *Soviet Strategic Forces: Requirements and Responses* (Washington, D.C.: Brookings Institution, 1982), pp. 147–50.

16. Berman and Baker, *Soviet Strategic Forces*, p. 65; and U.S. Department of Defense, *Soviet Military Power* (Washington, D.C.: Government Printing Office, 1983), pp. 18–21.

17. Jake Garn, "The SALT II Verification Myth," *Strategic Review* 7, no. 3 (Summer 1979): 21–22.

18. See, for example, President Carter's rationale for cancellation of the B-1 bomber (*Facts on File, 1977*, p. 514).

19. Edward N. Luttwak, "Ten Questions About SALT II," *Commentary* 68, no. 2 (August 1979): 21–32; Colin S. Gray, "The SALT II Debate in Context," *Survival* 21, no. 5 (September–October 1979): 202–5; and Coalition for Peace Through Strength, *An Analysis of SALT II* (Washington, D.C., 1979).

20. U.S. Arms Control and Disarmament Agency, *A Chronology of United States Arms Reduction Initiatives, 1946–1982* (Washington, D.C., 1982).

21. See Chap. 11 in this volume; S. J. Lukasik, "Die Dynamik des Gleichgewichts: Beziehungen zwischen Technologie und Rüstungskontrolle," in Uwe Nerlich, ed., *Die Einhegung sowjetischer Macht* (Baden-Baden: Nomos Verlag, 1982), pp. 143–218; and William C. Potter, ed., *Verification and SALT: The Challenge of Strategic Deception* (Boulder, Colo.: Westview Press, 1980).

22. M. Collins, *American and Soviet Military Trends*, pp. 133–41.

23. Werner Kaltefleiter, "Entspannung und Eskalation: Konfliktlösungsmuster im internationalen System," *Zeitschrift für Politik* 23, no. 1 (1976): 33–36; and idem, "Der systemische Konflikt in den internationalen Beziehungen der Gegenwart," *Aus Politik und Zeitgeschichte* 41 (16 October 1982): 29.

24. Henry A. Kissinger, statement before the Senate Committee on Foreign Relations, in *Détente* (Washington, D.C.: Government Printing Office, 1975), p. 240.

25. Werner Kaltefleiter, "Aussenpolitische Willensbildung in der Demokratie," *Geschichte und Gegenwart* 1, no. 3 (September 1982): 213–17.

26. E. Scherr, "Perceptions of U.S. Strength: A Factor in Reagan's Election," *Wireless Bulletin* (Washington, D.C.), no. 238 (19 December 1980): 6–7; and P. Losche, "Die amerikanischen Präsidentschaftswahlen 1980: Eine Analyse aus deutscher Sicht," *Zeitschrift für Parlamentsfragen* 12, no. 4 (1981): 573–88.

27. Werner Kaltefleiter, "Entspannungskonzept und aussenpolitische Strategie der USA," in G. Brunner, et al., eds., *Moderne Welt: Jahrbuch für Ost-West-Fragen, 1983* (Cologne: Markus Verlag, 1984).

28. Ulrike Schumacher, ed., *Nulllösung oder Nachrüstung: Argumente aus drei Kontinenten* (Kiel: Institute of Political Science, Christian-Albrechts-Universität, 1983).

29. F. J. Schulze, "NATO's Strategic Planning," in Kaltefleiter and Schumacher, *Conflicts, Options, Strategies*, pp. 133–39.

30. Schumacher, *Rüstungskontrolle*, p. 66.

31. Alexis de Tocqueville, *Democracy in America* (Garden City, N.Y.: Doubleday & Co., 1969), pp. 231–35.

6

STRATEGY AND ARMS CONTROL: POLITICAL WILL AND PUBLIC DIPLOMACY

W. Scott Thompson and Robert E. Kiernan

Arms control and public diplomacy have separately been among the most controversial and least understood of the Reagan administration's foreign policy programs. As such, it is nearly impossible to discuss the nexus of arms control and public diplomacy without first defining, or perhaps redefining, arms control and public diplomacy. Since neither arms control nor public diplomacy can be understood outside the wider context of national strategy, we hope to use the principles of strategy to illuminate the nature and purpose of U.S. foreign policy in these areas.

ARMS CONTROL, POLITICAL PRINCIPLE, AND STRATEGY

The interests of the United States are preserved, protected, and advanced through the exercise of strategic principles that together constitute a "grand" strategy. Although these principles represent discrete political, economic, and military contingencies, together they may be defined in terms of the realization of a more fundamental objective. Professors Robert Strausz-Hupé, William Kintner, and Stefan Possony succinctly summarized this objective long ago: "The priority objective of any American grand strategy is, by a broad margin, the preservation and enhancement of our political system rather than the maintenance of peace."[1]

Although this may appear rather blunt, if not pugnacious, objectively it must be considered the first tenet of statecraft, even in a nuclear age, so long as our world comprises more than one sovereign state. Peace, after all, comes in many forms, including those imposed by one's adversaries; it can never be more than a function of U.S. strategy, as opposed to an end in itself. The preservation and consolidation of the United States' political system, however, must be stated in terms of the shared values and principles that constitute the system if that system is to be compelling. These values and principles have been summarized by Secretary of Defense Caspar Weinberger in his fiscal 1984 *Annual Report to Congress*, which prescribes the larger objectives of the Department of Defense as

— To preserve our freedom, our political identity, and the institutions that are their foundation—the Constitution and the rule of law.

— To protect the territory of the United States, its citizens, and its vital interests abroad from armed attack.

— To foster an international order supportive of the interests of the United States through alliances and cooperative relationships with friendly nations; and encouraging democratic institutions, economic development, and self-determination throughout the world.

— To protect access to foreign markets and overseas resources in order to maintain the strength of the United States' industrial, agricultural, and technological base and the nation's economic well-being.[2]

In short, the United States' goals are the defense of freedom, territory, the world political order, and the world economic order. While the protection of these values is easily asserted, the Reagan administration in particular has explicitly recognized the importance of former secretary of defense James Forrestal's observation to the Congress: "It is our duty to see that our military potential conforms to the requirements of our national policy; in other words, that our policy does not outstrip our power."[3] Clearly, military power, like political power, can never be absolute. The wars of the first half of the twentieth century alone have demonstrated the verity of Edmund Burke's epigram that "there are no permanent victories." By recognizing such limitations on military power, arms control policy—when it serves larger, strategic objectives—can be an effective component of grand strategy, both conceptually and practically.

Conceptually, the goals, direction, and execution of arms control policy represent a means by which strategic goals are realized. The immediate objective of arms control policies is to establish and maintain an international environment in which strategic goals can be advanced. Such an environment rests on the paradoxical and antinomical concepts of "stability" and "deterrence." The condition of stability, a descriptive term, requires a matrix of incentives and disincentives that inspire states to avoid the use of force in the event that political circumstances become obstacles to their policies. Deterrence, on the other hand, is an operational term and requires that the survivability and capability of rival states' forces be so counterbalanced as to guarantee that attack would be a losing proposition for either side. Thus, in the most acute sense, arms control policy is a means of seeking to reduce the risk of war without increasing the risk of defeat were war to occur.[4]

Practically, arms control policy is a political instrument. In the international political arena, it is the instrument by which we seek to affect stability and deterrence by the enhancement and/or reduction of armaments—conventional and nuclear—as the requirements for stability realized through deterrence demand. In the domestic political arena, it is currently an expression of the will of the American people to preserve their vital interests while minimizing the economic cost and maximizing the military effectiveness of security.

But the short history of arms control policy, both in theory and in practice, has been a confused and unproductive one that has undermined sensible definitions of "stability," "deterrence," and indeed, "arms control" itself.

The theoretical roots of arms control policy are found in the evolution of nuclear strategy. When economists first applied their discipline to the problems of nuclear strategy in the early 1960s, they discovered that the paradox of deterrence was unresolvable, even by the calculus of economic theorems. However, by applying mathematical "game theories" to political relations in a thermonuclear age, they found that the incentives and disincentives that preserve stability could be factored into formulas. From these equations, they inferred that limitation of the various types and quantities of nuclear arms yielded a situation in which the likelihood of their use was *relatively* diminished.[5]

In a very short period of time, however, the economists' formulas for increasing stability, which relied on the quantitative reduction of nuclear arms, departed from the fundamental antinomies of deterrence *per se* and took on a new meaning: arms control, as an expression of these formulas, became an end in itself, separate and distinct from the strategic principles it had originally been designed to serve. In a strategic environment turned on its head, the limitation of arms was the first principle from which all other strategic principles flowed. This was complicated, at the same time, by a blurring of the political distinctions that differentiate the essential goals of the major nuclear powers. The political strife of the 1960s and 1970s distorted the perceived purposes of U.S. military power, leading to a new, rather specious, moral equation that, while quite aside from the technical changes that the new economic thinking had generated, prompted the reconsideration of the military balance strictly in terms of destructiveness, without concern for the practical purpose of the military in defending the political principles that constitute the state.

The result of all this was that realization of the condition of stability became the principal, rather than the subordinate, goal of strategy, fracturing the essential relationship between principle and power. Indeed, during the SALT I negotiations "stability" (redefined) was considered "a truly divine goal."[6] This shift, which replaced the operative with the descriptive, has had two rather dramatic effects on strategy. First, arms control policies—not as a means for seeking to reduce the risk of war without increasing the risk of defeat were war to occur, but rather as a means for reducing the quantity of nuclear weapons, delivery systems, and so on—supplanted the political objectives that previously had inspired national strategy. Thus, arms control agreements became an end in themselves, to which strategic and political principles accommodated themselves.

Second, once policymakers became captivated by this objective, the arms control agreements in which the condition of stability was supposedly codified came to discount, if not exclude entirely, the operational aspects of strategy that formerly maintained the paradox of deterrence. Moreover, after deterrence was discarded, this development undercut the definition of arms control as an attempt to reduce the risks of war without increasing the risk of defeat should war occur.

Herein lies the essential problem with arms control policy as conceived and practiced. By the nature of the political principles that define the character of the republic, the United States has long maintained, and under the Reagan administration continues to maintain, a defensive posture in its military strategy. Moreover, this defensive posture is realized at the least possible cost to the economy of the nation. However, the unprecedented destructiveness of nuclear weapons has made it difficult if not impossible to discuss operational defense—which includes a credible and thereby operational offensive capability.

"The core of the whole disarmament problem," writes Liddell Hart, "lies in convincing the aggressor that victory is unattainable from the start. The most effective means is to annul the chances of successful attack. To sterilize offensive potency is to sterilize war itself."[7] Yet because the distinction between offense and defense is at the root of the deterrence paradox, arms control must serve to complement, rather than stifle, operational aspects of U.S. strategy that serve to sterilize the adversary's offensive potency. Because both effective arms control policies and effective operational offense serve this goal, the point that arms control policies must consider the risk of defeat in war becomes of primary importance.

Indeed, the reigning notion that made the condition of stability paramount and the undermining of deterrence that accompanies the realization of that condition have led Western policymakers to neglect the operational aspects of strategy— that is, offense to affect defense. The architects of arms control policies must be aware that "an adequate concept of stability has to be anchored in a prospectively effective theory of deterrence at the highest levels of violence."[8]

In practice, the history of arms control policy is equally confused. To repeat, in the international political arena, arms control is the instrument by which we seek to affect stability and deterrence by the enhancement and/or reduction of armaments; in the domestic political arena, arms control is an expression of the will of the American people to preserve their vital interests while minimizing the economic cost and maximizing the military effectiveness of security. Although the practical import of arms control policies is political, the history of arms control negotiations is a record of infatuation with technological developments that change the face of battle and of complete ignorance of the logical complement to arms reductions, which might well result from the political will for economically and militarily efficient security—arms building. One need not be reminded of the Reagan administration's commitment to this concept, nor of the fact that through the efforts of former secretary of defense Harold Brown, the Carter administration left office with the same concept affirmed. No one has put it as succinctly as Brown in his memorable testimony before Congress: "We build, they build. We stop building, they build."

But this is merely the technical side. In practice, the political side suffers in the same way. "Arms control," writes Lawrence Freedman, "has become an incompetent and inadequate alternative to the reappraisal of strategic objectives and the honest confrontation of political differences."[9] That is to say, arms control, as manifested in negotiations to date, has long been an apolitical exercise, an exercise that has not been founded in concert with the primary objectives of the United States' national strategy: the preservation and consolidation of its political system. This is in large part because "arms control negotiations cannot but reflect the state of political relations."[10] And if the state of political relations is confrontational on the most fundamental questions of political principle, so too will be the tenor of arms control negotiations. The fundamental difference in the negotiating policies of the United States and the Soviet Union merely reflects the fundamental difference in the political principles that their respective national strategies preserve and consolidate. Lenin revealed an acute example of this reflection, when he wrote that advocacy of " 'disarmament' . . . is tantamount to complete abandonment of the class struggle . . . to renunciation of all thought of revolution . . . [and] arming of the proletariat to defeat, expropriate, and disarm the bourgeoisie . . . [which are] the only tactics possible for a revolutionary class." [11]

There is still no better explication of this fundamental political difference than that in National Security Council Directive 68 (NSC-68). What that document described was an irreconcilable asymmetry between the political systems of the West and the Soviet Union. It is worthy of lengthy quotation here:

> There is a basic conflict between the idea of freedom under a government of laws, and the idea of slavery under the grim oligarchy of the Kremlin . . . Thus unwillingly our free society finds itself mortally challenged by the Soviet system. No other value system is so wholly irreconcilable with ours, so implacable in its purpose to destroy ours, so capable of turning to its own uses the most dangerous and divisible trends in our society, no other so skillfully and powerfully evokes the elements of irrationality in human nature everywhere, and no other has the support of a great and growing center of military power. [12]

Given the fate of détente over the past decade and the fact that arms control is no longer considered a motor of that failed policy, it is now more possible than ever to reassert the fundamental political relationship between the United States and the Soviet Union as the point of departure for arms control negotiations. However, because of the high levels of social fear and anxiety that symbolically surround arms control negotiations, it is more likely that this will first be asserted in multilateral negotiations at places like the United Nations and the follow-ons to the Conference on Security and Cooperation in Europe (CSCE), where the Reagan administration has already made considerable headway in reasserting the obvious.

Still, it is in the realm of arms control negotiations that considerations of the relationship between political principle and military power will be most prominent. As a democracy, the United States' ability to exercise its will is considerably constrained compared to that of the Soviet Union. NSC-68 acutely defines the dilemma of the United States' situation, now as then: "The free society is limited in its choice of means to achieve its ends. Compulsion is the negation of freedom, except when it is used to enforce the rights common to all. The resort to force, internally or externally, is therefore a last resort for free society." [13] A resort to force, the document declares "cannot definitively end the fundamental conflict in the realm of ideas," a remark that emphasizes the importance of public diplomacy. [14]

Admittedly, arms control considered within the confines of this political dichotomy is a far more imposing project. Yet by forcing reference to the fundamental political differences between the two superpowers, it tends to concentrate the mind on the issues of strategy, properly defined, that should rightly serve as milestones in negotiations.

But it is better to understand the arms control *calculus* as such than to delude oneself with arms control *arithmetic* into believing that agreements that ignore the strategic principles, political values, and international political context mentioned above are going to be effective instruments for reducing the risk of war without compromising the United States' ability to avoid defeat should war occur. We will not presume to explicate a new strategy nor burden the reader with detailed discussion of the technical aspects of "reducing the volume of violence," as Raymond Aron once defined *contrôle des armements*. The purposes of this paper are to make clear the political prerequisites such discussions of hardware demand and to understand those prerequisites as an expression of the political will of allies and adversaries as well. As Eugene V. Rostow writes, "The nuclear weapon is primarily a political, not a military force—a potent political force, generating currents of opinion that are transforming our world." [15]

PUBLIC DIPLOMACY, NATIONAL WILL, AND REASSURANCE

Clausewitz, discussing military genius, wrote:

> Truth in itself is rarely sufficient to make men act. Hence the step is always long from cognition to volition, from knowledge to ability. The most powerful springs of action in man lie in his emotions. He derives his most vigorous support, if we may use the term, from that blend of brains and temperament which we have learned to recognize in the qualities of determination, firmness, staunchness, and strength of character. [16]

This is a good point of departure for a definition of a public diplomacy policy for the United States that will have as its mandate the effective realization of a political consensus on the importance of the political values in front of which strategic principles stand and around which an effective arms control policy can be created. Simply put, effective public diplomacy involves presentation of a political idea in such a way that the leap from cognition to volition is effected.

This sort of presentation, however, has long seemed the province of Madison Avenue and public relations: an effective business practice, no doubt, but not quite the process for communicating notions such as freedom, liberty, and democracy. A distinction is called for at the outset. There are essentially four practices that are often confused with what we mean by public diplomacy. Three come from the world of commerce, the fourth from the world of diplomacy itself.

First, consider the most rudimentary form of communication (in the social scientist's sense of the word) for the merchant: *marketing*. This is a process by which the demand for a product is increased by communicating (some would say eliciting and soliciting) the desirability—perhaps in some cases, creating the illusion of necessity—of that product in the eyes of the potential consumer. This technique, applied to politics, is equally rudimentary and is commonly called *propaganda*. Because both marketeers and propagandists, such as the Soviets, have sometimes engaged less than scrupulously in this technique, marketing, advertising, and propaganda all have pejorative connotations. Both marketing and propaganda, as currently practiced, sometimes involve deception and sometimes lying. For this reason alone, the United States cannot practice either. The nature of a free society and the free press that accompanies it would simply not allow for such practices on the part of a government of, by, and for the people.

The word "propaganda" first gained wide usage following seventeenth century Pope Gregory XV's creation of the Congregatio de propaganda fide, whose mission was to propagate the faith beyond Rome. Obviously, faith, like political principle, cannot be instilled through deception or coercion. Thus, the modern analogue for the original objective of propaganda is *advocacy*. Advocacy is principally an information program in which the content and rationale of foreign policy is conveyed through diplomatic channels. The United States Information Service (USIS), for example, carries out this elementary objective abroad. This, however, is not what we mean by public diplomacy.

The second term of communications in need of clarification is *public relations*. In business this commonly refers to the task of placing the company's image in the best possible light with the public at large—that is, stockholders and consumers. This usually involves considerable flash and sparkle and is sometimes seen as rather contrived. Without intending animadversion, the analogue in affairs of state that most closely resembles this function is *politics* itself. The role of practicing foreign relations in a democracy almost exclusively falls upon the chief executive, who is responsible for relations with his constituents and, in the case of the leader of the free world, the constituency of his fellow heads of government. Although this is confused by the almost peculiarly American practice of combining the head of government and head of state in the same person, it is nonetheless the responsibility of the president and his representatives in the field—his ambassadorial appointments—to execute and maintain solid and credible political relations. Public diplomacy, while drawing on this and the advocatory practices mentioned above, is still something quite a bit more than the sum of those parts.

Third, we must discuss a term that has only recently entered the idiom, perhaps because of the negative connotation of public relations: *public affairs*. In the corporate world particularly, this term refers to the more basic aspects of representing a company's interests in interactions with other institutions—specifically, lobbying the Congress and providing funding to fulfill its social responsibilities. This, too, has an analogue in statecraft that might be most aptly described as the province of the career diplomat, whose responsibility it is to carry on the day-to-day relations between states, in theory never losing sight of the larger U.S. interest he represents. But if public affairs is *traditional* diplomacy, what then is public diplomacy?

This brings us to our final point of clarification, that is, public diplomacy is not traditional diplomacy conducted publicly. This common misperception is at the root of the problem of characterizing public diplomacy in terms of any of the activities described above, even though public diplomatic efforts draw on but do not comprise them. To understand public diplomacy, we must return to the political principles that constitute the objectives of strategy.

Public diplomacy, in a word, is most accurately described as an act of inspiring *political affirmation*—of, by, and for the body politic. In the present context, this is the animation of political will to engage in the fundamental political relationship that governs East-West relations. Its objective is to effect within the United States' national will and the national will of its allies (and in a certain sense, its adversaries) the transition from cognition to volition. The instruments of this exercise, however, are not those of the crusader, not those of the missionary, and certainly not those of the political organizer. Rather they are those of the active, rather than passive, the offensive, rather than defensive, public diplomatist who implements political principle as it manifests itself in public policy.

Here we must realign the terms of strategy—stability and deterrence—by recrafting them in terms of public diplomacy. Political affirmation occurs in the will of a state, the body politic, which reacts not to the calculus of strategy, but rather to the political and social expressions of strategy. Michael Howard, in a celebrated *Foreign Affairs* article, struck at the very root of this distinction when he described the nature of the U.S. military posture as one that included not just the

> *negative* role of a deterrent to Soviet aggression, but [also] the positive role of a *reassurance* to the West Europeans; the kind of reassurance a child needs from its parents or an invalid from his doctors against dangers which, however remote, cannot be entirely discounted. This concept of re-

assurance has not, as far as I know, hitherto been a term of art in strategic analysis, but it should be, and as far as we are concerned it is now.[17]

If the sum total of all military force structures is negative, in that they seek through the use of force to prevent the use of force, then the positive element of reassurance—directed as it is to the body politic and not governments *per se*—cannot be supplied by other than public diplomacy. This distinction between deterrence and reassurance becomes even more critical at a time when major public movements are expressing a lack of confidence in the deterrent policy that the West in general and the United States in particular are attempting to implement through the modernization of intermediate-range nuclear forces (INF). Clearly deterrence without reassurance will be ineffective; that is, the hardware to deter is useless without the political will to use it. This fact contributes both to the resolve of the West in its perceptions of itself and the ultimate effectiveness of its deterrent in the eyes of the Soviets.

However, it is obvious that public discussions of the operational elements of deterrence that produce the condition of stability are unacceptable to the body politic in a day when the proliferation of fear-mongering anti-nuclear groups has become one of the fastest growing cottage industries in the Western world. This does not mean that discussion of nuclear strategy should be avoided. To the contrary, it must continue as the body politic grows generally more sophisticated and reasonable in its discussion. However, this is not the area in which public diplomacy is most effective.

The incident of the Korean Air Lines flight 007 massacre demonstrated conclusively a truth that all but the most fervent Soviet apologist could not fail to admit: namely, that there is a political, moral, and cultural asymmetry between the West and the values its nuclear forces are deployed to defend and the Soviet Union and the values that its imperious oligarchy perpetuates. Professor Howard also sees this distinction, outlined above in the language of NSC-68, as rudimentary: "The requirement for effective deterrence remains, if only because the Soviet Union cannot be expected to observe a higher standard of conduct toward weaker neighbors than other states, whatever their political complexion, have shown in the past."[18]

Reassurance as a public diplomacy exercise, therefore, should primarily be directed to the character and nature of this asymmetry rather than to the actual technical requirements of maintaining the paradox of deterrence. This can be effected in several different ways, all of which have precedents in the United States' modern alliance relationships.

In the Helsinki Final Act (1975), a *quid pro quo* was struck; the West recognized Eastern Europe as a Soviet sphere of influence in return for certain guarantees of political freedom and pluralism for the peoples of those areas. In this instance, unprecedented in that it was the first time that security and political principles were directly linked in a multilateral covenant among nations, the foundation of a program for the evolutionary pluralization of the Soviet bloc can be found. It has been sustained, in form if not in substance, in the CSCE process. However, these government-to-government relations must be supplemented with programs developed by the Western alliance and nongovernment organizations that will have a more direct effect on the nature of the body politic itself, both in the West and behind the Iron Curtain. The goal of public diplomacy in all of this is, strangely enough, to move the discussion away from the technical points of arms control and nuclear war and into the area of the fundamental character of the political relationship between the West and the Soviet Union. Only *after* this is accomplished can arms control proceed along the political lines outlined in the first part of this essay.

What we are really talking about is not an engagement of conflicting governments' policies, but rather a contest of ideas that must be addressed by the body politic if we are to proceed. In a fascinating 1959 *Foreign Affairs* article written by (most agree in his own hand) Nikita S. Khrushchev, he argued that

> peaceful coexistence can and should develop into peaceful competition for the purpose of satisfying man's needs in the best possible way. We say to the leaders of the capitalist states: Let us try out in practice whose system is better, let us compare without war . . . We stand and will stand always for such competition as will help to raise the well-being of the people to a higher level.[19]

Despite the loss of flexibility that followed Khrushchev's less than natural departure, the Soviets have, more tenaciously than before, engaged unwilling Western partners in the competition for a better way and have, by default, been winning this ideological contest. By engaging them not as governments but as peoples, not in terms of defense policies but rather in terms of political philosophy, we will serve the larger context of the great debate and also, by no means incidental to the topic before us, provide the political prerequisite—that is, a consensus—for a properly executed and successful arms control policy.

There are already several groups and societies that convene to discuss the common interest in democratic forms of government. Whether they be parliamentarians or academicians or labor and business leaders, they will have a more profound impact on the problem of animating political will than can government-to-government relations. Still, what is needed is an escalation and consolidation of these efforts with the formation of, to borrow a construction from the communist movement, the Democratic International. The nature of the reassurance that the development of such organizations produce is essential to establishing the contrast between the two systems of government that lies at the root of the East-West conflict. This would serve to galvanize the resolve of the West, in its own perception of itself and in the eyes of the Soviets.

There is no more pertinent, nor more profound, question of politics today than that of the linkage of security and political principle. Its ramifications stretch far beyond current questions of arms control. Just as the neglect of operational aspects of strategy contributed to the debasing of arms control, the neglect of the fundamental political principles for which we have built defenses as well as the nature of the threat to these principles represented by their rival principles (if one may use that term) will serve to undermine the effectiveness of arms control agreements by disengaging the strategic elements—previously conceived in terms of defense, now in terms of will—that define the United States' purposes and objectives in the international order.

We can summarize the implications of reassurance for the political and strategic context in which arms control agreements are negotiated by referring again to the distinction made in NSC-68 with regard to the purposes of military power in the United States and the Soviet Union. The objectives of the two states' militaries, and therefore the armaments each employs, rounds out our discussion of the linkage between principle and security that defines the point of departure for future arms control.

> For us, the role of military power is to serve the national purpose by deterring an attack upon us while we seek by other means to create an environment in which our free society can flourish, and by fighting, if necessary, to defend the integrity and vitality of our free society and to defeat any aggressor. The Kremlin uses Soviet military power to back up and serve the Kremlin design. It does not hesitate to use military force aggressively if that course is expedient in the achievement of its design. The differences between our fundamental purpose and the Kremlin design, therefore, are reflected in our respective attitudes toward and use of military force.[20]

When this situation is recognized as a manifestation of the fundamental political asymmetry and when this is then *politically* affirmed in the collective will of the West—when the body politic has moved from cognition of the fundamental political relationships to volition in its desire to affirm the principles that underpin the Western tradition—then the public diplomacy battle will be won. But present research shows that we have still a long way to go.

THE PRESENT CONSTITUTION OF WESTERN WILL

Having discussed the prerequisites of arms control first in terms of operational strategy and then in terms of political will, we have arrived at the same conclusion: arms control is not a military but a political exercise predicated on the fundamental political relationships that are most acutely and vividly expressed in terms of national will. Given this conclusion, it is necessary to measure the degree of such understanding within the current bodies politic of U.S. allies in Europe. In large part, they instinctively confirm the conclusions arrived at analytically above, as a review of a compendium of polling data recently collected by the Research Office of the United States Information Agency (USIA) shows.

Consciousness of the asymmetry of the U.S. and Soviet political systems is manifest in public opinion polling that measures the degree of confidence, level of perceived sincerity, and credibility of the bargaining proposals of each superpower. In a 1981 survey of Europeans on the question of which superpower was more respected, the United States enjoyed a clear margin over the Soviet Union (ranging from 59 percent favorable in France to 67 percent in West Germany), although the United States' relative advantage has declined over the past few years. Yet the data support neither the suggestion that Europe is adopting a position of equidistance from both powers nor the more extreme suggestion that it is essentially proclaiming a pox on both houses. This is further offset by antipathy toward the Soviets, which has now reached an all-time high, with generally 75 percent of the survey population responding negatively.[21]

More fundamentally, when Europeans were queried whether each superpower's foreign policies promoted peace or war, their responses revealed that perceptions of the fundamental differences between the United States and the Soviets were even more acute; 41 percent (in the Netherlands) to 61 percent (in Italy) of the survey felt that the policies of the Soviet Union promote war.[22]

However, when questioned about the relative strength of the superpowers, the Europeans' reaction reflected the reality of the nuclear balance, a reaction that cuts two ways. First, it represents a recognition of a fundamental shift in geopolitical power. Second, it represents a challenge to the willingness of the Europeans to defend, in the face of a growing Soviet military superiority, the political principles on which their governments are founded. European public opinion confirms, with the exception of France and Italy, the empirical data supplied by such independent groups as the International Institute for Strategic Studies. On the other hand, no group sampled except Italians believed the United States was ahead of the Soviets.[23]

The answer to the challenge to defend political principles that stems from the question of military superiority is found in the response to a question of whether those queried would resist a Soviet attack, either conventional or nuclear. Although pacifist sentiment was not widespread in Europe (with the exception of France), 60–80 percent of the sample favored using military force if their country or any other member of the NATO alliance were attacked by the USSR. Those in favor of resisting conventional attack outnumber those opposed by large margins (3 to 1 and 4 to 1); majorities in Britain, Norway, and the Netherlands and pluralities in France and West Germany favored resisting nuclear attack by the USSR.[24]

These polls represent somewhat dated evidence, but continued USIA polling efforts have shown that with the exception of minor adjustments of negligible statistical significance, these conclusions still hold. Moreover, there is significant evidence showing that Europeans prefer a reduction in the number of ICBMs to a nuclear freeze (50 percent range in the Netherlands, West Germany, Italy, and Britain, with a 35 to 19 percent margin preferring reductions in France, but 46 percent with no opinion). And, the peace movement, while generally approved of, is seen in everywhere but Italy (43 to 53 percent) as ineffective in reducing the risk of nuclear war. In Italy, about half see it as reducing the chances of nuclear war.[25]

What this confirms in terms of a limited sense of realism and resolve in Europe is quite a different story than one might surmise from watching nightly news reports on demonstrations and anti-American feeling in Europe. And clearly, the intuition of the Europeans is far more sophisticated than the average American newspaper reader might deduce. The questions that now appear most pointedly, then, are What can the United States do together with its allies to galvanize the understanding of the fundamental political differences between the two superpowers and What are the strategic goals and implications of programs designed to animate political affirmation of philosophical principles in the context of security questions?

SOME CONCLUSIONS

Michael Howard's insight about reassurance has overwhelming implications for the future of arms control. In coining an operative term for the political complement of military deterrence, he is repeating a theme that has long been a favorite subject: the exposition of the elements of strategy as Clausewitz saw them. In a summer 1979 *Foreign Affairs* article, "The Forgotten Dimensions of Strategy," Howard argued essentially the same theme that appears in Clausewitz's description of the difference between the physical and the moral elements of strategy: "One might say that the physical seems little more than the wooden hilt, while the moral factors are the precious metal, the real weapon, the finely-honed blade." [26]

To leap from public opinion to a "moral factor" of strategy seems, on the face of it, quite a long leap indeed. Yet, in light of the conclusions of the preceding sections of this paper, it is a logical deduction. Supported by Howard and Clausewitz, we are asserting that the moral element of strategy is part of the context of public diplomacy, thus raising strategic issues to the level of national will and resolve and public diplomacy issues to the level of strategic planning. To reincorporate the moral, the national will, and the public opinion factors into the strategic matrix is the goal of Howard's efforts and indeed the goal of public diplomacy as well. The real question is how this might be accomplished.

The polling data above show that Europeans view many strategic questions in terms of the fundamental political asymmetry between the United States and the Soviet Union. Yet there is nowhere near the sort of support necessary to characterize the will of the alliance as solidly unified behind its stated defense policies. The real challenge now facing strategists, as Howard points out, is reconciling the often opposing objectives of deterrence and reassurance; that is, to "make it clear to the Soviet Union that in any attack on the West the cost highly outweighs the benefits, and to our own people that the benefits of such a defense will outweigh the costs." [27]

Commenting on Professor Howard's paper, Samuel P. Huntington addresses this problem and distills out of it a rather useful distinction between short- and long-term reassurance.

> Those whom weakness has made afraid of nuclear war want to be reassured that nuclear war will not happen; they seek that reassurance through nuclear freezes, no-first-use pledges, nuclear free zones and the like. Insofar as these actions impede the re-establishment of Western military strength, as well as possibly encourage Soviet adventurism, however, they obstruct long-term reassurance. They treat the symptoms but not the cause of uneasiness in the West. [28]

In addressing this distinction between short- and long-term reassurance, we have compiled additional polling data that strike at the heart of the problem. That is, What public diplomacy themes must be developed if deterrence and reassurance are to be reconciled? As one might expect, the polling data reflect commonsensical intuitions about public diplomacy that are already part of the USIA's programming.

For example, the most effective theme is that of the shared interests in the future security of the alliance. Polling indicates that, on average, the populations of the basing countries were 47 percent less likely to reject INF modernization if they understood that the modernization was in the mutual interests of their government *and* that of the United States.[29]

After shared interests, the second most productive theme is that of deterrence. When the populations of the basing countries understand that INF modernization will make the possibility of Soviet attack less rather than more likely, their opposition to modernization becomes 41 percent less likely. Other themes such as confidence in the United States' ability to deal responsibly with world problems, support of Reagan's INF negotiation proposals, and the likelihood that U.S. policy will promote peace rather than war are all productive elements of a public diplomacy that will animate national will to move from cognition to volition. But all of this forces reconsideration of a more basic question: How sincere are the public diplomacy efforts of the U.S. government?[30]

The data show that positive programming emphasizing the merits of Western political principles is far more productive than concentration on the failure of Soviet doctrine. The question in the minds, and therefore wills, of Europeans is one of belief, not awareness. Among those aware of the facts of the situation—for example, the Soviet monopoly in INF forces in Europe—there is considerably less opposition to modernization. But awareness is considerably low, even among the educated elite who have the information available to them.[31]

This makes nongovernmental information programs even more important, but on specific issues such as arms control as well as on more fundamental issues such as political principle. Not that governmental programs should not redouble their efforts to address this problem and increase credibility, but rather that their efforts must be complemented by those of indigenous and other nongovernmental groups if success is to be guaranteed.

With Professor Howard's assistance in pointing out what should have been obvious to all, we are on the verge of changing the idiom of security studies and realigning, by returning to its original meaning, arms control both in theory and practice. Raymond Aron has written that all of a nation's ability to provide security is reducible to capacity and will. Because capacity, once nuclear, becomes in this age problematic, will takes on a heightened importance. "All international politics involves a constant collision of wills," he writes.[32] We should begin to spend as much time studying and developing the will of the West as we have studying and developing the capacity of the West. Each is useless without the other.

NOTES

1. Robert Strausz-Hupé, William R. Kintner, and Stefan T. Possony, *A Forward Strategy for America* (New York: Harper, 1961), p. 402.

2. Caspar Weinberger, *Annual Report to Congress, Fiscal Year 1984* (Washington, D.C.: Government Printing Office, 1983), p. 15.

3. James Forrestal, *First Report of the Secretary of Defense* (Washington, D.C.: Government Printing Office, 1948).

4. This formulation is not our creation; see Raymond Aron, *Paix et guerre entre les nations* (Paris: Calmann-Levy, 1962); trans. from the French by Richard Howard and Annette Baker Fox, *Peace and War: A Theory of International Relations* (Garden City, N.Y.: Doubleday, 1966).

5. See, for example, Thomas C. Schelling, *The Strategy of Conflict* (London: Oxford University Press, 1960).

6. John Newhouse, *Cold Dawn: The Story of SALT* (New York: Holt, Rinehart, & Winston, 1973).

7. Basil Henry Liddell Hart, *Defense of the West* (New York: William Morrow & Co., 1950), p. 307.

8. Colin S. Gray, "Strategic Stability Reconsidered," *Daedalus* 109, no. 4 (Fall 1980): 150.

9. Lawrence Freedman, "Arms Control: No Hiding Place," *SAIS Review*, Winter–Spring 1983, p. 4.

10. Ibid., p. 8.

11. V. I. Lenin, "The Military Program of the Proletarian Revolution" and "The 'Disarmament' Slogan," *Collected Works*, vol. 23, *August 1916–March 1917* (London: Lawrence & Wishart; Moscow: Progress Publishers, 1964), pp. 81, 96–97.

12. NSC-68, as reprinted in *Naval War College Review* 26, no. 6 (May–June 1975): 54, 56.

13. Ibid., p. 58.

14. Ibid., p. 59.

15. Eugene V. Rostow, "Arms Control Fever," *National Review* 35 (1983): 994.

16. Carl von Clausewitz, *On War*, trans. and ed. Michael Howard and Peter Paret (Princeton, N.J.: Princeton University Press, 1976), p. 112.

17. Michael E. Howard, "Reassurance and Deterrence: Western Defense in the 1980s," *Foreign Affairs* 61 (1982–83): 310; reprinted in *Adelphi Paper*, no. 184 (Summer 1983).

18. Ibid., p. 321.

19. N. S. Khruschev, "On Peaceful Coexistence," *Foreign Affairs* 38 (1959–60): 1–18.

20. NSC-68, p. 59.

21. Stephen M. Shaffer, "West European Public Opinion on Key Security Issues,

1981–1982," Study # R-10–82 (Washington, D.C.: USIA, Office of Research, 1982), p. 6.

22. Ibid., p. 7 (revised 19 September 1983).

23. Ibid., p. 10.

24. Ibid., p. 17.

25. "Research Memorandum," # M-11/30/82 (Washington, D.C.: USIA, Office of Research, 30 November 1982).

26. Clausewitz, *On War*, p. 185.

27. Ibid., p. 322.

28. Samuel P. Huntington, "Broadening the Strategic Focus: Comments on Michael Howard's Paper," *Adelphi Papers*, no. 184 (Summer 1983): 27–28.

29. Leo Crespi, "Most Promising Themes for Strengthening West European Support for INF," Study # R-15–83 (Washington, D.C.: USIA, Office of Research, August 1983), p. 2.

30. Ibid.

31. Ibid., p. 5.

32. Aron, *Peace and War*, p. 47.

7

DISCUSSION

Robin Ranger

Professor Kaltefleiter has made the most important and most neglected point that can be made about arms control; namely, the totally different domestic political structures of democratic and totalitarian societies create fundamentally opposing and incompatible political and military objectives. The objectives of democratic societies in arms control negotiations and agreements, therefore, must be opposed to those of totalitarian states. Democracies have sought, and will seek, technically effective arms control agreements. Totalitarian states have rejected, and will continue to reject, such agreements in favor of those furthering their quite different objectives: the weakening of democracies' will and capability to resist totalitarian expansion.

Experience before as well as after World War II shows that these differences between democratic and totalitarian societies have had three main effects on the conduct of arms control negotiations and on the observance of the agreements reached.

First, in regard to verification and compliance, the verification capabilities of democratic societies have proved insufficient to enforce compliance with arms control agreements. No democracy has ever imposed sanctions on totalitarian violators of arms control agreements, even when these violations were clear, continuing, and militarily significant. This has been true of the interwar agreements, especially those on naval arms control, from 1919 to 1939, and of the arms control agreements reached between 1959 and 1983. The national technical means (NTM) for verification by democracies have proved moderately successful at identifying some, though not all, of the violations occurring, but they are a total failure for the purpose of enforcing compliance or offsetting the effects of noncompliance. This is because, in democracies, evidence of violations must meet the grand jury bill of indictment test. The evidence must be, when declassified, sufficient to convince the public, the media, and the legislature that violations are so likely to have been committed that the violator(s) can be indicted and sanctions imposed. No democratic government, not even the Reagan administration, has felt that evidence of violations would prevent it from suffering adverse and unacceptable domestic political consequences if it imposed sanctions on totalitarian states known to have violated arms control agreements in both letter and spirit.

Second, democracies always expect too much from the arms control and disarmament process. Since the vast majority of their citizens are peace-loving, they impute their desire to reduce or eliminate weapons to totalitarian governments. The existence of a significant, permanent public constituency for disarmament and, since the 1950s, for arms control as well, creates pressure on elected representatives to substitute popular arms control measures for unpopular defense budgets and weapons purchases. Members of the media, most of whom are traditionally supporters of arms control, have encouraged this process. But once excessive expectations for arms control have been created, two developments occur. One is that as negotiations and agreements produce much less than the public expected, they expect more, not less, of arms control, producing increasingly millennial and unachievable demands. Those for the nuclear freeze are typical. The other development is that these increasing expectations for arms control create an increasing barrier to acceptance of the evidence that totalitarian regimes are violating arms control agreements and not negotiating for effective arms control.

Third, both of these factors encourage totalitarian governments to continue their exploitation of the hopes for arms control on the part of publics in the democracies. They do so by exploiting arms control negotiations for political effects, by engaging in a policy of political arms control, to create illusions of détente and arms control. At the same time, they violate, with impunity, what the democracies believe, often incorrectly, to have been the substance of such arms control agreements as have been reached.

The policy prescriptions from Dr. Kaltefleiter's incisive diagnosis of the problems caused by the asymmetries in arms control expectations between democratic and totalitarian states are clear. First, although arms control negotiations for democracies are not *un*productive but *counter*productive, their termination is politically undesirable until it can be justified to the public. Second, while such negotiations must therefore be continued, it is important that democratic governments, especially that of the United States, recognize their objectives. Their first objective must always be the achievement of meaningful arms control. Their second objective must be the explanation of the first to the publics in the democracies, currently the United States and its allies. Such an explanation is owed to both current and future generations, so that they may understand both that the United States and its allies have sought real arms control and that it has been the totalitarian states that have rejected it: currently the Soviet Union, and in the interwar period, Hitler's Germany, Mussolini's Italy, and Japan. The third objective must be to educate the publics, the legislatures, and the media in the democracies about the real obstacles to arms control: the totalitarian states. This process of public education should be furthered by an open discussion about the evidence of totalitarian violations of arms control agreements, especially in substantive rather than legal terms—legalistic quibbles over whether Soviet actions violate the letter, for example, of the SALT agreements obscure the real issues posed by their noncompliance. Public education in the new, and old, realities of arms control should include the United States' allies.

Finally, Professor Kaltefleiter's analysis suggests the following safeguard for American democracy to ensure compliance with arms control agreements, existing and future. The executive and legislative branches should agree to a legally binding reservation that no such agreements will be binding, vis-à-vis a particular government, for more than a year unless that government is certified as being in substantive compliance with what the United States understands to be its terms by all of the following: the president, the Senate and House Armed Services and Foreign Affairs committees, as well as the full Senate and House. Democratic government could, thus, provide safeguards against the problems created by democratic domestic political systems engaged in the arms control process.

Harriet Fast Scott

LINKAGE, SECRECY, AND VAGUENESS IN ARMS CONTROL

Professor Kaltefleiter has written a most thoughtful paper. He correctly begins with the utopian ideal of a world without arms. For anyone, politician or statesman, to disbelieve in arms control is like damning motherhood and apple pie. But again and again throughout Kaltefleiter's paper, the question of verification comes up. The Soviet Union talks a great deal about struggling for peace. As the great Prussian military theoretician Karl von Clausewitz noted more than a century ago,

The aggressor is always peace-loving; he would prefer to take over our country unopposed. To prevent his doing so, one must be willing to make war and be prepared for it. In other words, it is the weak, those likely to need defense, who should always be armed in order not to be overwhelmed. This decrees the art of war.[1]

All attempts at arms control in the 1950s broke down over demands for on-site inspection. However, with deployment of reconnaissance satellites capable of photographing rather small objects on earth, the way out of this dilemma seemed at hand. This condition did not last for long. As anyone knows who has been to Moscow, where microphones are omnipresent, listening to one's every breath 24 hours a day, the system can be deceived and manipulated. Thus, as soon as the satellites were launched, deception blighted the hope of a breakthrough. It was back to square one. Verification still remains the sticking point in any serious arms control agreement.

Ambassador Staar's paper, which concentrates on one set of arms control talks—the Mutual and Balanced Force Reductions (MBFR) talks—shows us the difficulties and opportunities he had in this most unique of all negotiations. They were the only multilateral talks being conducted between NATO and the Warsaw Pact. Twelve Western and seven Eastern bloc countries were involved in a veritable nightmare of procedure. Its goal, a slippery one at that, was to establish a conventional manpower force balance between East and West in Central Europe. Ambassador Staar's paper is a model of logic and reasonableness, reflecting the patience and determination, not to mention diplomatic skills, that he brought to the task of chief U.S. negotiator in Vienna.

As for the Soviet Union, did it ever want to reduce manpower in Central Europe? Let us look at what led up to the MBFR talks.

In March 1971, at the Twenty-fourth Congress of the Communist Party of the Soviet Union (CPSU), Leonid Brezhnev unveiled his Peace Program. This statement appeared under point four: "We stand for the dismantling of foreign military bases. We stand for a reduction of armed forces and armaments in areas where the military confrontation is especially dangerous, above all in Central Europe."[2]

Shortly after this congress, the Mansfield amendment threatened to remove U.S. troops from Europe. Brezhnev responded by including the following passage in a May 1971 speech at Tbilisi:

In connection with the reaction of the West to the proposals put forward by the [Twenty-fourth] Congress, I want to mention one detail: some of the NATO countries show an evident interest and even nervousness over the question of reduction of armed forces and armaments in Central Europe.

Their spokesmen ask: What armed forces—foreign or national? What armaments—nuclear or conventional—are to be reduced? Or perhaps, they ask, the Soviet proposals concern all this taken together? In connection with this, we, too, have a question: Don't these curious people resemble a person who tries to judge the flavor of wine by its appearance alone without imbibing it?[3] If anything is not clear to somebody, very well then, we can make it clear. But you have to muster the resolve to try the proposal you are interested in by testing it. Translated into diplomatic language this means—to start negotiations on this question.[4]

So we tasted the wine, thus beginning one of the longest wine-tasting sessions in history.

Before turning to the preliminary meetings and their results, there must be a pause here to look at the larger framework of negotiations in Europe, of which those at Vienna represent only a part.

The Soviet Union had actively been promoting an All-European Conference on Security and Cooperation in Europe (CSCE). Representatives from 35 countries started meeting in Helsinki on 22 November 1972 for preliminary talks. NATO had wanted the agenda to include military reductions. The Soviet Union opposed this because it was certain that discussion would be lengthy and drag out the conference. It suggested that the topic should be the subject of a separate meeting. NATO agreed, provided that the talks on "mutual and balanced force reductions" would be held simultaneously. The USSR objected to this "linkage" as vehemently as it objected to inclusion of the word "balanced" in the name.[5] NATO had defined "balanced" as meaning the Soviet Union would have to withdraw more troops from Central Europe because of its proximity to the area. The USSR wanted all European countries represented in order to show that these were not "bloc-to-bloc" negotiations between NATO and the Warsaw Pact. One of the prime unspoken aims of the Soviet Union in the CSCE was to supersede NATO and the Warsaw Pact with an all-European security system, so that both military organizations could be dissolved.[6] The MBFR talks admittedly would be much more difficult than the ongoing SALT II negotiations and might last for years. To have them identified with NATO and the Warsaw Pact at the beginning, the Soviets felt, would prolong these organizations for the life of the talks, if not turn them into permanent entities.

Elections took place in November 1972 both in the United States and West Germany. Richard M. Nixon was re-elected president, and within a week NATO invited the Warsaw Pact to meet at Geneva on 31 January 1973 for preliminary consultations to open negotiations on "mutual and balanced force reductions." Bulgaria and Romania, both Warsaw Pact members but not in Central Europe and without Soviet soldiers stationed on their territory, were not among those invited.

The SALT II negotiations started in Geneva on 21 November 1972, and the following day preparatory talks for CSCE opened in Helsinki. Notes dated 18 January 1973 from the Warsaw Pact countries announced their willingness to participate in preparatory consultations on negotiations for the mutual reduction of armed forces and arms (MFR) in Central Europe.[7] A week later NATO responded to the Warsaw Pact note of acceptance. Within two days, the cease-fire began in Vietnam. That same day, the USSR informed NATO that Soviet representatives would arrive in Vienna on 31 January to begin MFR consultations.

U.S. and other Western delegates had been arriving at Geneva in early January. The last-minute switch by the Soviet Union from Geneva to Vienna caused a rush for suitable facilities and quarters in the Austrian capital. Despite these difficulties, the first plenary session did convene at the famous Hofburg Palace on schedule—without a chairman, agenda, or seating arrangement. A technician from the domestic broadcasting system had to switch on the microphones before delegates could speak.[8]

Nineteen countries were represented—the Soviet Union, East Germany (GDR), Poland, Czechoslovakia, the United States, Canada, the United Kingdom, Belgium, the Netherlands, Luxembourg, West Germany (FRG), Hungary, Romania, Bulgaria, Norway, Denmark, Italy, Greece, and Turkey. A Portuguese representative also appeared. Nobody seemed to know what to do with him, so he became an unofficial observer. France was not invited to the talks in Vienna since it was no longer a member of NATO's military organization. Neutral Austria, the generous host for the proceedings, had no representative at the talks.

This first meeting lasted only 35 minutes because no agreement could be reached over who should take part. Marathon bilateral and multilateral consultations extended over more than a hundred days before a compromise could be reached over the status of Hungary. Only after this had been settled was the first plenary session held, or the second, if one counts the initial 35-minute meeting.

The talks soon broke up into regular quadripartite meetings: the Soviet Union and Hungary across from the United States and the Netherlands. By 13 April, this group had met thirteen times, with almost as many cocktail parties or "meetings on the social level," as observers have described them.[9] In fact, about 150 bilateral and multilateral meetings of the delegations were held during the hundred days between 30 January and 14 May, when the sessions finally got under way. Many of these were "meetings on the social level." It was at a "plenary cocktail" that British delegate J. A. Thomson was chosen chairman by lot, and it was agreed that his successors would be selected alphabetically in English. Even at this point, the British delayed consultations for a week by questioning one of the items of the agreement. Perhaps this was what Leonid Brezhnev had in mind when he had asked the West to "taste the wine" during his speech two years before at Tbilisi.

However, considerable action took place behind the scenes. Diplomats were busy setting up visits for Brezhnev to Bonn (May 1973) and Washington (June 1973). The latter visit concluded with a joint communiqué announcing that the Vienna talks would begin on 30 October 1973. That agreement at the summit cleared the way for preparatory consultations to end on 28 June. And five days later, the CSCE opened at Helsinki.

The MBFR talks have continued over the past decade, and both NATO and the Warsaw Pact still exist. They appear to be turning into permanent organizations, as the Soviet Union anticipated.

It is sometimes asked: Does the USSR really want disarmament? To quote from an authoritative Soviet source,[10]

> The position of the Communist Party of the Soviet Union is clear and plain: the Soviet Union has made and is making every effort to force the imperialists to general and complete disarmament. At the same time, we are giving and will give all possible aid, including military, to peoples struggling against the not-yet-disarmed imperialists. At the same time, any victory in the cause of disarmament immeasurably facilitates the struggle of the proletariat of capitalist countries and people fighting for their independence, the waging of the struggle against imperialism whose policy to an enormous degree depends on military force. Each concrete victory in the cause of disarmament means assistance to the liberation movement, to the forces struggling for social progress and national liberation.[11]

How right Clausewitz's prophetic words were.

Disarmament is one tactic of communist strategy. Secrecy is another. One final point will be made, a point brought out in the investigation of the wheat deal made in 1972 with the USSR. Outwitted by shrewd Soviet buyers, the U.S. government discovered too late that it had been taken advantage of. What made the deal possible was secrecy. Two missions arrived from Moscow in June 1972, one looking for credits and the other buying grain. In each case, the Soviets are said to have sworn the individual company to secrecy. They need not have bothered since the companies needed secrecy to buy up grain. Only the USSR knew how much it would buy. When all was said and done, the United States had sold the Soviet Union so much that Americans themselves ran short, raising already inflated food prices and adding to economic woes.[12]

This same secrecy plays havoc in negotiations. While the Soviet side is orchestrated by one small group of coordinators in Moscow, U.S. negotiators flounder in isolation with the right hand not knowing what the left hand is doing. Policy planners from leading Soviet research institutes lobby for their latest project with visiting U.S. senators and other dignitaries, having invited them to Moscow for the red carpet treatment. Then they hold conferences and symposiums with different groups from abroad, in turn accepting invitations to go abroad and meet with foreign individuals or groups. In this fashion, policy in many countries is influenced. Were the groups and VIPs to compare notes, they would find they were all being sold the same bill of goods. The highly centralized Soviet system, operating with great discipline, gives the Kremlin an advantage.

The ten years of talks in Vienna have not been entirely fruitless. As Ambassador Staar points out in his paper, the East's views are close to those of the West on certain elements of the package. But the associated measures, so vital to the verification of any reductions agreement, remain an area of basic disagreement. We can hope, along with Ambassador Staar, that the new Kremlin leadership may finally understand that both East and West have a vital interest in lowering tensions and enhancing stability in Central Europe. However, the possibility exists that the talks will deteriorate into a "most bizarre form of ritual," repeating the events of the first hundred days of preliminary negotiations.

NOTES

1. Carl von Clausewitz, *On War*, trans. and ed. Michael Howard and Peter Paret (Princeton, N.J.: Princeton University Press, 1976), p. 370. In the Russian-language translation (Moscow: State Military Publishers, 1934), p. 311, Soviet editors have added that when Lenin copied this section into his notebook, he wrote in the margin, "Ha-ha! Very clever!"

2. *24th Congress of the Communist Party of the Soviet Union* (Moscow: Novosti Press, 1971), p. 38.

3. Brezhnev gave the address at Tbilisi, the capital of Soviet Georgia, famous for its fine wines.

4. *Pravda*, 15 May 1971, p. 1. This speech came six weeks after the party congress.

5. Yuri Zhukov, "A Truly Urgent Matter," *Pravda*, 14 September 1972, p. 1. This author wrote that NATO was talking of holding a conference in October for the purpose of "establishing links [!] between the all-European security and cooperation conference and negotiations on a considerable reduction in armed forces." He added that "W[alter] Stoessel [U.S. assistant secretary of state], for his part, deemed it necessary to declare: 'We and our allies believe that a multilateral study of the possibility for mutual and balanced troop reductions must also be made before, or simultaneously with, the multilateral preliminary negotiation.'"

6. *24th Congress*, p. 38. Brezhnev's Peace Program included the following: "We affirm the readiness expressed jointly by the participants in the defensive Warsaw

Treaty to have a simultaneous annulment of this treaty and of the North Atlantic Alliance [NATO], or—as a first step—dismantling of their military organizations."

Since the East European countries are tied to Moscow through bilateral agreements, dissolving the Warsaw Pact would have had little effect on the Kremlin's control over the area. At a Warsaw Pact meeting, held in Prague on 25–26 January 1972, the final communiqué stated that at "the all-European conference, its participants could work out practical measures for the further easing of tensions in Europe and begin the construction of a European security system." The CPSU journal *Kommunist* (February 1972) again called for the abolition of NATO and the Warsaw Pact or, as a first step, their military organizations.

7. Tass in *Krasnaya zvezda* [Red Star], 19 January 1973. Also underlying the tentative negotiations in Europe was the final recognition of the existence of two Germanys. The first formal treaty between these countries, signed on 26 April 1972, was ratified six months later. Diplomatic relations were agreed on in December and went into effect on 21 June 1973. Moscow was careful to orchestrate each diplomatic move, corresponding to these dates.

8. A. Rayzacher, *Zycie Warszawy* [Warsaw Life], 1 February 1973.

9. Ibid., 15 May 1973. Delay was caused by several external events, chiefly the preliminary talks for a CSCE at Helsinki. Debate centered around the question of the free flow of people and ideas. It proceeded slowly because there was no progress in Vienna. NATO wanted to include Hungary in the latter talks, but Moscow objected that all of its troops in Europe would be subject to reduction while only part of U.S. forces would be included. In the end, Hungary was not included in the troop reductions area.

10. The authoritative Soviet source was Academician N. N. Inozemtsev (1921–1982), head of the Institute of World Economy and International Relations (IMEMO) from 1966 until his death. A member of the CPSU Central Committee and a deputy in the USSR Supreme Soviet, Inozemtsev was a member of the Soviet Peace Committee and the Soviet Committee for European Security and Cooperation and chairman of the Peace and Disarmament Research Council (established in 1979). These positions made Inozemtsev a dominant figure in the Soviet peace establishment.

11. N. N. Inozemtsev, chief ed., *Mezhdunarodniye otnosheniya posle vtoroi voiny* [International Relations After World War II] (Moscow: Politizdat, 1965), 3:99.

12. William Robbins, "It Looked Good but It Went Bad," *New York Times*, 15 July 1973.

8

DEFENSE: RETALIATION OR PROTECTION?

Edward Teller

Nuclear bombs produce total destruction.

Prevention of total destruction requires retaliatory deterrence.

Retaliatory destructiveness necessitates arms limitations.

Arms treaties lessen the danger of nuclear war.

For more than two decades, these four statements have been the implicit basis for U.S. defense policy. Yet each is flawed. Policies once set in motion seem to acquire their own momentum. Breaking out of the fatal circle of these conclusions—in spite of all the evidence of their falsity—will not be easy. This essay offers a series of questions rather than clear, unambiguous answers. The questions are meant to raise some long overdue doubt about assumptions that affect the survival of the United States.

THINKING ABOUT UNTHINKABLE NUCLEAR WEAPONS

Few peoples, with the exception of the Aztecs and the Incas, have ever been faced with weapons as terrifyingly strange as the two exploded over Japan. In this case, however, almost everyone—not just those attacked—was ignorant of the nature of these weapons. But the shock of what may have been the greatest single surprise people ever experienced was overwhelmed by relief that a long, horrible war had ended.

The bombs that exploded over Japan had a most profound effect on the men who had helped to design and build them—particularly those who had advocated their use without warning.[1] Part of the scientific community found a hope to escape its fear: no other power would have an atomic weapon for a long time. However, four years later, the Soviet Union exploded its first atomic bomb. Work on the hydrogen bomb in the United States was finally seen as unavoidable. Both countries succeeded in developing the latter almost simultaneously.

The atomic bomb is a thousand times more powerful than the largest conventional bomb; the hydrogen bomb is a thousand times more powerful than the atomic bomb. The public awoke to a nightmare: weapons were becoming more powerful at an exponential rate; the world could be destroyed in a single explosion, or so it was thought.

The fusion bomb was a natural sequential development of the fission bomb. Three decades later, no further major developments in bombs have occurred. The explanation is simple. An explosive force much larger than that produced by the hydrogen bomb could not be confined by the pressure of the atmosphere. Damage from the blast would not extend laterally, and most of the radioactivity would pass into outer space. Such a bomb would have no military advantage.

Nonetheless, the apocalyptic vision continued: radiation poisoning would wipe out all life, or at least all human life. This and similarly easily disproved speculations have repeatedly become focal points of discussion. The actual horrors are sufficient. World War I cost 10 million lives; World War II 50 million. Reasonable estimates of what would occur in a nuclear war currently set the number of victims at between one hundred million and one billion people.[2] Believing that nuclear war would cause the end of the world makes it unnecessary to consider the actual terrible damage that could occur. Unfortunately, lack of thought does not solve problems or prevent war.

THE ORIGINS OF RETALIATORY DETERRENCE

During the 1960s, a new hope arose. Since these weapons were so horrible, a balance of terror would prevent their use. The systematic mind of Robert Strange McNamara (coupled with the exigencies of budget considerations) devised a policy that has come to be called—not without justification—MAD, an acronym for mutual assured destruction. Civilian vulnerability would prevent war.

The idea that deterrence must be based primarily on retaliation exercised against innocent bystanders was based on the fact that the first (fission) and second (fusion) generation of nuclear weapons were indiscriminately destructive. However, by 1965, nuclear weapons resulting in steadily decreasing peripheral damage were being developed. For more than a decade, it has been possible to achieve military objectives without extensive civilian destruction.

Even before the advent of nuclear weapons, World War II had profoundly affected military thinking about the superiority of offense. World War I had established the idea that defense (by means of trenches and machine guns) had an overwhelming advantage. But, in 1939, Germany introduced the *Blitzkrieg*, a form of offense so unusually rapid and successful that Genghis Khan's innovative development of disciplined mounted attack forces may be its only parallel.

Technically superb airplanes, tanks, and motorized artillery overwhelmed a nation with an army of 2.5 million in a few days;[3] a second strike, eight months later, expelled all Allied forces from the European continent within 45 days. The advantages of aggressive attack over defense came to be seen as overwhelming. But how much validity did this assumption possess even then?

World War II was not won by the aggressor. During the 1930s, while the appeasers were busy limiting Hitler's ambitions by concessions, a small group of British scientists began defense preparations. Among them was a mathematician, Alan Turing, who asserted that whatever a human brain could accomplish, a machine could do faster and more reliably. The only proviso was that the required mental activity be defined with mathematical accuracy.

When the British acquired the Nazi encoding-decoding device, they had models of all the possible codes the enemy could use. But given the huge number of possibilities, even an army of cryptographers could not have identified the correct code in time for the message to be useful. A score of dedicated men using Turing's prototype computer were able to do so. This technology changed history at the Battles of Britain, of the Atlantic, of El Alamein, and of Midway.

Creating a balance of terror could not have become a national policy without the more dramatic experiences of World War II. The shock of the atomic bomb obscured the destructiveness of earlier civilian bombing. More people died in Dresden than at Hiroshima. A single attack on Tokyo devastated almost three times the area that was destroyed by the first atomic attack. On seventeen occasions bombing attacks on Japanese cities devastated an area at least as large as that destroyed in Nagasaki. Incidentally, in Nagasaki, the people in a well-built conventional bomb shelter only one-third of a mile from ground zero survived, unharmed, the effects of a nuclear weapon explosion.[4]

Innocent bystanders have suffered in countless wars, but in World War II extensive damage was deliberately inflicted on urban areas. This innovation—distinct from that of nuclear weapons—was in large part due to the inability of contemporary technologies to achieve accurate bombing, a situation that is totally different today. A morally reprehensible strategy—developed during wartime under other technological conditions—deserves reexamination. Has this been done?

THE EFFECTS OF TECHNOLOGY ON WARFARE

Two accepted characteristics of technological warfare are the advantage it appears to give the aggressor and the horrors that it produces. However, technology has had another effect. Innovation can produce totally unexpected results. Attempts to utilize (and avoid) technical surprise have produced a great amount of secrecy.

Secrecy in weapons development within a dictatorship, where everything depends on central planning, is natural. In a democracy, however, its effects are apt to be harmful and can even be deadly. In a free society, secrecy impedes cooperation, on which innovative technology depends, and repels scientists, whose work demands the open exchange of ideas. Secrecy counteracts the great advantage that individualism can produce.

To see this truth in action, one need only compare the development of nuclear weapons technology with that of the computer industry. In the first, erecting barriers of secrecy, the United States began with an enormous advantage, which it has lost to the Soviet Union. In the second, where governmental secrecy played almost no part, the United States has maintained worldwide leadership and is unquestionably far ahead of the Soviet Union.

A second, more important effect of secrecy is that a free nation cannot select a proper course of action without public information. To wage war or peace effectively, the U.S. government must have the wholehearted support of the people for its policies. As long as citizens are not fully informed about the facts and principles affecting their fate, reasonable decisions will be rare. Yet this harmful practice continues, unaffected by common sense.

The long-held belief that defense against nuclear weapons is impossible cannot be refuted except by examples. Offering them would run up against security restrictions. Saying that defensive systems could be explained if this were permitted is necessarily an ineffective argument. Yet, this is the case. All that can be offered are the fringes of a case that at its core is sound but on its periphery must seem unimpressive. Because of secrecy, the best-publicized defense systems are those that are rather primitive or will not work at all.

CURRENT DEFENSE TECHNOLOGY

In the past few years, a remarkable number of brilliant ideas connected with potentially effective defensive weapons—some non-nuclear, some nuclear—have emerged. In any discussion of defense proposals, one essential requirement must be kept in mind: the protective system must cost less than the means that could defeat it. This is the crucial criterion for judging the soundness of any defensive plan.

Under proper conditions, lasers can emit sharply focused beams of electromagnetic radiation at amazing intensities, hardly modified over long distances. The beams can be directed against specific targets, such as incoming weapons. The best-known type of defense in this category has infrared lasers deployed in space, ready for action in case of attack.[5] Deploying space laser stations is expensive, but shooting them down is both cheap and easy. Furthermore, relatively simple modifications could protect the attacking weapons against infrared lasers.

Defensive lasers should not be predeployed in space. Appropriate mirrors located above the atmosphere can redirect laser beams generated on the ground. An excellent possibility exists that such mirrors can be deployed with sufficient speed after an attack begins. This in itself is an intricate new technology, full of problems that any astronomer can guess, but the difficulties show promise of being overcome.

Three further facts are pertinent to laser defense. Longer wavelength beams (such as infrared light) must be reflected by larger mirrors if they are to acquire a directionality comparable to that of shorter wavelength beams. In addition, the shorter the wavelength, the more efficient the laser becomes in defense. However, the difficulty of developing lasers increases as the wavelength used grows shorter. Since laser defense research has not received much attention, this field alone offers almost unlimited possibilities.

If space battle stations are expensive to deploy and difficult to defend, another problem should be clear. How can observation satellites, crucial to a warning system, be defended? Only a few reconnaissance stations are needed, but even the defense of these is difficult. Observation stations can probably be defended against rockets, and, at least to some extent, they also can be hardened against laser or nuclear weapon attack in space. In addition, each observation satellite can be accompanied by inconspicuous silent replacement stations, activated only if the original is destroyed. These "black" satellites in turn could be accompanied by numerous inexpensive decoys. The enemy's job of sweeping the sky could become far more expensive than defense of these objects. Still, the question of reliable early warning remains one of the most crucial protective defense questions.

Another class of defensive weapons has been described as third-generation nuclear arms. Although the second-generation fusion explosives were a thousand times more powerful than atomic bombs, they could also be made considerably cleaner—that is, emit much less radioactive fallout. The third-generation weapons continued the trend toward limiting damage. They were constructed to serve precise purposes—to generate extremely concentrated energy for a special, limited effect. Concentrated energy—for example, temperatures approximating those in the center of stars—produces unusual, novel effects.

One of these effects is called an electromagnetic pulse (EMP)—an emission of intense electromagnetic radiation of a much longer wavelength than infrared light. This type of pulse interferes with communications. Shorter wavelength emissions (still longer than infrared) can affect electronics—increasingly used in manufacturing, computers, and military weapons. An EMP weapon is but one of the new possibilities.

In 1962, scientists in the United States were surprised to run into intense manifestations of EMP following a weapons test. Shortly thereafter, they were amazed to find that these unanticipated effects had already been described in open Soviet literature.[6] It would be a great mistake to consider American scientists technical wizards with whom the Soviets can never compete. The Soviet Union has given primary emphasis to the military component of technology.

Another promising form of nuclear defense is also based on third-generation weapons. If incoming nuclear missiles penetrate the atmosphere, they still can be stopped without harmful ground effects. Small nuclear devices, exploded in proximity to the missiles, can destroy the attack weapons without detonating them. In this terminal phase of defense, enemy decoys accompanying the warheads are no longer effective. If the decoys are to be inexpensive, they must be light. If they are light, the upper atmosphere will slow them, so that they can easily be distinguished from warheads.

Terminal defense using non-nuclear weapons suffers from several problems. Some methods—for instance, using metal darts against the warheads—employ heavier objects. This means the defensive objects are less maneuverable and more expensive to deploy. The most important problem, however, is that warheads can be armed to explode on contact with any object. Even if this occurred far enough above ground to minimize the blast damage, the resulting electromagnetic disorder would blind detecting radar. Small nuclear explosives are much more difficult to counter and would not cause substantial interference with ground-based observation.

Deterrence of a conventional attack, while less in the public mind than ballistic missiles, is of vital importance to maintaining peace. Another (badly misunderstood) defensive nuclear weapon is the so-called neutron bomb—a very small nuclear explosive designed to be detonated a few hundred feet above ground.[7] Heat and fallout from these weapons cause no damage, and the shock waves, at worst, would break a few windows. These weapons produce a brief intense burst of radiation. Crews in armored tanks within a thousand feet of the explosion would be vulnerable.

Because the neutron bomb would be so effective against conventional attack, Soviet opposition to its deployment has been intense. In contrast to the artillery shelling that it would effectively replace, the neutron bomb causes no property damage in the defended area. Furthermore, because of its precise and limited effects, the neutron bomb would sharply limit injuries among the defended populace. People only one-half mile from the explosion would not be harmed. Even those unable to leave the immediate path of the invasion would be safe in a deep cellar with protective layers of sandbags over the floor.

However, the invading personnel—in planes, tanks, or armored personnel carriers—would be defenseless against these precisely targeted, small defensive weapons. The Soviets have no need for the neutron bomb, not because it is a "capitalistic" weapon, but because they fear no invasion.

Another argument against this weapon suggests that once the nuclear firebreak is crossed, a full-scale nuclear exchange cannot be stopped. Why this should be true remains unanswered. There is a marked difference between an offensive and a defensive weapon. The West should arm itself with this excellent deterrent and, at the same time, announce that its forces will never use nuclear weapons first *on enemy territory*. A potential invader then would have three choices: to be defeated by the neutron bomb; to be first to use nuclear weapons on enemy territory (and thus risk full-scale nuclear retaliation); not to attack.

ANOTHER FORM OF DETERRENCE

The 1972 Anti-Ballistic Missile Treaty between the United States and the Soviet Union limited protective defense installations to two sites per country (later reduced to one). No limits were placed on research because such stipulations could not be verified. The United States set up a system near Grand

Forks, North Dakota, to protect its retaliatory missiles but abandoned the effort after a short time. Research in the United States languished, in part because democratic people try to abide by the intent as well as the detailed stipulations of a treaty. Other, more important problems involved the amount of funding and the interest scientists had in a project that probably would not be deployed.

The Soviets built their defensive system around Moscow. In the past few years, they have upgraded it substantially. There should be little doubt that none of the possibilities that U.S. weapons laboratories are now considering have escaped Soviet attention, nor should one doubt that actual development and deployment of a system adds to knowledge about how to improve it. While retaliation has provided great deterrent strength in the past, its major flaw (aside from moral bankruptcy) is that it assumes the absence of new technology. What would happen if truly effective defensive systems against nuclear attack weapons were achieved?

On 23 March 1983, President Reagan had the courage to cast doubt on some of the concepts underlying current defense policy: "Would it not be better to save lives than to avenge them?"[8] The question implicitly challenges the validity of the first two statements of this essay, assertions that by repetition seem to have become absolute truth.

Although President Reagan never mentioned the word *space* or any special form or system of protection, the media promptly labeled the speech "Star Wars" and began an intensive campaign to obscure the real issues. Were there reasons other than political bias? What are the objections to a humane proposal that might protect civilian populations?

Many claim that nuclear defense is absurd because nothing less than completely impenetrable defense will do. If only one warhead escapes destruction, the effect will be so terrible as to render defense useless. The argument has deceptive simplicity and, therefore, great persuasive power. Nevertheless, it is wrong. The main purpose of defense is not to win a war but to deter it.

In 1969, at a conference in Glacier National Park, the moderator in his introduction gently chided me about the insufficiency of current defensive possibilities. He described a walk we had taken a few hours earlier during which I had picked up a stick. When asked why, I replied (not truthfully), "For protection against grizzly bears." When asked if I didn't know that a stick was inadequate, I replied, "I know, but I hope the grizzlies don't." The moderator concluded, "Dr. Teller will now talk to us about antiballistic missile systems."

The quality of sticks has improved markedly since 1969, but the bears in the Kremlin, now as then, are extremely cautious. They embark on adventures only when the odds are overwhelmingly in their favor. They do not strike aggressively if they are not sure of their success. With such an adversary, deterrent strength, whatever its basis, has value.

Decades ago, opponents of the H-bomb argued that the weapon should not be developed because it was too horrible. Today, opponents of protective defense claim that such measures should not be developed because they may make nuclear war less horrible and, therefore, more acceptable. While the sets of opponents are separated by one-third of a century, their membership has considerable overlap. Both points of view used by the same people cannot be entirely correct.

There is no tolerable level of destruction should a major nuclear war break out. If deterrence fails, protective defense, at best, might reduce the level of sacrifice and suffering to one similar to other major wars. The difference may still save hundreds of millions of lives. But, more important, the deterrent effect of protective defense might prevent war, while its absence only adds to the probability of war.

THE ARMS LIMITATION ALTERNATIVE

The last and probably most popular argument against defensive systems is: "Why bother? End the arms race now. Technological development can be stopped by negotiating a treaty."

At least a quarter century ago, in hopes of setting limits on the race in offensive nuclear weapons, a series of arms limitation negotiations were begun. Has the probability or potential destructiveness of nuclear war declined in that period?

Negotiations have included the demand that the agreements be verifiable. Clearly the number and kind of nuclear explosives could not be verified, so the number of fixed missile sites was substituted as the control. Even the verification of this incomplete component has been proved to rest on an insecure foundation. SALT I failed to specify that missile sites should be able to fire only a single missile. The Soviets, but not the Americans, used this oversight to their advantage.

The only post–World War I arms limitation treaty that survived World War II was the 1925 Geneva Protocol outlawing chemical and biological warfare. In 1972, many countries, including the United States and the Soviet Union, signed a treaty forbidding the production or stockpiling of biological and toxin weapons. In 1981, the U.S. State Department issued a well-documented report about the more than 10,000 people in Laos, Cambodia, and Afghanistan who had died from the effects of toxin weapons originating in the Soviet Union.[9] Two years earlier, an accident involving anthrax—a most dangerous disease in its pulmonary form—had occurred in Sverdlovsk in the Soviet Union. The American press raised the suspicion that the Soviets were preparing biological weapons in the area.[10] The responses from the Soviet Union have not been enlightening. No one from outside has been allowed—even this many years later—to examine any of the locations in question.

A 1975 agreement guarantees certain simple human rights. Although the Soviets signed the Final Act of the Conference on Security and Cooperation in Europe, commonly known as the Helsinki Accords, they do not even pretend to comply with it. In this case, continuing negotiations in hopes of obtaining more lenient treatment of those—such as Anatoly Shcharansky—held in harsh imprisonment for seeking these rights is understandable.

It seems that where treaties can be verified, they are clearly violated; where verification is more difficult, violations (because they cannot be fully identified) are ignored. One of the psychological complications of making treaties that cannot be verified is that by holding out hope, such treaties make facing unpleasant truths more difficult. What would happen if the United States issued an ultimatum on the Sverdlovsk incident: either permit inspection so that bacteriological experts can assure that the 1975 production and stockpiling agreement was not violated, or the treaty will be terminated?

How would active U.S. research on biological weapons and their countermeasures affect the probability of biological warfare? The development of bacteriological weapons rests on the science of genetics. Until the 1940s, the Soviet Union had a splendid assembly of geneticists. Then Stalin, advised by Academician T. D. Lysenko that Mendel's theories were wrong, not only approved redirection of all genetic research in the Soviet Union and its satellites but also destroyed the best of a whole generation of geneticists. The effects on agriculture and on mutations research were so profound that the USSR has not yet recovered. The Soviets would be in a clearly inferior position should they attempt biological warfare—if the United States were prepared.

Work on countermeasures to biological warfare agents automatically benefits medical science, and freedom of information in this area of defense should be absolute. Dangerous microorganisms can be produced, but they also occur spontaneously. Wartime and peacetime activities, as this case demonstrates, can never be distinguished sharply. The dangers produced by lack of preparedness are clear.

Why negotiate treaties where verification is uncertain? Such treaties increase suspicion and tension and, if not observed bilaterally, weaken deterrence. Treaties whose verification is simple and straightforward could have good results. International tensions could be decreased by negotiating about topics that would make the consequences of a war, should it come in spite of all good efforts, less terrible. This type of negotiation has time-honored models going back almost one hundred years, an example being the prohibition of exploding bullets.[11] When the combatants have had equal technologies, the 1925 Geneva Protocol forbidding chemical or biological warfare has also been effective. Such treaties do not affect military strength but do reduce unnecessary suffering.

Negotiations to diminish the useless pain, suffering, and destructiveness from a nuclear war are not only justified but even necessary. Radioactive fallout could produce varying amounts of damage and suffering. Present preliminary calculations indicate that the average fallout that would occur outside the combat zones from an all-out nuclear war would be in the range of 20 to 30 R units.[12] This would occur in the general latitudes in which combat takes place, most probably between 30 and 70 degrees latitude in the Northern Hemisphere, the place of residence of the majority of the world's people.

Statistically, 20 or 30 R units cannot be proved harmful because the effects are small enough that the sample size is impractically large.[13] However, this amount is likely to have some harmful effects. The actual problem, however, is that fallout does not disperse evenly, and varying weather conditions will tend to concentrate it in hot spots—areas where the radioactivity may be ten times greater. Unprotected people in the hot spots would suffer ill effects, and many would die.

But a worse scenario is possible. Electricity-generating nuclear reactors can be put out of operation by bombing, without serious additional consequences. However, if the radioactivity contained in the world's reactors and in nearby cooling ponds were dispersed, the fallout over the immense area included in the latitudes of combat could go up threefold.[14] No military advantage would be gained, but the number of additional victims could approach 100 million. The average radiation would be 60 R units, and in the hot spots, at least half of the people would die. Why not attempt to negotiate an agreement to avoid dispersing reactor materials? Clearly, such a treaty would be in the best interest of both sides.

Ten years ago, studies conducted at Lawrence Livermore National Laboratory indicated that powerful nuclear weapons have the effect of depleting the ozone present at high altitudes.[15] The ozone layer filters out ultraviolet radiation, which causes skin cancer and possibly eye damage and is harmful to biologically sensitive plants. The increase in skin cancer is unlikely to be a serious problem, but the effect on eyes and on the ecosystem has not been thoroughly studied. It is quite unlikely that the effects would be tolerable.[16]

The amount of damage that the ozone suffers is closely related to the size of the nuclear explosives used. The ozone layer will be damaged only if the individual nuclear weapons are at least half a megaton (500 kilotons) in explosive power. A one-megaton weapon will cause much more damage to the ozone layer, and several megatons even more. Damage is not just proportional to megatonnage, but is related to the distance that the fireball penetrates into the ozone layer, a factor that increases sharply with greater explosive power.[17]

The United States has almost no nuclear weapons that would produce ozone damage.[18] The United States found that weapons of 100 to 200 kilotons have the greatest military usefulness, and almost all of its weapons are concentrated in this range. The USSR controls the vast majority of the warheads of a size that might bring about this atmospheric effect.

The average size of the Soviet nuclear weapons seems to have begun to decrease. It may be that Soviet leaders have started to understand that what they are doing is not militarily useful. An agreement to decrease the size of nuclear weapons would not reduce military effectiveness, but it would have a considerable effect on peripheral damage.

A final and most interesting type of possible negotiation involves the bombing of cities. When a city burns, it produces smoke of a different composition from that of a forest fire. Smoke from burning cities is dirty and absorbs solar radiation, lowering the temperature on the surface of the earth.

Lawrence Livermore National Laboratory calculations suggest that, incredibly enough, if the major cities in the Soviet Union, Europe, and the United States were burned, the temperature in the combat latitudes would drop by approximately 20 degrees F for a period of at least 90 days.[19] Calculations by a Soviet scientist indicate very large temperature changes—60 degrees F and more—over mid-continental areas.[20] The effects of such climatic changes would be extremely serious.

Before any negotiations can be initiated, the accuracy of the calculations must be improved as much as possible. At the 1983 Ettore Majorana Centre's International Seminar on Nuclear War held in Italy, the Soviets were represented by E. P. Velikhov, a vice-president of their Academy of Science and an excellent plasma physicist. By a very informal agreement, Velikhov, Antonino Zichichi of the European Organization for Nuclear Research (CERN), and this writer agreed to look into these questions and try to arrive at factual agreement on them. For such work, negotiations are not necessary.

If the Soviets recognize that the indiscriminate destruction of cities outside the USSR might damage their own climate, that the size of their weapons would damage the ozone layer, and that fallout damage can be minimized to mutual advantage, negotiations with mutually beneficial results seem possible. Agreement on these vital issues could contribute to a lessening of tensions. In fact, refusing such agreements would be impossible unless a government acknowledges in public that it wants to kill as many people as possible.

THE REQUIREMENTS OF DEFENSE

Requirements for offense and defense are radically different. An attacker has the advantage of surprise and will be helped by massive expenditures, great effort, and by secrecy. The defender needs only one thing: intelligence and more intelligence. In fact, infinite intelligence would be required to be prepared for all eventualities.

The chance of success, for either a defender or an attacker, is increased by following behavior appropriate to each role. In a technological era, research is limited by the number of talented minds applied to it. A strong defense cannot be developed unless the largest possible number of excellent scientists are devoted to this task. The highest possible degree of intelligence can be obtained only if the free world works together.

That both scientific talent and technological ability are much greater in the West than in the Soviet Union is obvious. Talking openly, at least sharing the non-nuclear defense work—for instance, lasers and aiming systems—with U.S. allies, is an absolute necessity if the alliance is to survive and be strong.

Many countries whose stable purpose is to preserve peace are already cooperating within the framework of NATO. More states can be added, without raising any doubt that pursuit of power will take precedence over pursuit of peace. The United States' main negotiations should be with its allies and potential allies and should be aimed at decreasing secrecy and increasing cooperative protective defense work. The cooperative development of defensive weapons could weld together all advanced free countries long before the work of creating this defense had neared completion. Such cooperation could turn out to be the strongest deterrent of all.

At the same time, negotiations with the Soviets should focus on agreements that might lead to a further increase in mutual security. These agreements should involve issues on which compliance will be obvious and the effects of noncompliance clear. Since these treaties cannot put either side at a military disadvantage, they offer a far more productive course of action. But even without negotiations, the emphasis in military preparedness can probably be shifted toward defense.

Defensive deterrence has suffered three decades of neglect. Restoring the balance is a crucial immediate need. Twenty-five years of disarmament negotiations have been frustrating and sad, indeed, almost disastrous. Today, we have the opportunity, both to develop protective defense and to turn negotiations to good ends—to save lives and protect people, those in the free world and in the rest of the world as well.

NOTES

1. Edward Teller, "Seven Hours of Reminiscences," *Los Alamos Science* 7 (Spring 1983): 192.

2. The variance in the estimates results from different assumptions about strategy and the number of countries involved in direct attack.

3. By the sixth day, Poland's military forces were so shattered that only pockets of resistance remained. Seventeen days after the German attack, the Soviet army also invaded. By the end of the month (September 1939), the valiant but hopeless fight was over.

4. David Irving, *The Destruction of Dresden* (New York: Holt, Rinehart & Winston, 1964), p. 210; U.S. Office of Air Force History (Wesley Frank Craven and James Lea Cate, eds.), *The Army Air Forces in World War II*, vol. 5, *The Pacific: Matterhorn to Nagasaki, June 1944 to August 1945* (Chicago: University of Chicago Press, 1953), pp. 636–43, 674–75; and Francis X. Lynch, "Adequate Shelters and Quick Reaction to Warning: A Key to Civil Defense," *Science* 142 (8 November 1963): 665–67.

5. Angelo Codevilla, "Defense from Space," *Policy Review* 25 (Summer 1983): 67–69.

6. A. S. Kompanees, "Radio Emission from an Atomic Explosion," *Soviet Physics JETP*, 1959, pp. 1076–80; and O. I. Leitunski, "Possible Magnetic Effects from High Altitude Explosions of Atomic Bombs," *Soviet Physics JETP*, 1960, pp. 219–21.

7. This is more accurately called an enhanced radiation weapon.

8. Ronald Reagan, "Peace and National Security: A New Defense," *Vital Speeches of the Day*, 15 April 1983, pp. 386–90.

9. U.S. Department of State, Bureau of Public Affairs, Office of Public Communication, "Chemical Warfare in Southeast Asia and Afghanistan: Report to the Congress from Secretary of State Alexander M. Haig, Jr., 22 March 1982," Special Report no. 98 (Washington, D.C., March 1982).

10. "Anthrax Fever: New Report on Germ Research," *Time*, 23 June 1980, p. 14.

11. The First Hague Conference Declaration on Expanding Bullets was signed in 1899.

12. J. B. Knox, "Global Scale Deposition of Radioactivity from a Large Scale Exchange," in *Proceedings of the International Seminar on Nuclear War, Third Session: The Technical Basis for Peace* (New York: Plenum Publishing, forthcoming).

13. Committee on the Biological Effects of Ionizing Radiations, *The Effects on*

Populations of Exposure to Low Levels of Ionizing Radiation: 1980 (Washington, D.C.: National Academy, 1980), pp. 139–40.

14. Knox, "Global Scale Deposition of Radioactivity."

15. J. S. Chang and W. H. Duewer, "Possible Effect of NO_x Injection in the Stratosphere Due to Atmospheric Nuclear Weapons Tests," UCRL-74480 (Livermore, Calif.: Lawrence Livermore National Laboratory, May 1973).

16. Committee to Study the Long-Term Worldwide Effects of Multiple Nuclear-Weapons Detonations, *Long-Term Worldwide Effects of Multiple Nuclear-Weapons Detonations* (Washington, D.C.: National Academy of Sciences and National Research Council, 1975), pp. 8–9, 14, 178–79.

17. F. M. Luther, "Nuclear War: Short-term Chemical and Radiative Effects of Stratospheric Injections," in *Proceedings of the International Seminar on Nuclear War.*

18. U.S. Department of Defense, "The United States Nuclear Weapons Stockpile," News Release no. 424–83 (Washington, D.C., 25 August 1983).

19. M. C. MacCracken, "Estimated Climatic Effects of Nuclear Exchange," in *Proceedings of the International Seminar on Nuclear War.*

20. V. V. Alexandrov, "Climatic Response to Global Injections," in *Proceedings of the International Seminar on Nuclear War.*

9

THE FUTURE: CAN THE ISSUES BE RESOLVED?

Mark B. Schneider

The most fundamental task facing all Americans today is the preservation of their national security, peace, and freedom. One of these cannot be achieved at the price of the other two. Americans need to maintain all three if their country is to prosper and they are to preserve the heritage of freedom and the American way of life in an increasingly hostile and dangerous world.

The most basic national security problem is how to deal with the Soviet Union. The issues and alternatives are fairly well drawn. The Reagan administration stands for "peace through strength." It follows a prudent and responsible policy of attempting to negotiate effective and *verifiable* arms control agreements with the Soviet Union. Many critics of this approach have consistently campaigned for "détente"-style unequal, ineffective, and unverifiable agreements.

The Reagan administration recognizes that the USSR has achieved a dangerous margin of military superiority over the United States and its allies. This has resulted from a decade of defense underfunding in the face of a steady, large-scale Soviet buildup of military power. During the 1970s, the USSR outspent the United States in military spending by $400 billion.

The Soviet effort in developing strategic nuclear forces is enormous. In 1982 and 1983, the USSR began flight-testing two new ICBMs and probably will test two additional ones before the end of 1984. The Soviets have continued to deploy improved fourth-generation weapons systems that now threaten the survivability of the U.S. ICBM force. The USSR is developing a new heavy strategic bomber, the Blackjack, while continuing to produce the formidable Backfire. Under construction are the Typhoon-class submarines, the largest ballistic missile submarines in the world. The Soviets continue to deploy SS-20 intermediate-range missiles at the rate of about one launcher per week. They have under way an extensive modernization of air defense forces and are deploying a new ballistic missile defense system around Moscow.[1]

The Soviet military buildup involves more than strategic nuclear forces. Ground and air forces are being modernized at an alarming rate. T-64, -72, and -80 advanced tanks exist in large numbers, while the United States is just beginning to improve its outnumbered inventory. The USSR recently introduced a 152-millimeter nuclear artillery shell and a new generation of advanced tactical fighter aircraft. The Soviet naval construction program features construction of four new classes of advanced surface warships as well as nuclear attack and cruise missile submarines. This last category includes the Oscar-class submarines, which carry no fewer than 24 launch tubes for 500-kilometer-range antiship cruise missiles. The Soviets are now building a large nuclear-powered aircraft carrier.[2]

While modernizing the United States' nuclear deterrent forces, the Reagan administration has begun a series of arms control negotiations with the Soviet Union. These negotiations differ somewhat from those of the past. The United States is making a serious effort to achieve genuine reductions instead of merely negotiating supposed limits on future deployments.

While in office, Secretary of State Alexander Haig outlined the Reagan administration's principles of the arms control.

— Our first principle is that our arms control efforts will be an instrument of, not a replacement for, a coherent allied security policy.

— Our second principle is that we will seek arms control agreements that truly enhance security.

— Our third principle is that we will seek arms control bearing in mind the whole context of Soviet conduct worldwide.

— Our fourth principle is that we will seek balanced arms control agreements.

— Our fifth principle is that we will seek arms controls that include effective means of verification and mechanisms for securing compliance.

— Our sixth principle is that our strategy must consider the totality of various arms control processes and various weapons systems, not only those being specifically negotiated.[3]

More specifically, the Reagan administration has adopted four principles that have shaped the content of its arms control proposals:

1. Significant reductions in the arsenals of both sides;
2. Equal force levels on both sides since unequal levels can encourage coercion and aggression;
3. Effectively verifiable agreements; and
4. Enhanced U.S. and allied security by actual reduction in the risk of war.[4]

In the fall of 1981, the Reagan administration announced a new program to modernize the U.S. nuclear deterrent and reduce the vulnerability of its key elements to nuclear attack. Under this program all parts of the triad are to be improved over the next decade. The government also increased research and development efforts on strategic defensive forces. This program is of vital importance to U.S. arms control efforts. Without it, there will be little if any incentive for the Soviet Union to agree to the type of arms control constraints the United States has proposed.

The topic of the future of arms control has certain advantages. Nothing I say can be proved wrong in the immediate future.

The only way I know of attempting to predict the future is to study the past, determine the direction of events and their causes, and extrapolate this into the future. Past experiences with arms control are hardly heartening. Some of Sir Winston Churchill's comments on the 1935 Anglo-German Naval Agreement have a rather contemporary ring to them:

> The Foreign Secretary dwelt upon the advantages which the Naval Agreement confers upon us. Those advantages are very doubtful. Of course, it is quite wrong to pretend that the apparition of Germany as a formidable naval Power, equipped with submarines and all the other apparatus of war, is the result of the Naval Agreement. That would have happened anyhow. The deep purposes of great nations are not, I am afraid, governed by the ebb and flow of political discussions or by temporary agreements which are made. It has for some time been evident that Germany intends to embark upon a gigantic process of rearming by land, sea and air, which will make her the most formidable military Power in the whole world. I am not blaming upon this Agreement these events and the misfortunes which will follow from them, but when the Prime Minister says, and he did the other day, that he hoped this would be a great measure of disarmament, let me tell him that I am afraid it will not.[5]

Few today would quarrel with Churchill's profound and insightful assessment. Unfortunately, one could have said almost the same thing about arms control in the 1970s.[6] This does not exactly make for optimism about the future.

The future of arms control will depend on negotiations between the two most powerful sovereign states. Whether there will be effective arms control agreements in the future depends at least as much on Soviet acts as it does on U.S. policy. An agreement with the Soviet Union certainly can be achieved through a series of unilateral concessions by the United States, but such an agreement would represent little more than "cosmetic" arms control—an agreement that merely legitimized a massive Soviet force buildup, unequal levels of forces, and unverifiable provisions.

Not the slightest reason exists for the U.S. government to be defensive concerning its attitude toward arms control. Every U.S. administration since 1969 has proposed to the Soviet Union far-reaching arms control agreements, which, if they had been accepted by the USSR, would have improved the security of both parties significantly. It is not the fault of the United States that these proposals were rejected.[7]

The Reagan administration has still less cause to be defensive about its arms control record. It has proposed a series of very sound arms control concepts to the Soviet Union. It has called for agreements that would result in mutual and verifiable arms reductions. Even in the aftermath of the Korean Air Lines massacre, it has continued these negotiations without a break.

Much of what can be achieved in the future will depend on the attitude of the Soviet government toward arms control. Unfortunately, there is no reason to believe that these attitudes will be much different in the future from what they have been in the past. Not much effort is required to document consistent Soviet opposition to effective limitations involving Soviet armed forces, equal levels, precise agreements, and cooperative verification, particularly of the intrusive variety.

It is also not very difficult to document that the existing strategic arms control agreements, SALT I and SALT II, have done little if anything to limit the increase in the number of Soviet nuclear weapons aimed at the United States. A threefold increase has taken place since 1972 when SALT I was signed, and a 75 percent growth since the 1979 SALT II agreement.[8]

American force levels also have risen during this period, although at only a small fraction of the Soviet increases. There has been virtually no increase since 1979 in the number of U.S. strategic nuclear weapons aimed at the Soviet Union. The United States froze the number of its ballistic missiles in 1967 and reduced the number of its heavy bombers significantly. Indeed, from the mid-1960s to 1983, the total U.S. nuclear stockpile dropped by 8,000 weapons, and the megatonnage of these weapons has decreased by 75 percent.[9]

When the United States began the SALT negotiations in 1969, all three legs of the U.S. deterrent were invulnerable to Soviet attack. Today, almost all U.S. ICBMs could be destroyed by the USSR utilizing only a fraction of its ICBM force. The United States' strategic bomber force is also vulnerable under certain circumstances. The Soviet Union, on the other hand, has a much more survivable deterrent today than it did in 1969. The basic reason for this can be attributed to U.S. restraint. The United States clearly has the technical capability to threaten every leg of the Soviet deterrent to a greater extent than the USSR has threatened the U.S. deterrent. It has not done so.

The United States has complied most scrupulously with the letter and intent of arms control agreements. The Soviet Union clearly has not. The Reagan administration has taken the Soviet compliance record into account in formulating its approach to arms control. To have failed to do so would have been reckless in the extreme. It is no longer possible to argue that acceptance of a bad agreement will result in a good agreement in the future. There is clear evidence that acceptance of bad agreements results in bad future agreements and encourages further deterioration in the United States' relative strategic posture.

Verification and compliance are of critical importance to effective arms control agreements in the future. In the words of President Reagan, "Simply collecting agreements will not bring peace. Agreements genuinely reinforce peace only when they are kept. Otherwise, we are building a paper castle that will be blown away by the winds of war." [10]

Back in 1979, many of us believed that the Soviet compliance record was bad. Today, earlier issues look almost trivial compared with those we now face, and these issues have direct relevance for the future of effective arms control.

In March 1983, President Reagan told the Los Angeles World Affairs Council: "I am sorry to say there have been increasingly serious grounds for questioning their [Soviet] compliance with arms control agreements that have already been signed and that we have both pledged to uphold." [11]

Among the most disturbing issues today is the Soviet use of chemical and biological weapons. As President Reagan told the United Nations Special Session on Disarmament, "The Soviet Union and their allies are violating the Geneva Protocol of 1925, related rules of international law and the 1972 biological weapons convention. There is conclusive evidence that the Soviet government has provided toxins for use in Laos and Kampuchea, and are themselves using chemical weapons against freedom fighters in Afghanistan." [12]

Concerning the 1974 Threshold Test Ban Treaty, which limits nuclear testing to 150 kilotons, President Reagan commented, "We have reason to believe that there have been numerous violations. And, yet, because of the lack of verification capability, we could not make such a charge and sustain it." [13]

A number of compliance issues have arisen involving SALT II. Regarding the Soviets' testing of two new ICBMs, President Reagan said, "We have reason to believe that very possibly, they were in violation of the SALT agreement."[14] Then-director of the Arms Control and Disarmament Agency Eugene Rostow addressed the same subject with the following words: "Certainly evidence has come along that causes great concern about whether the SS-16 provisions of SALT II are being respected."[15] On the issue of Soviet telemetry encryption, Secretary of Defense Caspar Weinberger has observed that "there may be a violation, indeed, and this would not be the first time."[16]

There are also serious questions about Soviet compliance with the 1972 Anti-Ballistic Missile (ABM) Treaty. During its last days in office, the Carter administration revealed that "Soviet phased array radars, which may be designed to improve impact predictions and target handling for ABM battle management, are under construction at various locations throughout the USSR. These radars could perform some battle management functions as well as provide redundant ballistic missile early warning coverage."[17] One of these radars is of particular concern. As the U.S. Department of State has announced, "the existence of this radar does raise serious questions with respect to its consistency with the ABM treaty."[18]

The bipartisan Scowcroft Commission report voiced concern about the possibility of a "Soviet rapid breakout from the ABM treaty by a quick further deployment of current ABM systems, or the deployment of air defense systems having some capability against strategic ballistic missiles."[19]

It is vital to the United States that future arms control agreements be more carefully drafted to provide a better legal basis for challenging Soviet actions and that treaties include effective mechanisms for verification. Based on previous experience with the USSR, the United States can only expect the Soviets to continue to oppose both of these efforts.

This, of course, creates a dilemma for the United States. Does it simply accept predictable Soviet acts of misconduct without any response? How can it? In the words of President Reagan, after the Korean Air Lines massacre, "What can be said about Soviet credibility when they so flagrantly lie about such a heinous act?"[20]

What does this mean for verification? After the acceptance by the Soviets of two strategic arms control agreements that prohibit deliberate concealment that impedes verification, they seek to justify shooting down a civilian airliner because it crossed the "sacred" borders of the USSR, "overflying our critical strategic facilities." Even if one believed the fairy tale that this aircraft was on a reconnaissance mission, what does the Soviet statement imply about Soviet willingness to accept any type of cooperative verification in the future? The USSR deliberately shot down an airliner for overflying a remote area of the country at night, above what they admit was heavy cloud cover, when even a real reconnaissance plane could not have photographed anything of significance. Would a regime that does not hesitate to kill hundreds of innocent people because a commercial airliner strayed off course agree to cooperative verification?[21]

Verification is not the only issue involved in the future of arms control. Substance is at least as important as verification. It does little good to verify expansion, under an agreement, of dangerous and destabilizing weapons systems. Compliance issues, as important as they are, should not obscure the fact that most of the Soviet buildup has taken place within both the letter and the spirit of SALT I and II.

The Reagan administration is often accused of a lack of "seriousness" concerning arms control because it is attempting to do better than past administrations have done in negotiating with the USSR. Yet, as Assistant Secretary of Defense Richard Perle has observed,

> Is it a sign of seriousness to make concessions to the Soviet desire to accumulate and preserve significant advantages in nuclear weapons? Is the ease with which we abandon our objectives and make "progress" toward an agreement—any agreement—a sign of seriousness? Is there any relationship between seriousness and the content of the agreements we seek to negotiate?

Stripped of the rhetoric about *seriousness*, the core of the criticism against U.S. proposals, Perle continued,

> amounts to little more than that we modify our proposals so as to permit the Soviets to retain a vastly larger strategic arsenal than the levels the administration has proposed. According to this view, seriousness is to be found on the side of the big guns—or, in this case, the big missiles.[22]

Curiously, those who equate seriousness with a willingness to accept a bad agreement that permits force expansion and higher Soviet force levels somehow reject the argument that the USSR's willingness to accept meaningful limits will depend on its perception of how serious the United States is in meeting the threat the USSR poses to it. The extent to which Congress will fund administration programs in this area is one of the fundamental uncertainties today. Yet it has very profound implications for any assessment of the Soviet willingness to agree to equal and verifiable agreements in the future.

The core of the bipartisan Scowcroft Commission report on strategic forces asserts that the United States will have to proceed with the MX and other elements of its strategic force modernization program if there is to be a chance of Soviet acceptance of substantial arms reductions. The commission went even further and noted that the real lever the United States has to obtain Soviet acceptance of such reductions is the threat that it would deploy several hundred MX missiles if the USSR refused to bargain in good faith.

Hopefully, the Korean Air Lines massacre has destroyed the notion that in dealing with the Soviets we are really dealing with Americans who wear funny fur hats. If there is one consistent element throughout the history of the USSR, it is the respect for power and especially Soviet military power as the foundation of national strength. The Soviets will accept significant limitations only if they are convinced that they are dealing with a serious competitor. The United States must take the actions necessary to preserve its security if it is unable to achieve this objective through equitable and verifiable agreement. If the Soviets are convinced that the longer they wait, the more concessions the United States will make, the more strategic programs Congress will terminate, and the more likely that electoral pressures will result in unilateral concessions, then the USSR will have every incentive to avoid an agreement.

If we can identify a critical weakness in the United States' approach to arms control, it is the tendency to pre-negotiate agreements within the bureaucracy to assure *fairness* vis-à-vis the Soviet Union. The proposals that the Reagan administration has made to the USSR have been more than fair. The Soviets, on the other hand, particularly in the area of intermediate-range nuclear missiles (INF), have yet to make a serious proposal. To date, only the United States has offered compromises in these negotiations. The Soviets have merely repackaged the same basic inequitable and ineffective proposal. The basic elements of the Soviet INF proposal are

1. The USSR should have a monopoly on INF missiles in Europe; the United States should have none.

2. British and French bombers and missiles should be counted on the side of the United States;

3. Soviet missiles and bombers outside the European part of the USSR should not be effectively limited, despite their ability to strike targets in Western Europe; and,

4. U.S. but not Soviet, tactical fighter aircraft should be limited in Europe.

As President Reagan has observed, "I've also repeated our willingness to consider any serious alternative proposal. Their failure to make such a proposal is a source of deep disappointment to all of us who have wished that these weapons might be eliminated or at least significantly reduced." [23]

In the area of strategic weapons, the Soviet Union's position at the Strategic Arms Reduction Talks (START), while somewhat more equitable than its INF position, still contained virtually all the defects of SALT II. In 1979, these defects made the Senate Armed Services Committee conclude that SALT II was "not in the national security interest of the United States of America."[24] Some of the initial Soviet proposals in START seemed little more than ploys to curtail vital U.S. programs, such as the Trident missile, while allowing the Soviet force buildup to continue. Like SALT II, the Soviet START proposal would allow a continued expansion of the most threatening type of Soviet strategic nuclear missile systems and would preserve the many inequalities of SALT II that favored the Soviet Union.

In the chemical weapons area, the USSR is asking for a complete ban on these weapons, without effective verification, and this in the face of irrefutable evidence that the Soviets are violating existing agreements on chemical and biological weapons.

In the nuclear testing area, the USSR is asking for an unverifiable comprehensive test ban, while refusing to negotiate effective verification procedures for the Threshold Test Ban Treaty.

One could go on listing other examples, but the common characteristic of all Soviet proposals is opposition to effective verification, effective limits on Soviet forces, weapons reductions, and equal force levels. The basic Soviet position seems to be "What's ours is ours, and what's yours is negotiable."

As Richard Perle has observed, "In our view, seriousness requires clear-sighted objectives, militarily significant outcomes, and agreements that are equal and verifiable."[25] To achieve them, the United States must have patience and courage. These results cannot be attained quickly, for the simple reason that the Soviets will not permit it. Results that can be arrived at quickly are, in most cases, simply not worth the effort. They would, in fact, prove harmful with regard to U.S. aims, that is, real reductions and improvements in national security. The Soviets clearly prefer to wait and see whether they can achieve agreements like those they have made in the past, agreements that leave their military programs largely unimpeded and that will allow their buildup to continue. We must remember that it took seven years to negotiate a *fatally flawed* SALT II treaty.

If the United States is to achieve effective arms control with the Soviet Union, it must show patience and determination. Congress must fund the strategic force improvements that the Reagan administration has proposed. The USSR must be convinced that the United States will respond to new Soviet programs and to circumventions or violations of arms control agreements. Only then will the Soviet Union have a compelling incentive to negotiate in good faith. Only then will the United States have any chance of obtaining effective and verifiable arms control.

NOTES

1. U.S. Department of Defense, *Soviet Military Power*, 2d ed. (Washington, D.C.: Government Printing Office, 1983), pp. 15–31.

2. Ibid., pp. 33–63.

3. Alexander Haig, "Arms Control for the 1980s: An American Policy," *Current Policy* (Washington, D.C.: U.S. Department of State), no. 292 (14 July 1981): 1–2.

4. U.S. Department of State, "Arms Control and the Nuclear Freeze Proposal" (Washington, D.C., April 1982), p. 2; and Richard Burt, "Evolution of the U.S. START Approach," *Current Policy*, no. 436 (1982): 2.

5. Robert Rhodes James, ed., "Consequences in Foreign Policy, July 11, 1935, House of Commons," *Winston S. Churchill: His Complete Speeches, 1897–1963*, vol. 6, *1935–1942* (London and New York. Chelsea House Publishers in association with R. R. Bowker Co., 1974), p. 5656; see also Martin Gilbert, *Winston Churchill: The Wilderness Years* (Boston: Houghton Mifflin, 1982), pp. 136–37.

6. Compare John F. Lehman and Seymour Weiss, *Beyond SALT II Failure* (New York: Praeger, 1981), pp. xv–xxi.

7. Walter B. Hendrickson, Jr., "An Interview with Chief START Negotiator Edward L. Rowny," *National Defense* 62, no. 386 (March 1983): 37–51; William R. Van Cleave, "Implications of Success or Failure of SALT," in William Kintner and Robert L. Pfaltzgraff, eds., *SALT: Implications for Arms Control in the 1970s* (Pittsburgh, Penn.: University of Pittsburgh Press, 1973), p. 319.

8. U.S. Department of Defense, *Soviet Military Power* (Washington, D.C.: Government Printing Office, 1983), pp. 19–20; Richard Nixon, *U.S. Foreign Policy for the 1970s: The Emerging Structure of Peace* (Washington, D.C.: Government Printing Office, 1972), p. 173; Jake Garn, "Exploitable Strategic Nuclear Superiority," *International Security Review* 5, no. 2 (Summer 1980): 173–89; U.S. Congress, Senate, Foreign Relations Committee, *The SALT II Treaty* (Washington, D.C.: Government Printing Office, 1979), p. 310; *Has America Become Number 2?* (Washington, D.C.: Committee on the Present Danger, 1982), pp. A3–7.

9. U.S. Secretary of Defense, *United States Nuclear Weapons Stockpile* (Washington, D.C.: Department of Defense, 25 August 1983), pp. 1–2.

10. "Text of the Address by the President to the Second United Nations General Assembly's Special Session on Disarmament" (Washington, D.C.: White House, 17 June 1982), p. 3.

11. "Text of Remarks by the President to the Los Angeles World Affairs Council," 31 March 1983, p. 2.

12. "Address by the President," p. 5.

13. "Remarks of the President in Interview with Reporters . . . 29 March 1983," p. 9.

14. "President's News Conference on Foreign and Domestic Matters," *New York Times*, 18 May 1983, p. A20.

15. "Key U.S. Words in START: Reductions, Verification," *San Diego Union*, 3 October 1982, p. C-1.

16. *Today Show*, 6 April 1983, p. 4. At the United Nations, President Reagan stated: "We have negotiated arms control agreements, but the high level of Soviet encoding hides the information needed for verification" ("Text of President's Address at U.N.," *New York Times*, 27 September 1983, p. 16).

17. David C. Jones, *United States Military Posture for FY 1982* (Washington, D.C.: Government Printing Office, 1981), p. 101.

18. Thomas D. Brandt, "U.S., U.S.S.R. Seek Way Out of Obsolete 1972 ABM Treaty," *Washington Times*, 17 August 1983, p. 3. At the United Nations, President Reagan stated: "A newly discovered radar facility and a new ICBM raise serious concerns about Soviet compliance with agreements already negotiated" ("Address by the President").

19. *Report of the President's Commission on Strategic Forces* (Washington, D.C.: Government Printing Office, 1983), p. 22.

20. "President Reagan's Statement," *Washington Post*, 3 September 1983, p. A22.

21. Viktor Linnyk, a Soviet official attempting to rationalize the destruction of KAL flight 007 stated: "The fact was that the U.S. reconnaissance planes were flying over the area all the time." He continued, "They were about to monitor the would-be tests of the Soviet intercontinental missiles. And the tension that the pilots in that area are telling about is so intense, is so high, that I was not surprised they reacted in this trigger-happy manner." ("Soviet Official Acknowledges Pilots Erred," *Washington Post*, 22 September 1983.)

22. "Testimony of the Honorable Richard Perle, Assistant Secretary of Defense for International Security Policy, Before the House Armed Services Committee" (Washington, D.C.: Department of Defense, 12 July 1983), p. 2.

23. "Statement by the President on Intermediate-Range Nuclear Forces Negotiations" (Washington, D.C.: White House, 10 March 1983), p. 2.

24. U.S. Senate, Armed Services Committee, "Military Implications of the Proposed SALT II Treaty" (Washington, D.C.: Coalition for Peace Through Strength, 20 December 1979), p. 19.

25. "Testimony of the Honorable Richard Perle."

10

DISCUSSION

Joseph D. Douglass, Jr.

Dr. Staar's discussion of multilateral negotiations has been especially illuminating. Certainly the difficulties involved in counting forces is an enormous one, as are the problems of coordinating multinational views throughout the negotiating process.

The principal question concerning Mutual and Balanced Force Reductions (MBFR) that troubles me involves the equipment side of force capabilities. Forces are composed of both personnel and equipment. Thus, it is somewhat surprising to learn that most attention by far has been placed on counting people. It seems more logical to look toward moving both personnel and equipment out of the reductions area to stabilize the situation. It is far more difficult to transport a 50-ton tank, for example, than its four- or five-man crew. At some point in time, it seems to me, NATO will have to count and verify equipment levels as well as people; this will add another difficult problem, considering the Soviet capacity for storing equipment in underground installations.

According to a wide variety of refugee and émigré reports, there are hundreds of underground installations in Eastern Europe and the USSR. How does one corroborate these rumors, which include reports of storage areas for tanks, trucks, medical supplies, ammunition, and even factories to produce bullets and shells? The problem has been illuminated recently in the Middle East. As reported in July 1982, when Israeli forces went into Lebanon, they uncovered in underground installations, caverns, and galleries enough material to equip ten Soviet divisions. This included not merely arms and ammunition but also heavy equipment, helicopters, and command and control facilities. The amount of material totaled ten times more than Israeli intelligence had estimated.

The problem of counting personnel is certainly complex, considering the different categories of Soviet military forces. However, I would submit that the problem of evaluating force levels, where forces include both equipment and personnel, will be much more difficult and constitute a problem that we are a long way from resolving.

In regard to the difficulties of multilateral negotiation that Dr. Staar laid out so clearly, despite its many problems, this process may have significant advantages that we should not discount. Three recent examples come to mind in comparing MBFR with SALT I and SALT II. First, it appears that because of their multinational character, talks are carried on by appointed representatives without back-channel negotiations in addition to the formal negotiation process. The second advantage is that since the various national elections remain uncoordinated, the pressure to reach accommodation for political purposes stays low. Perhaps this is one of the reasons why the MBFR negotiations have extended over ten years without achieving any agreement, even on the number of personnel involved. By comparison, in the SALT talks agreements were reached on an interim basis for what can only appear to be political reasons. The third advantage is that when many countries participate, one is not confronted with pressure from nonparticipating states to reach accommodation or agreement. Everybody is part of the process and working on it and cannot complain about the lack of progress by others. It would seem that these and other advantages associated with the multinational approach to negotiations may be a very strong benefit and one that might be considered seriously for other negotiations in which there are strong multinational interests. An example is INF, the intermediate-range nuclear force talks in Geneva.

The theme that appears to be increasingly stressed by the U.S. administration is the need for equitable and fully verifiable treaties. This theme has been consistently stressed throughout Dr. Schneider's paper. Certainly, both attributes were lacking in the past and contributed to many of the disappointments associated with the arms control process. The importance of these measures, as the United States works on a new agreement, cannot be overestimated.

At the same time, caution is appropriate to avoid allowing the significance of these two items to detract from the more immediate problems of compliance. Without meaning to degrade the importance of equitableness and verifiability, I would like to point out that there are times when the strong rhetoric associated with equitableness and verifiability appears more intended to camouflage the lack of progress in and attention to the more immediate problems of compliance. In this regard, let me move to a specific example of violations in the chemical and toxin areas.

After five years of unsuccessful protests, the United States' response to the Soviet use of lethal chemical warfare agents and toxins ("yellow rain") in Afghanistan and Southeast Asia now appears to have fallen back to the old standby, "What we really need is a better treaty." Under Secretary of State for Political Affairs Lawrence Eagleburger explained in congressional hearings in the spring of 1983 that the conclusion to be drawn as a result of the Soviet actions is that "real, equitable and fully verifiable arms control is an absolute necessity. It is not that arms control is pointless; it is that we have to do a better job of it."

One of the most disturbing aspects of this position is that it directly follows a specific recognition that the policies of the United States "cannot be based on a benign or naive view of the Soviet Union and its intentions" and the almost unbelievable assertion that "with a realistic appraisal of the Soviet goals and an appreciation that they are not constrained by many of the values we support, we can proceed with caution and prudence to help build a world eventually free from chemical, biological and toxin weapons."

The use of yellow rain in Southeast Asia and Afghanistan, in direct violation of the 1925 Geneva Protocol and the 1972 Bacteriological and Toxin Weapons Convention, provides an unusually good microcosm within which to examine Soviet intentions and the faulty logic that officials of Western states continue to apply in pursuing arms control negotiations with the Soviet Union.

In seeking not to upset the arms control process, a questionable objective considering the lack of progress in this process over the past twenty years, Mr. Eagleburger begs the real issue and attempts to focus attention on issues of verification and the need for better arms control agreements. The real issue is What use can any treaty be, however well written, with the Soviets, unless their intentions are to comply with both the spirit and letter of the treaty? In the case of the chemical and biological areas, this is clearly applicable. Obviously, the unspoken concern is how these Soviet violations add further credence to the alleged Soviet violations and circumventions in the various nuclear arms control areas.

The 1972 Bacteriological and Toxin Weapons Convention is probably one of the best treaties that has ever been written. It is good because everything is outlawed—development, production, and storage of agents, as well as development of weapons and any types of related assistance to other parties involving biological agents and toxins. Under the 1925 Geneva Protocol, the use of poisonous gas and biological agents in war is prohibited.

And it has become quite clear over the past few years that the Soviet Union has violated both the spirit and the letter of both treaties.

Nor is it appropriate to blame verification. It is quite true that there are no effective provisions for verification in either the Geneva Protocol or the Bacteriological and Toxin Weapons Convention. However, the violations have been so extensive and blatant that no provisions have been needed to establish the case of deliberate noncompliance. While initially there were some concerns that the United States might have been overly sensitive in its claims of violations and might have been using the data to support its own chemical weapons rearmament program, these possibilities have been dispelled as other countries examined that data and reached the same conclusions: that chemical and toxin weapons are being employed and that the only plausible explanation is that the Soviet Union and its allies are directly violating the treaties.

Sterling Seagrave, who, more than any other individual, deserves credit for discovering Soviet atrocities in Southeast Asia and Afghanistan, in his recent testimony before the U.S. Congress discussed the governments that have examined the data to reach the above conclusions. His list included Canada, France, West Germany, England, Israel, South Africa, Australia, Norway, Sweden, Denmark, China, Thailand, Singapore, and New Zealand. The only glaring deficiency at this time is the absence of strong, public pronouncements by these governments against Soviet actions and in support of U.S. analyses.

The problem, therefore, is not the absence of a "real, equitable, and fully verifiable" arms control agreement. The problem is compliance. And no treaty, however well written, will be any better than the current one unless the Soviets are motivated to comply with the treaty. They have demonstrated clearly that they have no such motivation.

One of Dr. Teller's numerous talents is his ability to cut through to the heart of the problem and express it clearly and concisely. I believe he has really done that in discussing defensive measures by pointing out that, without some good examples, defense will continue to be subjected to the criticism that there is nothing one can do to alleviate the consequences of nuclear war. Certainly one of the tasks that is essential, if we are to achieve any type of increased focus of attention on defense and survivability, is a variety of examples of what can be done. Dr. Teller himself presents perhaps one of the simplest and the most effective examples, when he states that a group of civilians in a well-built conventional bomb shelter survived without effect the Hiroshima blast one-third of a mile from ground center. This is a graphic illustration of the effectiveness of shelters.

The effectiveness of other simple preparations were described in a congressional hearing in March 1982 by Mr. T. K. Jones from the Department of Defense. He stated that Soviet leaders have prepared to survive and to continue operating the country during the course of a nuclear war, that they have built bunkers and communications centers adequate to outnumber the surviving U.S. weapons available to target these facilities. Moreover, he indicated that the U.S. capability to target Soviet power projection forces and nuclear reserves had been negated by Soviet practices of mobility and that simple industrial protective measures had, in effect, reduced the lethal area of destruction for large weapons by as much as 99 percent. Still further, Mr. Jones indicated that in the event of nuclear war the immediate casualties that the population of the Soviet Union would suffer, as a result of modest civil defense measures, had been reduced to less than half the casualties they suffered during World War II. It certainly appears that although any nuclear war would entail unimaginable destruction, there is still a great deal that can be done to alleviate the consequences.

Another aspect of the problem, which Dr. Teller concisely identified, concerns the response by the U.S. media to President Reagan's words in March 1983 on the need for defense. This response portrayed the concept as one of "Star Wars." The discouraging aspect to me of the response to the president's call for providing for the survivability of the United States in the event of nuclear war is not so much the media's reaction, however, as that of his own administration. Since President Reagan's speech, two actions have emerged. One has been a sequence of speeches and papers that, in effect, seem to be designed to damn with faint praise the idea of defense. The other has been to focus attention on technological developments that might produce something in twenty years as opposed to asking what can be done now. The president called for defensive measures. Yet it is very difficult to see that there has been any substantial response within his administration to ask what can be done now in terms of building an integrated, active, and passive defense system—not a perfect one, not an expensive one, but one that could provide the country with a dimension of survivability within the next five to ten years. This, to me, is far more discouraging than the media's characterization of the president's proposals as "Star Wars."

Professor Kaltefleiter has presented one of the most intellectually honest papers I have read in years. His logic builds up to a conclusion. He states the conclusion clearly and without qualification, namely, that arms control appears inconsistent with the national security interests of the West. His rationale is quite simple. There are no mutual interests. To have a meaningful treaty, Dr. Kaltefleiter explains, one has to have an area of mutual interest. Insofar as the USSR is concerned, its approach is dominated by the attempts, first, to foreclose any efforts to check on verification of treaty violations and, second, to achieve substantial military advantages for the Soviet

Union. Thus, he concludes there is no mutual interest. Soviet motivations are the very antithesis of those of the West.

Over the past several years, I, too, have asked myself where are the areas of mutual interest—areas where both countries could work productively as opposed to just exchanging views. Given the Soviet ideology, doctrine, strategy, and the results of this ideology and doctrine that we see in the aftermath of SALT I, SALT II, and the other treaties, there are only two areas where I have detected possibly strong mutual interests. Those are the areas of proliferation and accidental war. Proliferation, for reasons similar to those proposed by Dr. Kaltefleiter, I have subsequently concluded is not so mutual and could at some time be to the disadvantage of the United States. That leaves the area of accidental war. Certainly one would like to believe that both countries would like to prevent accidental war. The problem about dealing with accidental war is, however, that it is tied in, perhaps inextricably so, with surprise and first strike. It is clear to many defense analysts that a surprise attack is the Soviets' preferred strategy for war and one to which they devote a great deal of attention. It is also clear to most that such a first strike is highly unlikely to be a U.S. option, either now or in the foreseeable future. While this does not mean that accidental war ceases to be an area of mutual interest, it does indicate the need for extreme care on the part of the United States in dealing with the issue and particularly in evaluating any proposals.

Few people here today would question the need to continue talking with the Soviet Union and to work diligently to achieve arms control treaties in all areas. However, it seems essential that that be done with our eyes open and that one not put forth false promises or create false expectations that cause treaties to be negotiated without fully understanding the consequences or Soviet interests or U.S. interests. To date, our experience in evaluating Soviet interests has been deficient, and statements that attribute to the Soviets interests and motivations of the United States should be regarded with the greatest possible skepticism.

11

Breaches of Arms Control Obligations and Their Implications

William R. Harris

Irrespective of their military significance, breaches of arms control obligations involve disregard of binding commitments under international law. Scholars like Louis Henkin in a qualitative study, *How Nations Behave*, and Peter H. Rohn in a quantitative study, *Treaty Profiles*, have demonstrated that compliance with binding international obligations is the rule and not the exception. Admittedly, many treaties create few incentives for breach; for example, those for bilateral military assistance, collective self-defense, and friendship. While arms control agreements may create stronger incentives for their breach, almost all of the parties comply with their obligations without committing a material breach of binding obligations.

Consider the Geneva Protocol (1925) or the Non-proliferation Treaty (1968) or the Bacteriological and Toxin Weapons Convention (1972).

The Geneva Protocol, ratified by at least 119 governments, prohibits the use of "asphyxiating, poisonous or other gases" and "the use of bacteriological methods of warfare." Italy, a party to the protocol, violated it by using lethal chemical gas in Ethiopia in 1935. Various other countries have circumvented its restrictions in China, Mongolia, Yemen, Laos, Kampuchea, and Afghanistan. However discouraging the disregard of the ban against chemical and bacteriological weapons, the community of nations generally complies with the specific protocol limits: at least 95 percent of the signatory states have apparently observed its terms as well as underlying object and purpose.

The Non-proliferation Treaty, in force with some 116 governments, binds states both with and without access to nuclear weapons to halt their spread. Undoubtedly the public has paid greater attention to efforts by a few states to acquire nuclear weapons than to efforts by a far larger number to stop proliferation. Many governments that seek nuclear weapons, or the freedom to acquire them later, have not ratified or acceded to the Non-proliferation Treaty. Almost all that have agreed to be bound do, in fact, comply with their treaty obligations.

The Bacteriological and Toxin Weapons Convention, signed by over ninety countries, prohibits development, production, stockpiling, or trans-fer of biological agents, toxins, and associated weapons and means of deliv-ery. Apparently all of the signatories claim that they are in compliance, and almost all of them, in fact, appear to be.

Under most conditions, parties to binding international agreements (in-cluding arms control agreements) comply with their obligations. Hence, the detection of a *material breach*, defined as an act or acts that defeat the ob-ject or purpose of the obligation, is a pathological event within the interna-tional system. A material breach is a warning of disequilibrium, a challenge to the rule of law and to the ethos of self-restraint, even if the specific gains to the violator appear modest.

Beyond challenging the rule of law, a state that materially breaches an arms control agreement uproots expectations of reciprocity in benefits. A government deliberately committing acts that defeat the objectives of other parties to an arms control agreement signifies indifference, disregard, con-tempt, or antagonism in regard to sharing benefits of participation. Hence, detection of one or more material breaches of arms control obligations is a warning that the stake of the breaching party in the agreement is insufficient to deter acts that deprive other parties of a share in the benefits of the undertaking, the *quid pro quo* that gave rise to the original mutuality of commitment.

Unless the violator of an arms control agreement is confident that viola-tions will remain covert and undetected, a *deliberate* material breach or an *inadvertent* material breach that remains uncorrected after inquiry signifies a phenomenon even more disturbing than the abandonment of a commit-ment to reciprocal benefits: the violator's indifference to detection signifies the violator's anticipation of a failure of will or capability on the part of victim-states. The prospective violator has assessed the will and responsive capabilities of affected states and found them wanting.

More than two decades ago, Fred Iklé illuminated the dilemma of the victim-states. In an article entitled "After Detection—What?" (*Foreign Af-fairs*, 1960–61), Iklé emphasized the potential for failure of what he termed "restorative measures" and other sanctions, in part because the breaching state has already anticipated responsive measures and has not been deterred by them. Hence, the victim-states face the challenge of reshaping the violator's assessment that the responsive will and capabilities of the victims are inadequate.[1] In September 1961, just eight months after Iklé's article appeared, the Soviet Union breached its legally binding obligations under a nuclear test moratorium, even while a draft treaty to ban atmospheric testing was under negotiation in Geneva. The violator's discounting of victim responses is of greater concern than the violation itself because the detected violation relates to a *past* decision, while the signaled failure of anticipated responses to deter violations relates to the entire range of anticipated *future* conduct of victim-states.

A nation breaching its arms control obligations may discount the consequence of restorative measures in part because it anticipates that the detection of violations will be incomplete, untimely, or insufficiently persuasive to compel effective response. From the perspective of a victim-state, the detection of an arms control violation raises legitimate concerns that what is detected is incomplete, untimely for adequate response, or unpersuasive regarding the facts of what is under way or the benefits anticipated from responsive measures.

A pattern of breaches is of concern, therefore, because the violator signifies by such acts a discounting of the adequacy of the victim's *compliance intelligence* to pierce the veil of military concealment and deception, diplomatic chicanery, and illusions embedded in the arms control process.

In the United States, the public literature on arms control emphasizes verification at the expense of compliance intelligence. In an important pamphlet drafted by Dr. Carnes Lord, then at the U.S. Arms Control and Disarmament Agency (ACDA), the Verification Bureau, at the time directed by Amrom H. Katz, defined *verification* as "the process of assessing compliance with the provisions contained in arms control treaties and agreements. It is the attempt to ascertain whether states are living up to their international obligations." (ACDA Publication 85, March 1976.)

In contrast, compliance intelligence should encompass not only verification of the fact of compliance or noncompliance, but also the assessment of the materiality of the breach, the motives and causes of the breach if known, and the likely consequences of responsive measures and other actions to implement a strategy that would restore compliance. Compliance intelligence is a rarity within the U.S. intelligence community. Without such intelligence, decisionmakers within victim-states tend to postpone responses to arms control breaches. Such postponement of an effective response may embolden the violator to extend defense programs that breach arms control commitments. A pattern of recurring arms control breaches, particularly breaches of increasing military significance, should raise concerns that the rituals of verification have thwarted the development of an adequate compliance intelligence capability and delayed the formulation and implementation of an arms control compliance strategy.

The symbiosis between observer and observed includes opportunities for a party to arms control agreements to utilize the verification and disclosure process of other parties to fine-tune evasions and concealments of strategic significance. The detection of arms control breaches raises concern that what remains undetected may be of greater military significance than what has been discovered or that the missions and capabilities of illicit armaments remain beyond the understanding needed to implement an effective response. Hence, detection of breaches leads to the question "Is what has been detected merely the tip of the iceberg?" Amrom Katz states succinctly: "We have never found anything the Soviets have successfully hidden." [2] National technical means of verification are a double-edged sword: they may verify compliance or noncompliance with arms control obligations, but they may instead demonstrate apparent compliance or nonmaterial breaches while missing a pattern of arms control breaches of military significance.

Of greater concern than the military significance of detected and undetected arms control breaches is that breaches of arms control obligations have, in the past, been precursors to war. The causes of war remain somewhat of a mystery even to historians. We cannot be sure that breaches of arms control obligations and inadequate responsive measures have aggravated the momentum toward war. On the other hand, we cannot be sure that the failure of responsive measures did not embolden violators, hasten the collapse of self-restraint and loss of international respect, and lead to war.

FAILURE OF RESPONSES BEFORE WORLD WAR II [3]

The final report of the Inter-Allied Military Control Commission, which supervised the disarmament provisions under the Treaty of Versailles, concluded: "Germany has never disarmed, has never had the intention of disarming, and for seven years has done everything in her power to deceive and 'counter-control' the Commission appointed to control her disarmament." [4] The report was an inconvenience to the Allies, who suppressed and largely ignored it.

Before its demise, the Inter-Allied Military Control Commission provided a forum for discussion of German disregard of the Versailles Treaty. Prior to departing, a British naval inspector told his German counterpart:

> It is now time for us to separate. Both you and I are glad that we are leaving. Your task was unpleasant and so was mine. One thing I should point

out. You should not feel that we believed what you told us. Not one word you uttered was true, but you delivered your information in such a way that we were in a position to believe you. I want to thank you for this.[5]

After the Allied inspectors left, Germany expanded the scope of its covert rearmament, utilizing the Council at the League of Nations to forestall and divert restorative measures by the stronger League powers. Following his appointment as chancellor in January 1933, Hitler arranged for German pilots to train secretly with the Italian air force and imposed obligatory "national labor service" to evade the Versailles ban on military conscription. Hitler issued a secret order for rearmament the following year. In the absence of countermoves, Germany repudiated the disarmament provisions (Part V) of the Versailles Treaty in 1935 and Article 43 on demilitarization of the Rhineland in 1936. The League of Nations condemned German renunciation of the demilitarization clauses and the Rhineland provisions of the Versailles Treaty as breaches of binding obligations under international law.

Meanwhile, in violation of the 1922 Washington Naval Treaty (United States, Great Britain, Japan, France, Italy), Japan constructed four Atago-class heavy cruisers, from 1927 on, with displacement about 45 percent greater than declared. Since there were no responsive measures to these covert breaches, Japan renounced the treaty in December 1934, with termination to occur after two years. Even before the 1935 Anglo-German Naval Treaty, Hitler supported construction of Scharnhorst-class battleships in the guise of "improved 10,000-ton ships," with actual and illegal tonnage more than three times greater. The subsequently constructed *Bismarck* was even larger and also illegal. The Washington Naval Treaty lapsed before the victims ever condemned the violators.[6] Perhaps more important, the appearance of general compliance with this agreement discouraged the other signatories from building submarines and other vessels that remained unregulated.[7] Germany also violated the 1935 naval treaty before renouncing it four years later.

Italy, a party to the 1925 Geneva Protocol on chemical weapons, used banned chemical weapons during the invasion of Ethiopia ten years later and just one month after Ethiopia had acceded to the protocol. The League of Nations condemned the violator but recommended only limited economic sanctions. With the failure of verbal and economic sanctions in a case of demonstrated violation, it is scarcely surprising that Japan, a nonparty to the protocol until 1970, used bacteriological weapons in China (1939) and Mongolia (1940–1942).

Barton Whaley summarizes the effects of arms control breaches and the failure of responsive measures before World War II as follows:

. . . national leaders were easy prey for deception. By failing to demand rigorous verification of alleged infractions they showed apathy. By failing to apply sanctions when Intelligence did occasionally bring undeniable proof of infractions to their attention they showed themselves impotent as well. And the opponent's perception of this impotence was a spur to even more audacious infractions.[8]

Delay in detection, including the lapsing, refusal, or failure of on-site inspection; suppression of information from public view; dependence on verbal sanctions, words not deeds; and resignation to the continuation of treaty violations together signaled a tolerance of arms control breaches and a collapse of the interwar regime. The decline by 1938–1939 in publications on treaty breaches and sanctions implied a sense of futility that preceded war.

Those who would keep the public ignorant of contemporary arms control breaches should ask themselves whether the resulting conduct of treaty violators brings us closer to or further from war.

MATERIAL BREACHES

The Vienna Convention on the Law of Treaties (1969), signed by the United States but not ratified and neither signed nor ratified by the Soviet Union, codifies and reformulates the standards for suspension, withdrawal, or renunciation of a treaty. Such rights and other self-help measures are privileged under condition of a material breach, defined in Article 60(3) of the treaty:

   a. a repudiation of the treaty not sanctioned by the present Convention; or
   b. the violation of a provision essential to the accomplishment of the object or purpose of the treaty.

Material breaches may include the following:

— *Violations* of bilateral or multilateral treaties or other agreements binding under international law, when the act or acts defeat a provision essential to a treaty object or purpose.[9]

— *Breaches of unilateral commitments* authorized to bind a state and relied upon by another state, whether that commitment is written or oral and whether resulting from reciprocal commitments or from unilateral obligation.[10]

— *Evasions defeating an essential object or purpose*, whether constituting fraud or other abuse of rights, but not breaching a specific
provision of a treaty or other agreement.

[A] state is guilty of an abuse of rights when it seeks to evade its
contractual obligations by resorting to measures which have the
same effects as acts specifically prohibited by an agreement.

— *Acts which would defeat the object and purpose of a signed but unratified treaty or other international agreement*, unless the state shall
have made its intention clear not to become a party to the treaty or
unless entry into force is unduly delayed.[11]

— *Customary international law*, whether established by state practice
or by peremptory norm through treaty codification.[12]

These are the main sources of obligations whose breaches concern participants in the arms control process and also those with a memory of earlier wars after arms control failed. There should also be concern about disregard of unilateral statements that are not legally binding, as a breach of
the duty of good faith incumbent on all nations.

How widespread is the practice of breaching provisions of arms control
commitments so as to defeat an essential object or purpose of agreements?
Before World War II, the practice of breaching obligations that were essential to other countries spread like a cancer within the community of nations.
What is the situation today?

Based on the public record of treaty practices, it appears that the vast
majority of governments meet their arms control obligations. If there is a
cancer within the body politic of arms control, surgical remedies should still
be feasible.

The United States can be proud of an admirable record of compliance
with outstanding arms control obligations. The February 1978 review of
SALT I compliance through 1977 illustrates a recurring pattern: instances
of noncompliance are not deliberate and are of a magnitude and import that
do not constitute a material breach of obligations.[13] There is always room
for improvement, for better interagency coordination, but the track record
of the United States in arms control compliance has been excellent.

Other nations have done far worse. Vietnam, for example, not only
breached its armistice arrangements with the United States but in contravention of the Bacteriological and Toxin Weapons Convention used toxin
weapons in offensive operations against both Laos and Kampuchea.[14] The
convention specifically prohibits storage of toxins and associated weapons,
but Vietnam has violated these provisions recurrently. Despite this regret-
table situation, it is the Soviet Union that is the source of these and various
other arms control breaches.

THE PUBLIC RECORD OF SOVIET BREACHES

In testimony before the Senate Foreign Relations Committee on 15 June 1983, Secretary of State George Shultz commented that "Moscow's continuing practice of stretching a series of treaties and agreements to the brink of violation and beyond" was of increasing concern. In particular, "Soviet practices— including the recent testing of ICBMs"—raised "questions about the validity of their claim of compliance with existing SALT agreements." [15]

Official Washington has not always held the view that Moscow has gone to the brink of violations and beyond. Persons who consider arms control essential to peace and the finding of material breaches incompatible with that process still refuse to recognize Soviet breaches. An example can be found in the text of the February 1978 compliance report transmitted to the Senate Committee on Foreign Relations by then ACDA director Paul C. Warnke. [16] In a June 1978 publication (no. 8947), the Department of State asserted, "In the SCC [Standing Consultative Commission of the United States and the USSR], we have promptly raised with the Soviets any unusual or ambiguous activities which were, or could become, grounds for more serious concern. In every case, either the activity ceased or we obtained a satisfactory explanation."

As recently as August 1979, the same agency indicated a satisfactory Soviet record of compliance, while SALT II lay before the Senate:

We have raised such [compliance] issues promptly with the Soviets, and in every case the activity has ceased, or subsequent information has clarified the situation and allayed our concern. [17]

However, as Senator James McClure has pointed out:

While it is true that the SCC has "resolved" all U.S. compliance concerns about the Soviets, these concerns have been "resolved" by American acquiescence. At a Senate Foreign Relations Committee hearing in 1979, Ambassador Paul Nitze was asked how Soviet treaty violations before the SCC were resolved. He replied, "They were resolved by accepting what had been done in violation." [18]

Three illustrations should suffice: (1) substitution of SS-19 intercontinental ballistic missiles for "light" SS-11s under SALT I; (2) movement of an experimental ABM radar from Sary Shagan in the central part of the USSR to Kamchatka in 1975; and (3) retention of as many as 50 excess launchers for SS-7 ballistic missiles in 1976–1977, despite the SALT I Protocol. Elaboration of these examples follows.

The SS-19 Missile Deployments

In August 1977, during the SALT II negotiations, the United States acquiesced in designating the SS-19 as the largest among the "light" ICBMs.[19] However, the Soviets defeated an essential U.S. objective and purpose of SALT I by increasing the throw-weight of the SS-19 by at least a factor of three over that of the SS-11, thus bringing closer the vulnerability of Minuteman missiles.[20] Public Law 92–448, enacted at the time of SALT I, set forth a U.S. goal of assuring "the survivability of the strategic deterrent forces." For the USSR to evade its commitment not to emplace a significantly larger missile in the SS-11 silos represented more than a circumvention of the specific terms of SALT I. It was an abuse of rights, to accomplish by evasion that which was contrary to an essential limit placed on heavy missiles. This involved no less than a material breach of SALT I and a violation of the second principle ("efforts to obtain unilateral advantage at the expense of the other") in the 29 May 1972 Principles Agreement. But after the United States acquiesced to an evasion of a qualitative limit under SALT I, should anyone be surprised that the Soviets attempted to deploy two new types of missiles under SALT II when only one had been allowed?

When asked about the testing of a new Soviet ICBM, considered a possible violation of SALT II's Article IV(9), President Reagan shared his concerns with the press on 23 February 1983: "You could say, 'I'm convinced that these are violations,' but it would have been very difficult to find the hard evidence to make it hold up in court. This last one comes the closest to indicating that it is a violation."[21]

Movement of Experimental ABM Radar

Common Understanding "C" of the 1972 Anti-Ballistic Missile (ABM) Treaty ruled out "the deployment of ABM launchers and radars which were not permanently fixed types." According to the February 1978 Department of State compliance report, in the fall of 1975 the Soviets moved an ABM radar (with NATO designation FLAT TWIN) from Sary Shagan to Kamchatka. The compliance report focused on whether the USSR had adequately announced a second ABM test range. The more important issue was whether the Soviets were preparing to develop movable radars for ABM systems that could be produced and deployed with a significant reduction in warning time, all in contravention of the limitation to "permanently fixed types" in Common Understanding "C." By 1978 the Soviets apparently knew not only that the United States would acquiesce in private but would apologize for the Soviet violation in a public report.[22]

What then would be the anticipated costs to the Soviets of taking further liberties with their obligations under the ABM Treaty? In the fiscal year 1982 *Military Posture Statement*, General David C. Jones, then chairman of the Joint Chiefs of Staff, asserted that "Soviet phased array radars . . . may be designed to improve impact predictions and target handling for ABM battle management" and are "under construction at various locations throughout the USSR" and expected to become operational in the 1980s (p. 101). On 1 August 1983, Senator McClure asserted that the Soviets have deployed a nonperipheral early warning radar in contravention of Article VI of the ABM Treaty.[23]

The 50 Excess SS-7 Launchers for ICBMs

The SALT I Protocol allowed the USSR to deploy as many as 740 ballistic missile launchers on modern submarines but required it to offset these additional submarine launchers by dismantling either older ICBM launchers or older-type submarine launchers. The Soviets did not comply with the SALT I Protocol by either method, despite attempts to gain credit for "dismantling" launchers to be retained in a ready reserve status. While 50 launchers for perhaps 50 to 100 older SS-7 ICBM missiles may not appear to be of strategic significance to some, the importance to the Soviets of retaining full coverage of the United States' land-based strategic targets should not be dismissed. The Soviets reportedly violated the SALT I Protocol by retaining excess ICBM launchers in the 1976–1977 period until enough of the more accurate SS-17, SS-18, and SS-19 missiles could be deployed.[24]

After the failure of the attempt to gain dismantling credit and the March 1976 Soviet acknowledgment of "delays," anonymous U.S. officials who had disclosed the first undisputed evidence of a SALT I violation advised the press in May that "they were pleased that the Soviet Union had acknowledged the technical violation on its own . . . The issue, while apparently no more significant than a two-month delay in achieving a deadline, is a politically sensitive one to the Administration."[25] As late as February 1978, the Carter administration treated the problem of excess SS-7 launchers as "minor procedural discrepancies" and implicitly dismissed the notion of Soviet retention of a strategic reserve force comprising liquid-fuel missiles because the SS-7 launchers could not "be used to launch missiles" and could not be reactivated "in a short time" (never defined).[26]

If the Soviets retained in a strategic reserve force SS-9s and SS-11s displaced from silos in the late 1970s by SS-17s, SS-18s, and SS-19s, such reserve forces would be an evasion of the SALT I launcher limits and constitute an "abuse of rights" and a material breach of the SALT I obligation. But what was the cost to the USSR if it deployed away from declared silos equipment to launch older liquid-fuel ballistic missiles? How surprised should we be if the Soviets decided to retain excess ballistic missiles associated with soft-site launching equipment or undeclared missile launchers during SALT II? Senator McClure asserted that SS-11 ICBMs appeared at SS-4 medium-range ballistic missile (MRBM) sites and that SS-9 ICBMs appeared "operational" at test ranges.[27] Eugene Rostow, ACDA director during 1981–1982, expressed "great concern" about possible deployment of SS-16 launchers, banned by SALT II and the SALT II Protocol: "Q. It has been written that the Soviets have in excess of 100 SS-16 mobile ICBMs. Isn't that a prima facie violation of SALT II limitations? A. I wouldn't concede the number 100 in your question, but certainly evidence has come along that causes great concern about whether the SS-16 provisions of SALT II are being respected."[28]

Under Secretary of Defense Richard DeLauer has testified before the House Armed Services Committee that the USSR has a "large number" of SS-16 mobile intercontinental missiles that are not within SALT II limits. A recent article speculates that the Soviets seek missiles as well as launching capabilities beyond those allowed under SALT and conceal such capabilities to misdirect U.S. strategic targeting.[29]

The public record of Soviet compliance with SALT I, the ABM Treaty, and SALT II is murky. The perceived patterns are in considerable measure formed by views of strategy, Soviet-style, the resiliency of the arms control process when faced with material breaches of agreements, and the need for or hazards of candor in treating past compliance practices.

All that can be done in this review is to highlight aspects of the public record on arms control compliance. The U.S. government has a larger responsibility and the opportunity to determine whether Congress and the U.S. public should be advised about additional facts or interpretations of data. There has been no SALT compliance White Paper since 1979. A candid review could facilitate the implementation of a coherent strategy to strengthen incentives for arms control compliance.

In other sectors of arms control, there exists a considerable body of official information and independent assessment of the facts and legal obligations. In every year since 1979, the U.S. government has provided assessments and supporting information regarding Soviet transfer or use of chemical and biological weapons in South Asia. Other Soviet arms control breaches are so readily apparent as to enter the public domain almost immediately upon their occurrence. The decision to construct aircraft carriers at the Black Sea port of Nikolayev South virtually assures multinational observation of subsequent breaches of the 1936 Montreux Convention if carriers of the Kiev-class transit the Turkish Straits in contravention of that treaty.[30]

The record of Soviet practices with respect to arms control commitments is sufficiently complete to identify some of the patterns. The USSR appears to be interested more in implementing its five-year military plans or in lulling adversary defense efforts than in assuring substantial compliance with all of the arms control obligations it has assumed.

BREACHES OF TREATIES BOTH SIGNED AND RATIFIED

Examples of breached treaties include the 1963 Limited Test Ban Treaty (confirmed extraterritorial venting of radioactive debris on at least 30 occasions);[31] the 1972 Bacteriological and Toxin Weapons Convention (with documented use of banned toxins in Afghanistan and overwhelming circumstantial evidence of Soviet involvement in the transfer for use by client regimes in Laos, Kampuchea, and Afghanistan);[32] the previously discussed 1972 ABM Treaty; the 1936 Montreux Convention (with Kiev-class vessels constituting proscribed aircraft carriers).[33]

The Soviets have breached other international agreements in force. Examples include the SALT I Interim Agreement and Protocol mentioned above (also including deliberate concealment measures to impede verification); the 29 May 1972 Basic Principles of Relations (with the SS-19 deployments consituting a unilateral advantage); and probably the 22 June 1973 Agreement on the Prevention of Nuclear War (with Soviet military actions in the October 1973 Middle East war causing a U.S. strategic alert, and the lack of consultation prior to the 1 September 1983 shooting down of a civilian airplane); and the 1975 Helsinki Final Act (lack of notification to European states in connection with military maneuvers by 25,000 or more troops).[34]

The Soviets have also breached binding unilateral obligations. Examples include Khrushchev's pledge of a nuclear test moratorium, broken when the Soviets resumed atmospheric testing while a draft treaty banning such tests was under negotiation in 1961 at Geneva;[35] a pledge that there would be no offensive weapons in Cuba, breached by covert deployments of medium- and intermediate-range ballistic missiles (MRBMs and IRBMs) and launchers in 1962 on that island; a pledge that Soviet submarines armed with long-range missiles would stay out of Cuban territorial waters, breached during the 1970–1974 period;[36] and a pledge to halt the completion of operational SS-20 IRBM launcher sites in the European part of the USSR, reportedly breached when the Soviets finished 36 SS-20 launcher sites between May 1982 and 1983.[37]

The Soviets have committed evasions defeating an essential object or purpose. Such evasions constitute abuses of rights and material breaches of agreements. Examples include the previously mentioned emplacement of SS-19 ballistic missiles in SS-11 silos and transfer of toxins and other illegal biochemicals or chemicals for use against nonsignatories of the 1925 Geneva Protocol. The Red Army convicted twelve Japanese servicemen and officers for employing bacteriological agents in China (1939) and Mongolia (1940–1942) when neither Japan nor Mongolia were parties to that protocol.[38] By implication, the Soviets concede that such conduct is a crime in violation of the customary international law of war. If, however, the Soviet Union reserves the right to use banned weapons against nonsignatories, it is still an "abuse of rights" for the Soviets to transfer toxins and chemicals to the forces of client-states (which they have done in Vietnam, Laos, and Afghanistan) and to use such weapons without prior use of chemical weapons against such forces. The purpose of discouraging any use, especially first use, is defeated by a pattern of Soviet evasion of the protocol restrictions.[39]

Soviet conduct raises questions of compliance with signed but unratified treaties. Has the USSR entered into an arms control agreement with the intention of violating it, as the Germans did with the 1935 Anglo-German Naval Treaty? Treaties that appear to raise this issue include the Bacteriological and Toxin Weapons Convention, between its signing on 10 April 1972 and its entry into force for purposes of stockpile destruction on 26 December 1975; the Threshold Test Ban Treaty, in effect since March 1976; and the SALT II Treaty of 1979. Publicly available data do not permit an intelligent discussion of the issue or demonstration of a conclusion one way or the other.

The Soviets have breached obligations under customary international law. Specifically, the 1981 Conventional Weapons Convention codifies the international law of war by limiting the right to employ booby-trap mines or incendiary devices that unreasonably kill or injure civilians (Protocols II and III). Protocol I treats a novel subject, use of plastics resulting in fragments that are not detectable by X-ray devices. The obligations under Protocol I came into force on 2 December 1983, six months after the twentieth ratification. In the interim, the Soviets were reported in the press to have violated Protocols II and III, that is, codifications of customary international law.[40]

Soviet naval vessels have also breached customary international law by repeatedly transiting the territorial waters of other states without their consent. A Swedish Royal Commission reported in April 1983 that at least 40 illegal entries by foreign submarines into Swedish territorial waters had occurred during 1982 alone. In an incident involving the grounding of a Soviet diesel-powered Whisky-class submarine within their territorial waters, the Swedes detected radioactivity in the vicinity. An Oslo newspaper reported that Georgy Arbatov, director of the Institute for USA and Canada Studies in Moscow, had proclaimed, "If the Scandinavians are so naive that they believe this traffic is going to stop, they are living in a dream world."[41]

In August 1980, the USSR towed an Echo-class submarine of a type equipped for nuclear armaments through Japan's territorial waters without Japanese consent. Only after completing passage did the Soviets assert that no nuclear weapons were abroad.[42] The deputy U.S. ambassador to the United Nations, Charles Lichenstein, reported that there have been 75 Soviet violations of U.S. airspace.[43]

Whether or not this pattern of disregard for the territorial integrity of other countries violates the 1973 Agreement on the Prevention of Nuclear War, by increasing the risks of a serious incident, this conduct breaches the duty of good faith incumbent on all nations. The duty of a state with regard to arms control must include minimal standards of self-restraint in directing its military air and naval vessels near the territory of other nations. If the sacredness of Soviet territory justifies the death of 269 persons aboard an off-course civilian aircraft, it is assuredly an abuse of rights for the Soviet military to trespass recurringly on the territory of other states.

Any discussion of Soviet breaches of arms control obligations would, however, be incomplete without noting something positive: the Soviets appear to comply with arms control obligations designed to reduce the risks of accidental war, to halt the spread of nuclear weapons, and to prohibit extension of armaments to previously unarmed regions.

Agreements to reduce the risks of accidental war include the 1963 and 1971 Hot Line Agreements as well as bilateral accident agreements between the Soviet Union and the United States, the United Kingdom, and France. Agreements to halt the spread of nuclear weapons include the 1968 Nonproliferation Treaty, International Atomic Energy Agency guidelines for transfer of nuclear technology, and the Convention on the Physical Protection of Radioactive Materials. Agreements relating to armaments include the 1959 Treaty on Antarctica, the 1967 Outer Space Treaty, and the 1971 Seabed Treaty.

Those sectors in which the Soviets appear to have a good record of compliance tend to be those where a mutual interest exists between the USSR and its arms control partners. Sectors in which the Soviets appear prone to recurrent breaches include those where interests are not mutual and that involve, at best, reciprocal interests. While compliance might assure stability of a *quid pro quo* relationship, undetected noncompliance or detected noncompliance that is excused offers the Soviets an opportunity to take the *quid* without the *quo*.

IMPLICATIONS FOR THE FUTURE OF ARMS CONTROL

Some tentative thoughts follow from this preliminary review of arms control commitments and their breach:

1. It is important to distinguish between those arms control arrangements based on a substantial mutuality of interests and those which, at best, are based on a reciprocity of interests. The former may not require verification of compliance. The latter require verification. More important, they require that a potential violator anticipate that after detection, the parties deprived of reciprocal benefits have recourse to effective self-help, collective security initiatives, and other responsive measures.

2. Quantitative limits, qualitative limits, and operational limits on testing or employment of forces are generally sectors where interests are reciprocal at best. Without development and implementation of a strategy to restore substantial compliance, it will become increasingly imprudent to pursue such arms control agreements with the Soviet Union.

3. Even if it is not feasible to restore substantial compliance with these arms control agreements, some strategic confidence-building, accident avoidance, and nonproliferation measures as well as other agreements may, nonetheless, be prudent if based on a strong mutuality of interest.

4. To strengthen both incentives for compliance and disincentives for noncompliance, a program of anticipatory safeguards should be part of the design and implementation of arms control measures.

5. Following material breaches of arms control obligations, the victim's primary recourse lies in altering its own conduct and that of its allies, not in altering the conduct of the violator.

6. Even if further arms control agreements are not practicable, victims of material breaches of arms control obligations should continue the dialogue with violator-states, if only to restore the respect of the violator for victims who demonstrate a resolve to protect their interests.

7. Because the violator has already anticipated many of the responses of victim-states, post-breach remedies are likely to be limited and often ineffective. Hence, the victim or potential victim of arms control breaches needs to emphasize timely and effective compliance assessment over verification *per se*. Knowing whether there is a compliance problem is insufficient for sustaining a strategy of strengthening incentives for compliance. Causes of breaches and probable consequences of countermoves are appropriate topics of compliance assessment.

8. In a democracy, the foundation of strength is public knowledge. The support that an administration needs to pursue a more prudent course in arms control depends on a greater sharing of arms

control compliance issues with the citizens of the nation. Both the executive branch and the Congress should pursue opportunities to share essential information with the public.

NOTES

1. For an earlier consideration of the relation between detection and deterrence, see F. C. Iklé, *The Violations of Arms Control Agreements: Deterrence Vs. Detection*, Rm-2609-ARPA (Santa Monica, Calif.: Rand Corp., August 1960).

2. Amrom H. Katz, *Verification: The State of the Art and the Art of the State* (Washington, D.C.: Heritage Foundation, 1980). The United States has found out at a later date that the Soviets had successfully concealed strategic activities.

3. For detailed studies, see Historical Evaluation and Research Organization, *Responses to Violations of Arms Control and Disarmament Agreements: Study RIPOSTE*, 3 vols., Contract Report GC-177, for the U.S. Arms Control and Disarmament Agency (1964); Margaret P. Doxey, *Economic Sanctions and International Enforcement* (Oxford: Oxford University Press, 1971); George W. Baer, *The Coming of the Italian-Ethiopian War* (Cambridge, Mass.: Harvard University Press, 1967); Dan Maxim, Mary Walsh, and Barton Whaley, *Covert Rearmament in Germany, 1919–1939: Deception and Misperception* (Washington, D.C.: CIA, Office of Research and Development, and Mathtech, 1979); and Barton Whaley, "Covert Rearmament in Germany, 1919–1939: Deception and Misperception," *Journal of Strategic Studies* 5, no. 1 (March 1982): 3–39.

4. John W. Wheeler-Bennett, *The Nemesis of Power* (London: Macmillan, 1953), pp. 185–86, quoted in Whaley, "Covert Rearmament," p. 14.

5. Quoted in Whaley, "Covert Rearmament," p. 15.

6. Paul G. Johnson, "Arms Control: Upping the Ante," *U.S. Naval Institute Proceedings* 109, no. 8 (August 1983): 28–34, treats the Washington Naval Treaty as a model of arms control design and compliance.

7. On Japan's fortification of demilitarized islands, see Thomas Wilds, "How Japan Fortified the Mandated Islands," *U.S. Naval Institute Proceedings* 81, no. 4 (April 1955): 401–7.

8. Whaley, "Covert Rearmament," p. 37.

9. Christine Chinkin, "Nonperformance of International Agreements," *Texas International Law Journal* 6 (1982): 387–432.

10. In the *Nuclear Tests Case, Australia v. France* (1974), ICJ 253, and *New Zealand v. France* (1974), ICJ 457, the International Court of Justice determined that an authorized unilateral undertaking could be binding without a reciprocal benefit.

11. Article 18 of the Vienna Convention on the Law of Treaties, and Martin A. Rogoff, "The International Legal Obligations of Signatories to an Unratified Treaty," *Maine Law Review* 32 (1980): 263–99; R. D. Kearney and R. E. Dalton, "The

Treaty on Treaties," *American Journal of International Law* 64 (1970): 495; Robert F. Turner, "Legal Implications of Deferring Ratification of SALT II," *Virginia Journal of International Law* 21 (1981): 747–84.

12. V. A. Jordan, "Creation of Customary International Law by Use of Treaty," *Air Force JAG Law Review* 9 (1967): 38; and J. K. Gamble, Jr., "Reservations to Multilateral Treaties: A Macroscopic View of State Practice," *American Journal of International Law* 94 (1980): 373–94.

13. U.S. Department of State, *Selected Documents*, no. 7 (Washington, D.C., 1978).

14. See the White Papers issued by the U.S. Department of State in November 1981, March 1982 (Special Report no. 98), and November 1982 (Special Report no. 104) for details.

15. The phrases are quoted in a letter to President Reagan, dated 22 June 1983 and signed by 34 U.S. senators.

16. Department of State, *Selected Documents*, no. 7.

17. U.S. Department of State, *Verification of SALT II Agreement*, Special Report 56 (Washington, D.C., August 1979), p. 3.

18. *Congressional Record*, 19 May 1983, p. S7139; quoting *Washington Post*, 7 May 1983.

19. This was done "for planning purposes," according to Secretary of State Cyrus Vance (U.S. Department of State, *SALT II Agreement*, Selected Documents no. 12B [Washington, D.C., June 1979], p. 17).

20. David S. Sullivan, *Soviet SALT Deception* (Boston, Va.: Coalition for Peace Through Strength, 1979), especially section on "The SS-19 deception," pp. 1–3. Secretary of Defense James Schlesinger estimated the throw-weight as at least twice that of the SS-11 Modification 3 and at least three times the throw-weight of the SS-11 Modification 2 (see ibid., p. 14).

21. White House, Office of the Press Secretary, "Remarks of the President at Breakfast with the Godfrey Sperling Group," 23 February 1983, p. 16.

22. The February 1978 compliance report states: "This new system and its components can be installed more rapidly than previous ABM systems, but they are clearly not mobile in the sense of being able to be moved about readily or hidden. A single operational site would take about a half year to construct."

23. Press speculation includes "Soviet ABM Breakout," *Wall Street Journal*, 16 August 1983; *Washington Post*, 17 August 1983, p. 23; and *Baltimore Sun*, 19 August 1983, p. 2.

24. See the reference to 51 launchers in excess of the 740 baseline and explanation by the Department of State (*Selected Documents*, no. 7). David S. Sullivan, *The Bitter Fruit of SALT* (Houston: Texas Policy Center, 1982), asserts that the Soviets retained excess SS-7 launchers through the expiration of SALT I in October 1977.

25. Bernard Gwertzman, "Soviets Conceded Arms Violation," *New York Times*, 25 May 1976.

26. Department of State, *Selected Documents*, no. 7.

27. *Congressional Record*, 14 April 1983, p. S2948; and 19 May 1983, p. S7135.

28. *San Diego Union*, 3 October 1982.

29. *Soviet Aerospace*, 21 March 1983, p. 78; and Samuel T. Cohen and Joseph D. Douglass, Jr., "Selective Targeting and Soviet Deception," *Armed Forces Journal International*, September 1983, pp. 97–98.

30. See the annual *Jane's* volumes containing data for aircraft carriers of all naval powers. *Jane's* indicates that the *Kiev* first transited the Turkish Straits on 18 July 1976.

31. The 14 April 1983 speech by Senator James McClure provides references to at least 30 confirmed tests with extraterritorial radioactive venting (*Congressional Record*, p. S2948).

32. Department of State, White Papers of 1981, 1982, and supporting documentation in 1983. The natural occurrence of some mycotoxins is both irrelevant and not inconsistent with Soviet causation of the transfer and use of toxins in "yellow rain" and other illegal attacks. In the fiscal year 1983 *Posture Statement*, released in February 1982, Secretary of Defense Caspar Weinberger asserted: "The United States now has good reason for believing that the Soviet Union has violated the Biological Weapons Convention."

That same month, U.S. Ambassador Max Kampelman asserted that the Soviets operated a biological weapons research and production facility in Sverdlovsk and that "we are aware of five other such facilities in operation today" (*Baltimore Sun*, 17 February 1982, p. 5). Secretary of State George Shultz stated in November 1983: "I regret, then, to report that chemical and toxin weapons are nevertheless being used in Laos, Kampuchea, and Afghanistan by the Soviet Union and its allies" (Department of State, Special Report no. 104, November 1982, covering letter).

33. Annex II of the Montreux Convention defines aircraft carriers as "surface vessels of war, whatever their displacement, designed or adapted primarily for the purpose of carrying and operating aircraft at sea." Articles 10, 11, 12, and Annex II together prohibit passage of aircraft carriers through the Turkish Straits. The Soviets first called the *Kiev* an "antisubmarine cruiser" but published concurrently with transit in July 1976 a legal claim that Black Sea powers can transit aircraft carriers while others cannot (see the legally fallacious article of Captain V. Serkov, "The Legal Regime of the Black Sea Straits," *Morskoi sbornik* [Moscow: Krasnaya zvezda], no. 7 [July 1976]: 83–86). The 1983 edition of *Soviet Military Power* states that "in 1981, two Soviet *Kiev*-class aircraft carriers were operational. Now, three units are on the high seas; a fourth unit has been launched; and development continues on a newer, larger class of aircraft carriers."

34. After failing to provide so-called confidence-building notifications of military maneuvers (Soyuz-81 and Zapad-81) concurrent with the Polish crisis, the Soviets asserted that the provisions for notifications were "only 'guidelines,' not 'requirements'" (see the statement by Ambassador Max Kampelman in U.S. Department of State, *Madrid CSCE Negotiations, 1980–81* Selected Documents no. 20 [Washington, D.C., September 1982], p. 31). Before Soyuz-81 the Soviets failed to provide notice of troop strength. Prior to Zapad-81, *Izvestiia*, 3 September 1981, materially

misrepresented the numbers involved as "very limited." After the exercise had started, Tass conceded that there were "approximately 100,000 troops," the largest number since the Helsinki Final Act. The Soviets at least breached their duty of good faith and have destroyed the confidence-building aspect of the troop notifications by selective non-notification in crises.

35. In a legally binding declaration to the Supreme Soviet on 14 January 1960, with worldwide dissemination of the text, General Secretary Nikita Khrushchev declared: "I would like to stress again that in order to ensure the most favorable conditions for the early drafting of an agreement on the discontinuance of tests, the Soviet government will continue to abide by its pledge not to resume experimental nuclear explosions in the Soviet Union unless the Western powers begin testing atomic and hydrogen weapons." Khrushchev added, with regard to a proposed test ban treaty, "If a party violates its obligations, the initiators of the violation will cover themselves with shame and the peoples of the whole world will brand them." (*Current Digest of the Soviet Press* 12, no. 2 [1960]: 8.)

36. For one account, see Raymond L. Garthoff, "Handling the Cienfuegos Crisis," *International Security* 8, no. 1 (Summer 1983): 46–66. See the separate statements issued by the White House and by Tass on 13 October 1970. The U.S. statement appears to include territorial waters within the definition of Cuba for purposes of banning Soviet offensive weapons.

37. Leonid Brezhnev announced on 16 March 1982 a "decision of the Soviet leadership" to "introduce, unilaterally, a moratorium on the deployment" of SS-20 missiles in the European part of the USSR. On 18 May 1982, Brezhnev stated that the commitment "also envisions a unilateral freeze on the preparations for the ultimate deployment of missiles. Yes, it does envision this, including an end to the construction of launching positions." (See U.S. Arms Control and Disarmament Agency, *Soviet Propaganda Campaign Against NATO* [Washington, D.C., October 1983], p. 35.)

38. Records relating to a Red Army military tribunal in Khabarovsk, resulting in convictions, are contained in USSR, *Materials on the Trial of Former Servicemen of the Japanese Army: Trial of Otozoo, et al.* (Moscow, 1949).

39. At least 33 of the parties to the Geneva Protocol, including the Soviet Union, reserved the right not to be bound in relation to nonsignatories. The unusually high rate of reservations (28 percent, as of June 1983) may indicate that the protocol is only a peremptory norm when read in conjunction with the reservations of at least 33 parties. But if the Soviets can convict twelve Japanese servicemen for use of prohibited weapons when their nation was not even a protocol party, then Soviet use and transfer for use against nonparties to the Geneva Protocol is at a minimum an "abuse of rights" and a material breach of the object and purpose of the protocol.

40. The Soviet Union signed the Conventional Weapons Convention on 10 April 1981 and ratified it on 8 June 1982. Evidence taken at the People's Tribunal, founded by Bertrand Russell, led one participant to write: "After seeing booby-trap mines in the form of plastic toys, pens and pencils and valises, after holding in my hands gas masks removed from dead Soviet soldiers; after seeing photographs of the black,

bloated faces of dead Afghan women and children . . . I have no doubt that the Soviets have violated human rights and the rules of war" (Agah Khan, quoted in *New York Times*, 2 January 1983, sect. 4, p. 14). The USSR applied an incendiary chemical to at least 60 civilians, including children, in an incident on 13 September 1982, after Soviet ratification but before entry into force of the convention (Department of State, *Publication no. 104*, November 1982). Since Protocols II and III incorporate long-standing rules against unnecessary injury to civilians, a breach of these protocols is a breach of existing legal duties.

41. Svein A. Rohne, "Kremlin Boast About Submarines—Andropov's Friend Warns of New Cruises in Norwegian Waters," *Verdens Gang*, 11 May 1983, p. 5.

42. Robert J. Grammig, "The Yoron Jima Submarine Incident of August 1980: A Soviet Violation of the Law of the Sea," *Harvard International Law Journal*, no. 22 (1981): 331–54.

43. *Chicago Tribune*, 4 September 1983, p. 8.

12

DIPLOMACY AND CULTURE: NEGOTIATION STYLES

Richard Pipes

Foreign policy and diplomacy are clearly by-products of domestic political experience. A political culture tends to develop within the confines of a country and only then is applied to relations with foreign states. For this reason, there exists a close relationship between domestic policies and the way a government conducts foreign affairs in its imperial or colonial sphere. Many reasons account for this phenomenon. The most obvious is that individuals who rise to the top of a political system generally do so because of their skill in manipulating domestic forces; only when they have reached positions of national power do they deal with foreign countries. Except under extraordinary circumstances, such as periods of revolution or civil war, it is unthinkable that a politician could reach the highest positions on the basis of experiences in dealing with external affairs. Thus, the idiosyncracies of Russian political culture, accumulated over centuries, have as great a bearing on the conduct of foreign policy and diplomacy in the Soviet Union as they had in Imperial Russia.

The Russian political tradition differs in many fundamental ways from that of the West. For one, the latter attaches great importance to law, to abiding by contracts and treaties. The Western tradition derives in good part from a predominantly commercial background of arranging treaties to the advantage of both parties. In business dealings, it is inconceivable to have a contract benefiting entirely one side and giving nothing to the other: all commerical contracts presuppose gains for both parties. Hence, in all Western diplomatic negotiations, including those with the Soviets, attempts are made to anticipate the interests of the other party and often to satisfy them in advance. In return, the West expects that the Soviets will take its interests into account. For Western diplomats, negotiations are essentially a matter of splitting the difference and accommodating the legitimate interests of both sides. To this end, elaborate rules of diplomatic intercourse, dating to relations between medieval city-states in Italy and subsequently codified in the Peace of Westphalia (1648), have been worked out. Their fundamental premise is the acceptance by all parties of the right of other states to exist. No matter what the controversy, disputes must never affect the right to national existence: they always involve specific and limited issues such as territory, commercial rights, and so forth. A significant exception to that rule in the history of Europe was the partitions of Poland, which ended in the destruction of a large and ancient sovereign state, an event perceived at the time by farsighted observers like Edmund Burke as a dangerous violation of tradition and an ominous precedent.

The United States is heir to this European tradition, which holds that contracts are sacred, that treaties must benefit all parties, and that conflicts must not affect the right to existence of any sovereign state.

These elements are largely absent from the Russian political tradition. It was not influenced by Stoic philosophy, which had entered the mainstream of European thought mainly through the medium of Roman law and inculcated a deep respect for contractual obligations. Neither did Russia have a sizable middle class whose commercial habits played such a major role in the development of European attitudes toward laws and treaties. The background of its diplomacy was primarily Oriental, the reason being that the Russian state grew up on the fringe of Asia. Its attitudes toward both domestic policy and international relations were first developed vis-à-vis its sovereign, the Golden Horde, then its successor states, and until the early eighteenth century with diverse Eastern countries like the Ottoman empire, Iran, China, and various nomadic civilizations. The principles of this kind of diplomacy are very different from those of the West. There is, for example, no concept of the fundamental right of every state to exist. Asia never experienced anything similar to the Peace of Westphalia, and there conquest followed by eradication of states has not been uncommon.

History has taught Russian rulers to accommodate themselves to a superior power with cunning when they were weak and to act in an unmistakably imperial manner when they were strong. These men also developed a tradition that every individual and each country must take care of its own interests because no one else will do it for them. This same tradition teaches that it is not at all incumbent on one party to take account of the interests of the other because everyone takes care of his own and tries to get as much as possible for himself. Russia, unfortunately, also did not manage to develop a sense of belonging to an international community. In Europe this sense emerged during the Middle Ages, largely owing to a common religion whose head resided in Rome. Even after the Reformation had broken the unity of the Western church, the tradition survived. Russia, however, received its Christianity not from Rome but from Byzantium. After the fall of Byzantium in the middle of the fifteenth century, Russia remained for all practical purposes the only Orthodox Christian state in the world, other Orthodox Christians having come under Turkish rule. It found itself, therefore, psychologically and culturally in an isolated position. In the east, it bordered on infidel Muslims; in the west were Catholic and Protestant heretics. That sense of spiritual and cultural isolation, which events had imposed on the Russians, made it virtually impossible for them to feel part of the broader international community and tended to develop in them a sense of being *sui generis*.

In dealing with the Russian attitude toward the law, there is still another factor to take into consideration, and that is the psychology of the peasant. He has constituted in the past the overwhelming majority of the population, and from him today's Soviet leadership is largely descended. Students of peasant life in Russia have noted that the *muzhik* lacked a sense of law as something permanent, eternal, that is, something grounded in a higher rationality. What he had was a keen sense for the *living law*, which meant a decree or ordinance. When he was told to do something and he could not avoid doing it, the *muzhik* would carry out the order. But he never saw any underlying logic to these commands and obeyed only because he was under duress. Engelhardt, a brilliant essayist on peasant life, wrote over a century ago that the peasants did not even understand that they must pay taxes every year, even though they always had done so in the past. Every year, the peasants expected a new decree to be issued, ordering them to pay taxes; if no new decree came out, they would not pay.[1] This is in striking contrast to Western perceptions of law. It has sometimes occurred to me that when Soviet officials sign a treaty, for example on arms control, like their peasant ancestors they may intend to keep the provisions for the time being, but a year later, in view of the absence of a reinforcing act, they are strongly tempted to violate them.

The imperial diplomatic service came into being under Peter the Great. At the beginning of the eighteenth century, when Russia's attention shifted from the Orient to Western Europe, Russian diplomacy adapted itself quickly and at least superficially to European forms. Russians proved themselves extremely able diplomats. Eighteenth-century Europeans, who tended to regard them as barbarians, were amazed how clever, skillful, and patient they were in diplomatic intercourse. This first generation of diplomats negotiated excellent treaties with Sweden and even better ones with the Ottoman empire. They introduced an interesting technique that allowed them to interfere in the internal affairs of neighboring countries. Both Peter I and Catherine II used their arrogated rights to protect Orthodox Christians under Turkish rule as a pretext for intervening in the affairs of Turkey. In this manner, they initiated during the eighteenth century what today are known as "wars of national liberation." In the Treaty of Kuchuk-Kainardji, signed in 1774, they injected in a most subtle way provisions that they subseqently exploited to meddle in Turkish affairs. The Turks most probably did not even know what they were signing when they agreed to the terms of Kuchuk-Kainardji. Catherine II also used a similar pretext to intervene in the affairs of Poland in connection with her designs to partition and destroy that country.

For reasons that are not very clear to me, in the second half of the nineteenth century Russian diplomats lost their traditional skills and did rather poorly in defending the interests of their sovereign. It would be a most interesting inquiry to find out what had happened to the Russian foreign service after the Crimean War.

One might have expected the Bolsheviks, on coming to power, to develop their own diplomatic traditions and their own principles of foreign policy conduct. This did not happen. Marxism, which supplied the new Soviet rulers with their political philosophy, does not really have a theory of foreign policy, let alone one of diplomacy. Interestingly enough, Marx and Engels had written brilliant journalism on international affairs. Marx's work entitled *The Secret Diplomatic History of the Eighteenth Century* and Engels's essay on the principles of Russian foreign policy deserve special attention.[2] Although rabidly anti-Russian, both contain some interesting insights concerning the nature of the subject. These writers dealt not with relations between sovereign states but with revolutionary strategy and tactics and with future prospects of a socialist regime, but they provided little, if any, guidance to their followers in this area.

Once a socialist state had been established in November 1917, a foreign policy perforce had to be fashioned. It was viewed from the beginning as an aspect of class warfare. With the emergence of the first "socialist," "proletarian" state, class warfare moved in the eyes of Soviet leaders onto the international stage. Foreign relations became a form of class warfare. Riazanov, the leading Soviet expert on Marx and Engels, wrote in 1927 that war for the proletarian state meant transfer of revolution into the international arena.[3] This statement provides a valuable insight into the psychology behind the conduct of foreign relations by Soviet governments from 1917 to the present.

Because they realized that whatever their desire for an international revolution, they would have to deal with capitalist countries for many years to come, Soviet leaders established a diplomatic service to operate at the state-to-state level. The Commissariat of Foreign Affairs represented the first such department to be staffed almost exclusively with Bolsheviks; the others had a high percentage of officials inherited from the *ancien régime*. Even so, this commissariat almost immediately adopted the patterns of traditional Russian diplomacy. It is difficult to see how it could have done otherwise, given, as noted, the lack of guidance from the founders of Marxist theory. Nothing characterizes the continuity between Imperial and Soviet foreign policies better than the fact that the Soviet government to this day keeps the archives of the tsarist Foreign Ministry off limits to foreigners. Western scholars have been given access to the archives of all the other tsarist ministries, including the Department of the Police, but the tsarist Ministry of Foreign Affairs' archives are closed, presumably on the grounds that they contain state secrets of the Soviet regime.

When studying the foreign policy of Imperial Russia, one often runs into striking parallels with that of the Soviet Union. A remarkable illustration is found in a statement made by British foreign secretary Lord Palmerston in 1853 that has an utterly contemporary ring:

> The policy and practice of the Russian government has always been to push forward its encroachments as fast and as far as the apathy or want of firmness of other governments would allow it to go, but always to stop and retire when it was met with decided resistance, and then to wait for the next favorable opportunity to make another spring on its intended victim. In furtherance of this policy, the Russian Government has always had two strings in its bow—moderate language and disinterested professions at Petersburg and at London; active aggression by its agents on the scene of operations. If the aggression succeeds locally, the Petersburg Government adopts them as a "fait accompli" which it did not intend, but cannot, in honor, recede from. If the local agents fail, they are disavowed and recalled, and the language previously held is appealed to as a proof that the agents have overstepped their instructions. This was exemplified in the Treaty of Unkiar-Skelessi, and in the exploits of Simonovich and Vikovich in Persia. Orlov succeeded in extorting the Treaty of Unkiar-Skelessi from the Turks, and it was represented as a sudden thought, suggested by the circumstances of the time and place, and not the result of any previous instructions; but having been done, it could not be undone. On the other hand, Simonovich and Vikovich failed in getting possession of Herat, in consequence of our vigorous measures of resistance; and as they failed, and *when* they failed, they were disavowed and recalled, and the language previously held at Petersburg was appealed to as proof of the sincerity of the disavowal, although no human being with two ideas in his head could for a moment doubt that they had acted under specific instructions.[4]

One major difference between the conduct of foreign policy by the government of Imperial Russia and that of the Soviet Union lies in the function of the Foreign Affairs Ministry. The tsarist one did not differ either in structure or in responsibility from that of its West European counterparts, on which it had been patterned. In the case of the USSR, the ministry remains only an executor of foreign policy that is made elsewhere. The true center of decisionmaking is the Central Committee of the Communist Party of the Soviet Union and, specifically, its International Department. That division of responsibility between the ministry, which deals with foreign governments, and the Central Committee, which is a party institution, makes it much easier to pursue the kind of policy that Lord Palmerston had alluded to because it is quite simple for the party to disavow what Soviet diplomats do, and vice versa. In this connection, a statement by U.S. Secretary of State John Foster Dulles, who had considerable experience in dealing with the Soviets, has some interest:

> One point that always needs to be borne in mind is that, when you negotiate with the leaders of Communist-controlled states, you are not negotiating with the principals; you're negotiating with the second-class people, because the governments of these countries are all run by the Communist Party and, unless you bind that party, you haven't got any agreement which, as to broad policy, has any significance at all. I recall very well the Litvinov agreement, which we made at the time when we recognized the Soviet Union. The Soviet Government agreed that it would not tolerate the establishment on its soil of any group which was seeking to carry out subversive activities in the United States. Of course the subversive activities went on just the same, indeed were intensified. And we asked the Soviets "how come," and they said "Oh, those are being carried on by the party. The state is not carrying those on. Therefore, what we are doing is entirely consistent with our agreement." That is the kind of thing you are up against.[5]

The Soviet diplomatic service is the *crème de la crème* of the *nomenklatura*. Responsible positions are held only by those appointed to that select body. It is the most elite service of all: highly professional and impersonal. When we negotiate with the Soviets, we tend to send important national personalities, people who are in the news and who may have a personal stake in arriving at an agreement. The urge to reach an accord seizes virtually every U.S. negotiator. Everyone who negotiates with the Soviets and spends two or three years in exasperating talks wants to return home with a treaty that subsequently will be known as the so-and-so treaty, so-and-so being himself, of course. This is not true on the Soviet side. Even though Soviet diplomats are also engaged in negotiations for years on end, they remain faceless bureaucrats who have no personal stake in a treaty. Even if the negotiations are successful, they receive no credit for the results.

Second, the leeway given to Soviet negotiators is extremely small. They operate under tight instructions and have virtually no authority to go beyond them. Former British ambassador to Moscow Sir William Hayter wrote of negotiating with Soviet diplomats:

> Negotiation with the Russians does occur, from time to time, but it requires no particular skill. The Russians are not to be persuaded by eloquence or convinced by reasoned arguments. They rely on what Stalin used to call the proper basis of international policy, the calculation of forces. So no case, however skillfully deployed, however clearly demonstrated as irrefutable, will move them from doing what they have previously decided to do: the only way of changing their purpose is to demonstrate that they have no advantageous alternative, that what they want to do is not possible. Negotiations with the Russians are therefore very mechanical; and they are probably better conducted on paper than by word of mouth.[6]

Because I believe the foregoing to be correct, I am rather skeptical about the benefits of direct negotiations between heads of states or even between the foreign affairs ministries of the United States and the Soviet Union. What I know of the talks between U.S. secretaries of state and Andrei A. Gromyko seems to conform closely to Hayter's model: no real exchange of views, no give-and-take. Therefore, what really matters in dealing with Soviet diplomats is not diplomatic technique and well-prepared positions, but rather the strength with which one enters the negotiations. Only such a stance progressively closes to the Soviets all kinds of alternatives unfavorable to the United States and leaves them with few options, except those which the United States finds advantageous.

A third feature is the unorthodox quality of Soviet diplomacy, that is, its tendency to appeal above the heads of government to their citizens in order to manipulate them either by threats or promises. The negotiations in Geneva on reduction of nuclear weapons were originally intended to be strictly confidential. However, the Soviet side began to leak information immediately. Right now, the United States' real problem is not the Soviet negotiators but the mobs who threaten to take to the streets in Germany and elsewhere because they are informed, or rather misinformed, by the Soviet government about the progress of these negotiations.

A fourth element is the Soviet use of deception. In 1962, for example, when the Soviets were already far advanced in installing their missiles in Cuba, Soviet diplomats told the United States repeatedly and emphatically that they had no intention of placing offensive weapons on that island. Prior to the invasion of Afghanistan, Soviet diplomats also went out of their way to sow deception, in order to make us believe that no invasion would take place. To some extent this procedure was repeated in the case of Poland. We do not know whether the military preparations that the USSR made along the borders of Poland in December 1980 and again in March 1981 really were serious, that is, preparatory to an attack on Poland, or whether they were deception to divert everyone's attention from the planned internal crackdown. But there is no doubt that martial law in Poland had been preceded by a number of deceptive measures, such as negotiating with Solidarity, making concessions that no one had believed possible, in order to create the impression that the government was so weak that it could not possibly undertake an offensive against the trade unions. This deception worked not only with Western intelligence services but also with Solidarity itself.

In conclusion, the United States needs to develop a body of experts professionally knowledgeable in the art of negotiating with the USSR, people who know Russian history and literature and are well versed in the history of its foreign policy and diplomacy. Anybody who deals with the Soviets ought to be familiar with the documentation we have from the past. Particularly valuable are materials on the 1918 Brest-Litovsk Treaty, which the Bolsheviks had signed with the Germans. At that time, Soviet leaders spoke freely. In the debate on ratification of the treaty, to which there was great internal opposition, they revealed much about their thinking on both foreign policy and diplomacy. This event does not have purely historical significance because Soviet diplomatic authorities frequently cite Brest-Litovsk as a model. Another case would be the 1939 Nazi-Soviet Pact. Third, the materials and records of the SALT negotiations should prove most instructive. We need to have somewhere a school that conveys to specialists this knowledge. Any institution establishing such a school, with a rigorous program, would contribute greatly to avoiding the kind of mistakes in East-West diplomatic relations that have plagued us from 1917 to date.

NOTES

1. Aleksandr Nikolaevich Engelhardt, *Iz derevni: 12 pisem'*, *1872–1887*, 6th ed. (Moscow: Sel'knozgiz, 1960).

2. Karl Marx, *Secret Diplomatic History of the Eighteenth Century* [and *The Story of the Life of Lord Palmerston*], ed. Lester Hutchinson (London: Lawrence & Wishart, 1969); and Frederick Engels, "The Foreign Policy of Russian Czarism," in Paul W. Blackstock and Bert F. Hoselitz, eds., *The Russian Menace to Europe: A Collection of Articles . . . by Karl Marx and Friedrich Engels* (Glencoe, Ill.: Free Press, 1952), pp. 25–55.

3. In the symposium *Voina i voennoe iskusstvo* (Moscow and Leningrad, 1927), p. 23.

4. Evelyn Ashley, *The Life of Henry John Temple Viscount Palmerston, 1846–1865* (London: Richard Bentley & Son, 1876), p. 25.

5. John Foster Dulles, "The Role of Negotiations," *U.S. Department of State Bulletin* 38 (February 1958): 159–68; quoted in Library of Congress, Congressional Research Service, Senior Specialists Division, *Soviet Diplomacy and Negotiating Behavior: Emerging New Context for U.S. Diplomacy* (Washington, D.C., 1979), p. 297.

6. Sir William Hayter, statement in the *London Observer*, 2 October 1960; quoted in Library of Congress, *Soviet Diplomacy and Negotiating Behavior*, p. 249.

13

DISCUSSION

Samuel T. Cohen

INSPECTION, NOT VERIFICATION

Nuclear arms controllers have proclaimed nuclear arms control as the best way to nuclear peace. The U.S. government has declared nuclear deterrence the best way to nuclear peace and has attempted to use nuclear arms control to achieve stable nuclear deterrence. However, a careful look at U.S. deterrent strategy since 1960 reveals that it has been based on the assumption of assured destruction, not on nuclear war-fighting, which all U.S. presidents, when forced to the wall by public opinion, have claimed to be a hopeless proposition. When word got out that the Reagan administration was considering fighting and "prevailing" in an extended nuclear war, President Reagan was forced to back away and proclaim that there could be no winners in such a war, both sides could only lose.

Any president maintaining the contrary would have no basis in fact for his case, for a number of reasons. Not only would the present nuclear force imbalance in favor of the Soviet Union refute such claims, but in their current defenseless condition, the American people simply could not tolerate a nuclear war for any period of time. Not having active or passive defenses to reduce the casualties from Soviet nuclear attacks, the American people would collapse psychologically and sociologically in short order. Whether we like it or not—and even though U.S. presidents going back to Richard Nixon have professed not to like it—we are stuck with assured destruction unless the United States makes drastic changes in its nuclear posture, and this seems unlikely.

Assured destruction is such a subjective business that nobody, including U.S. presidents, can get a concrete handle on the problem. Next to God (whom we assume to be on our side—the Soviets being godless), all we have on which to gauge assured destruction criteria is our president, our commander-in-chief in charge of our nuclear forces; and if he's unlucky enough to be alive after a Soviet first-strike, God only knows what he might want to do to implement an assured destruction strategy. The last president to give a hint on the U.S. response required to maintain deterrence was Jimmy Carter, who saw the threatened discharge of one boatload of Poseidon missiles against Soviet cities as enough for deterrence. President Reagan (wisely) has said nothing so far to contradict his predecessor.

In this essentially unfathomable context of nuclear war and nuclear strategy, how relevant is the issue of verification of nuclear arms control treaties? How relevant are possible Soviet gains, through cheating on SALT or START, of, say, 50 percent or even 100 or 200 percent in increased military capabilities? The answer is that so long as the United States enters into arms control treaties where the bedrock on its side is assured destruction, there is no convincing way to prove that such Soviet violations, even if convincingly verified, are very relevant. In this respect, William Harris's presentation, while very scholarly and properly indignant over apparent Soviet perfidy, is basically little more than a well-delivered irrelevance.

It is basically irrelevant because it worries about essentially marginal increases in things the Soviets might be able to do to us over what they promised not to do in a treaty, when all that really counts to the United States is some unknown amount of damage that it can do to the Soviets if they attack. The magnitude of this ignorance dwarfs Soviet gains from violating treaties—gains that the United States thinks it can discover through verification techniques. If the United States is to engage in realistic arms control negotiations with the Soviets, it will have to look squarely at what the Soviets can do to it; and this means determining their true capabilities, not just worrying over verifying treaty violations.

This means gaining true knowledge about the Soviets that can be obtained only through inspection, not through national technical means (NTM). The United States must have full access to what it thinks or suspects the Soviets may be doing in developing, producing, and deploying nuclear weapons. In other words, the United States must do now what it tried to do in its first effort to control nuclear weapons: the Baruch Plan of 1946, which was unyielding on the matter of full on-site inspection. If it does not return to the principles of the Baruch Plan, nuclear arms control will become the most dangerous farce it ever has entered into.

President Reagan recently noted the inability of NTM to achieve concrete knowledge on Soviet ICBM developments. Referring to the flight testing of a new mobile ICBM, the president said, "We aren't sure that this is the same weapon or that they're not testing two weapons." If the United States' ability to monitor Soviet missile testing is that uncertain, on what basis can it say that it understands Soviet capabilities sufficiently to enter realistically into nuclear arms control treaties? In all probability, it does not have such understanding for a number of reasons, the most important being Soviet deception and disinformation.

To illustrate this point, take the notorious SS-20 ballistic missile, whose flight testing, as observed by U.S. NTM, led to the conviction that it is an intermediate-range ballistic missile (IRBM). This weapon so alarmed NATO several years ago that certain allies demanded that the United States develop and deploy missiles in Europe to counter this threat. This is also the weapon that has produced the intermediate-range nuclear forces (INF) negotiations at Geneva and has caused enormous political strains in NATO that threaten to divide the alliance.

Is the SS-20 really an IRBM? Maybe not, even probably not. If one examines the military requirements for such a theater nuclear weapon in the context of the panoply of theater nuclear weapons the Soviets already have developed and deployed, it is difficult to see why they would want to add the SS-20 to an already long list of weapons capable of destroying NATO many times over.

The Soviets are now deploying many hundreds of modernized, short-range, mobile ballistic missiles, having coverage over most critical targets— nuclear and non-nuclear—in Western Europe. In addition, they are deploying modernized, MIRVed, variable-range ICBMs by the hundreds that just as readily can target Europe as America. And we can add to this medium-range bombers and longer-range fighter-bombers, existing in the many hundreds, that have full coverage over all of NATO. So why would the Soviets have designed the SS-20 solely as an IRBM? Or is it possible, even probable, that from the beginning the SS-20 was intended to be a MIRVed mobile ICBM, which the Soviets have long needed to be able to have a survivable reserve force of intercontinental missiles for use in an extended nuclear war? Unfortunately, NTM is incapable of answering this question. If one tries to answer it in terms of logical Soviet military requirements, the answer would be affirmative.

As another case in point, consider the newest Soviet ICBMs (SS-17s, -18s, -19s), which the United States assumes are being deployed in hardened silos, which presumably gives it a sound basis for pursuing the START negotiations. In view of military logic (instead of claims based on NTM) and the enormous publicity the United States has given its efforts to achieve a nuclear counterforce strategy based mainly on attacking hardened silos (the primary justification for the MX), why would the Soviets be so obliging as to give the United States a known target system for implementing its strategy? Or is it possible, even probable, that these missiles actually are deployed elsewhere (hidden from NTM) and that Soviet silos have been constructed and increasingly hardened, with occasional launches presumably being conducted from them, all for the purpose of deceiving the United States in its targeting strategy and arms control efforts? The military logic of the matter would seem to dictate that the USSR has been deceiving the United States and (with a little help from the Soviets) the United States has been massively deceiving itself into believing that it has a credible targeting strategy and a sound basis for SALT and START.

Other examples could be brought out here, indicating that the United States may have been dangerously fooling itself into believing that nuclear arms control is the best way to enhance U.S. security. If it persists in this thus-far unrealistic effort, it must demand that the Soviet Union open itself up to full, unlimited inspection. Nothing short of this will suffice. President Reagan should explain this to the American people and at the same time make a public offer to the Soviets for full, mutual inspection of each side's nuclear capabilities.

If, indeed, Soviet deception has been successful in depriving the United States of a meaningful target system for its offensive nuclear weapons, its only hope for survival is to be able to defend itself against nuclear attack by active and passive means. In this connection, at the top of the list of U.S. defense priorities ought to be a crash effort to implement President Reagan's March 1983 proposal for attaining an ABM capability. The second-highest priority should be to construct a national civil defense system as quickly as possible. Next, air defenses should be revitalized to cope with the growing Soviet bomber threat. And then the United States can figure out what kinds and numbers of offensive weapons to build. In view of Soviet deceptive practices, this may be an exceedingly difficult task. Edward Teller has suggested that the ratio of strategic defensive-to-offensive capabilities might be 95 to 5. He may not be far off the mark.

Amrom H. Katz

AFTER DETECTION—SO WHAT?

Let us look at the cycle of events that begins with a treaty.[1] An arms control agreement usually will specify permitted and forbidden activities. Then, in the normal course of events, the United States' national technical means

(NTM) collect some raw data, which, after reduction to manageable form, are analyzed and collated with information secured earlier or by other means. The analyst may believe that these new data seem inconsistent with provisions of the treaty, that he has caught a violation. Being neither judge nor jury, he may not use the word "violation."

The next steps involve discussion within the intelligence community at successively higher levels of the government and a decision to raise the matter with the Soviets in the Standing Consultative Commission (SCC). It is assumed that Washington is considering what to do in the event nothing is achieved through the SCC. A court to assess damages and announce penalties, let alone enforce its decisions, does not exist. Nor does the United States seem to have compiled a list of responses, clearly correlated with unsatisfactory SCC discussions. In the first place, the proceedings of that commission are supposedly confidential; second, there is no compilation of responses. It is a good assumption that such preparations are nonexistent.

In an earlier work, I discussed these matters in a section entitled "Abrogation and Inertia."[2] One should recall the events and debate starting in September 1961, when the Soviets ended the U.S.-USSR moratorium and resumed atmospheric testing of nuclear weapons. Even in the face of such an action, the United States still did not find it easy to follow suit. That the Soviets had, indeed, resumed testing was clear; there was no question about the evidence. They announced it publicly, and the explosions provided sufficient confirmation. However, there was no treaty at that time, and inertia in the United States delayed resumption of tests.

One can only speculate about what might happen in other situations where the evidence may be equivocal, the facts are denied by one side, and corroboration is in a form that does not lend itself to public exposition or where disclosure of evidence might compromise the source. All evidence is not equally evidential; not all forms of evidence are equally clear, manifest, overt, or plain.

A well-known and often cited article anticipates the present:

> The current debate on arms control and disarmament puts great stress on the problem of how to detect violations . . . Yet detecting violations is not enough. What counts are the military and political consequences of a violation once it has been detected . . . If we focus all our attention on the technicalities of how to detect a violation, we are in danger of assuming that our reactions and sanctions will be adequate.[3]

A useful comparison of the relationship between detection and its aftermath is the movement of a roller coaster. Hard work pulls the cars to the top; once they reach the top, no further energy need be supplied. The train coasts the entire remaining route. Until a few years ago (keep the roller coaster in mind), I believed all the hard work existed at the front end of this problem; that when the detection-analysis-evaluation-agreement cycle inside the government concludes that a violation has taken place, the rest becomes automatic, inexorable, timely, and significant. I had thought that reaching a decision on a violation occurred at the peak of the ride. It seems that I was wrong. The process that seems to take all the work really moves us only about a third of the way up.

William R. Harris's paper should be required reading for all prospective travelers in the arms control treaty jungle. Milestones are rare, friendly guides unavailable, and accurate maps difficult to come by. Harris has taken the reader simultaneously on a *tour d'horizon* of the compliance problem and on a guided tour through a minefield. In so doing, he has invented a subject that he calls "compliance assessment." The paucity of sensible writing on the subject will attract, as it should, more attention to the interplay between verification and its consequences.

After noting the phenomenon described above as a roller coaster, Harris makes an important suggestion for "compliance assessment":

> . . . compliance assessment should encompass not only verification of the fact of compliance or noncompliance, but also the assessment of the materiality of the breach, the motives and causes of the breach if known, and the likely consequences of responsive measures and other actions to implement a strategy to restore compliance. Compliance assessment is a rarity within the U.S. intelligence community.

In my opinion, this function should not be performed by the intelligence community. I am not saying that it is incompetent at compliance assessment; rather, it is noncompetent. For example, net assessment is done in the Department of Defense and not by the intelligence community. However, I am not suggesting that the task of compliance assessment be given to Defense. It is an interdisciplinary task and cannot be fully defined or staffed after hasty discussion. Assignment of responsibility cannot precede recognition of a job to be done. In rebuttal to the above argument, it can be argued that this structure—from detection to decision and on to judgment—is conspicuously underpopulated. So, the analysts may figure that they must assume several roles, at least until the other players appear.

ON EVIDENTIALITY

President Reagan has been quoted as expressing concern over securing data on alleged Soviet violations of the unratified SALT II agreement, evidence that would stand up in court. By this he meant proof that could be explained to the public. No other court exists for matters of compliance with arms control agreements. Harris quotes the president's 23 February 1983 comments on Soviet testing of ICBMs: "You could say, 'I'm convinced that these are violations,' but it would have been very difficult to find the hard evidence to make it hold up in court. This last one comes the closest to indicating that it is a violation."

A thorough examination of this problem has been long overdue. Harris's paper gets us off to a good start. Of all the varied types of data available and used by intelligence analysts, the most persuasive to lay persons are photographs. Everyone has taken pictures, and almost everyone has looked out of windows of high-flying aircraft. What one sees are identifiable features and patterns, familiar from previous flights. Roads, fields, superhighways, bridges, airfields, cities, large manufacturing plants, are sensed directly. The director of the National Photographic Interpretation Center showed President Kennedy photographs taken by a U-2 flying over Cuba in October 1962 and explained them with confidence. The president did not see the objects being described, but he was convinced that they were there. Compare this with the "evidentiality" of an intelligence agent's report, an electronic pattern, or a radar-generated image. However important and unique these sources of data may be, they do not have the persuasive power of a picture.

Aerial photographs are persuasive, especially when an articulate analyst points out what they contain. However, at best they depict a fact or an assemblage of facts. These facts, even if clear and unarguable, do not carry with them an unequivocal interpretation. Writing about neither Cuba nor missiles, Dwight Macdonald stated:

> Americans often assume that facts are solid, concrete (and discrete) objects like marbles, but they are very much not. Rather are they subtle essences, full of mystery and metaphysics, that change their color and shape, their meaning according to the context in which they are presented. They must always be treated with skepticism and the standard of judgment should be not how many facts one can mobilize in support of a position but how skillfully one discriminates between them, how objectively one uses them to arrive at Truth, which is something different from, though not unrelated to, the Facts.[4]

The outstanding use of photography in the 1962 Cuban missile crisis has been discussed. However we should remember that almost everyone, except for a photo-interpreter, is a lay person, regardless of political or military position. McGeorge Bundy, former special assistant for national security affairs to Presidents Kennedy and Johnson, has commented on what he calls the technological revolution in intelligence, which started in the early 1960s:

> Unfortunately, there is a long and growing distance between what the intelligence analyst knows and what is immediately apparent to his political superiors. In the great case of the missiles in Cuba, it was the persuasive conviction of the experts and not the naked appearance of the first photographs which was immediately conclusive to President Kennedy on October 16. If he had not learned to know and trust these experts, he might well have doubted their story. This problem may be more acute today.
>
> If the danger of uncertainty and imperfect communication exists in the small circle of those who have full and current knowledge of the evidence, it is reasonable to suppose that the distance from that evidence to public understanding and confidence may be greater still. Moreover, at best, technical intelligence can show us only what exists and not what may be intended.[5]

Bundy makes two excellent points, still valid. The president and his immediate advisers are not photo-interpreters; they have become accustomed to trusting their experts. The latter have the advantage of doing their analysis from stereo-pairs, which allow separation of objects in the vertical dimension. Furthermore, for maximum separation of tones in the photographs, they usually employ transparencies. These allow a range of tone differences at least ten times greater than that available on ordinary paper prints. The briefing is usually based on monoscopic, that is, nonstereo enlargements.

Let us assume that photographs have been taken of some activities or objects and arouse suspicion on the part of the analyst. Suppose, further, that the matter turns out to be consequential and reaches high levels in the U.S. government. The matter will be debated in English by officials from various agencies who—despite their often fierce disputes—share the same values, goals, and perspectives. They are loyal, even patriotic, and broadly familiar with the subjects under discussion. Compare this with the quality of data needed to raise an issue in the SCC forum, let alone to go public, as Ambassador Adlai Stevenson did with the photographs of the missile sites in Cuba at the United Nations. Data can never be too good. Working at the threshold of interpretability may employ an expert's highest skills, but going public with such data is another matter.

In a memoir about the Cuban missile crisis, the president's brother said:

> I examined the pictures carefully, and what I saw appeared to be no more than the clearing of a field for a farm or the basement of a house. I was relieved to hear later that this was the same reaction of virtually everyone

at the meeting, including President Kennedy. Even a few days later, when more work had taken place at the site, he remarked that it looked like a football field.[6]

Ray Cline, at the time of the missile crisis, was deputy director of the CIA for intelligence. He reinforces the point that the high-altitude photographs were not self-explanatory. Expert tour guides were needed and, fortunately, were at hand.

> The undersecretary of defense . . . found time to have the key picture shown to him by military photo-interpreters from NPIC (which was a joint CIA-Defense Department facility). He was not too sure he could see what they saw in the print, but that was not surprising because the technicians worked with film and optical instruments that showed objects much more clearly than they appeared in a print for circulation. I worried for a long time that our evidence would be doubted, but it never was. A picture— however dim— is a compelling piece of reporting.[7]

These remarks should be kept in mind when thinking about the proposal, or perhaps it is a plan already, to give the United Nations a photographic satellite to enable so-called impartial nonaligned members to decide if alleged violations are real and founded in fact. I have been thinking and writing about these matters since at least 1946, and the idea of mounting a U.N. effort to achieve objectivity about treaty violations strikes me as either frivolous or mischievous. The current argument about "yellow rain" and the failure of the United Nations even to arrive at a conclusion should be enough to evaluate the idea of an international reconnaissance satellite.

ON AUTO-NEGOTIATIONS

Auto-negotiation is such a normal feature of the U.S. political scene that it no longer merits comments by either tourist or tour guides. I refer to the United States' behavior when it makes an arms control proposal to the USSR. By agreement, such proposals are supposed to be secret, as is discussion of their content. They are limited to the negotiating parties, but the press almost always publishes the essentials in a short time. Important exceptions to this blanket of confidentiality do occur. The president may choose to outline the proposals in public because of domestic political pressure to make them more attractive to the Soviet Union. When the USSR quickly rejects the new ideas, even as a basis for negotiations or as a point of departure, the proposals receive criticism from Americans! Invariably, the administration is accused of demanding too much from the Soviets. I call this "auto-negotiation." Washington finds itself engaged in debate, not with the USSR in Geneva, but with Americans on the banks of the Charles River in Cambridge or near Dupont Circle in Washington, D.C.

HOW TO TELL A MISSILE FROM A HOLE IN THE GROUND

Some of us thought that once the United States had deployed technical detection systems (NTM), the work of verifying a treaty would be relatively easy. Resolving problems that were uncovered or discovered would be done through the SCC. However, as William Harris has persuasively argued, the United States attempted to put into production what turned out to be a multiact play, with one written act.

Part of the problem comes from the desire for a treaty. I have elsewhere caricatured the two main categories of people involved in negotiations. Clearly, there are more types, but a more accurate delineation would blur the point. One group wears white hats, and it consists of the physicists; the other—the lawyers—wears black hats. The physicists would like precise language, the lawyers prefer elasticity. We can look at the results of this dichotomy if we imagine that these two groups—separately—were to design a chair. The physicists' design grabs you and holds you like a catcher's mitt holds a baseball; the lawyers' design has squirm room.

There is weakness and strength in each position. We need both physicists and lawyers. A different time and a different problem caused Shakespeare's Dick Butcher to say: "The first thing we do, let's kill all the lawyers." We do not intend to follow this advice, but it is worth remembering. I know that William Harris, who among several other competencies is a lawyer, disagrees with my stricture that intelligence analysts and data collectors should not pronounce the word "violation" any more than a police officer or a prosecutor presenting evidence to a grand jury should conclude that a crime has been committed.[8] In point of fact, even a grand jury does not do the latter. If it finds the evidence persuasive, the grand jury may indict. Then the matter is referred to a higher authority for prosecution and possible judgment of an alleged violation.

A LOOK AT CHEATING AND CIRCUMVENTION

Cheating is dirty; circumvention is clever. Cheaters cross over the line of illegality; circumventors find a loophole to drive through. Swindlers and con men cheat; lawyers circumvent. Cheaters evade taxes; circumventors avoid taxes. Cheaters laugh at their victims; circumventors smile at them. Cheaters eat steak tartar; circumventors eat quiche.

A single important example will illustrate the above descriptions. Consider a treaty limit on the number of fixed land-based ICBM launchers, such as found in SALT II. Building extra launchers secretly is *cheating*, but figuring out how to deploy missiles and launch them without using a standard launcher would get around the limits and hence would *circumvent* the treaty. We need to remember what the treaty is all about. It is an attempt to limit missiles. Since counting missiles is impossible, it limits the clumsy, immobile, long-in-building, easy-to-detect concrete silos that the treaty calls "launchers."

Not all "violations" are equally significant, portentous, or consequential. We can imagine some as misdemeanors, others as felonies. Our response cannot be to go for the jugular on everything. A proper response to this point is to ask whether not going for the jugular on *everything* may result in not going for the jugular on *anything*. Our behavior must certainly condition the reaction of our adversary.

The United States could have guessed that negotiating limits on ICBM launchers and treating launchers as dangerous objects would come back to haunt it. And it has. The largest and most significant nonviolation of the SALT process has grown from a distant shadow on the far horizon to a large cloud directly overhead. The United States was surprised and unsettled when the Soviet "showed" it cold-launch firings. Why should it have been surprised? After all, the United States invented the cold-launch technique. The Polaris SLBM is ejected from a submarine and ignited in the air. Soviet demonstrations of cold-launch firing of ICBMs came after the signing in 1972 of the so-called Interim Agreement and the ratification of the Anti-Ballistic Missile Treaty later that year.

It would take us far afield from these comments to go into a detailed discussion of the reasons for and benefits of cold-launch techniques. For our present purposes, it is sufficient to observe that ejecting a missile from the silo before igniting it helps to keep the silo relatively clean and undamaged so that it can be more readily prepared for re-use. The Soviets obligingly let the United States "observe" their preparations for refire, and a new factor in U.S. calculations immediately became evident.

Let me briefly divert from the discussion. For a long time, a few of us had been suggesting that the USSR could hide a significant number of ICBMs in near-deployable condition. We raised questions about the number of missiles produced, about what the Soviets do with their old missiles, etc. We were barely tolerated. Now we are told that "everybody knows that." This illustrates an old maxim: the larger the organization, the fewer the ideas it can hold at the same time.

Back to the refire problem. SALT II presumably took care of U.S. worries.[9] Article IV, paragraph 5, together with an Agreed Statement, covers this contingency:

> 5. Each party undertakes:
>   a. not to supply ICBM launcher deployment areas with intercontinental ballistic missiles in excess of a number consistent with normal deployment, maintenance, training, and replacement requirements;
>   b. not to provide storage facilities for or to store ICBMs in excess of normal deployment requirements at launch sites of ICBM launchers;[10]
>   c. not to develop, test, or deploy systems for rapid reload of ICBM launcher.
>
> Agreed Statement. The term "normal deployment requirements," as used in paragraph 5 of Article IV of the Treaty, means the deployment of one missile at each ICBM launcher.

Nobody in his right mind is going to store ICBMs near a hardened silo. To begin with, we do not know what "near" means. Besides, there is no agreement on the definition of "rapid." What this does mean is that if the United States finds a few missiles (or several dozen) stored in the woods, say, 50 miles from a known ICBM site, it has no complaint. It has a new target, and that is all. And if it does not find them, it could well be that the Soviets have developed TELs (transporter, erector, launcher) or otherwise made arrangements to launch from the area where the missiles are stored. All of a sudden, numbers do count.

An interesting observation about "old" missiles is found when we compare them with old aircraft. An old bomber, such as the B-52, may have perhaps 20 million miles on it. It is a used aircraft. An old missile is simply an unused one and, if maintained and stored properly, can be counted on to work. It is like a 1952 Chevrolet purchased new and never driven, mounted on blocks, carefully cleaned and serviced, with the engine started periodically. Anyone who has attended an old car rally can testify to the sight of beautifully maintained cars, all driven into the rally grounds, and some from considerable distances.

So here the United States has a real problem. If it believes that the Soviets are bent on reloading their empty silos, then it will probably consider that the silo is a target whether or not it contains a missile. We should not leap to this conclusion too quickly. Much more thought needs to be given this matter, but not here.

After detection, one would like to know whether there was some unobserved event or trend that, if recognized earlier, would have obviated the violation or circumvention that is found. The question "After detection, what?" begs the questions "Before detection, why?" and "After response, what then?"

NOTES

1. The author's opinions and judgments are his own, not necessarily being endorsed in whole or in part by his colleagues in or out of government. He regrets that his opinions are not shared by many, or even by a few individuals, who are in a position to make decisions and shape policy.

2. Amrom H. Katz, *Verification and SALT: The State of the Art and the Art of the State* (Washington, D.C.: Heritage Foundation, 1979), p. 8.

3. Fred Charles Iklé, "After Detection—What?" *Foreign Affairs* 39 (1960–61): 208.

4. Dwight Macdonald, "A Critique of the Warren Report," *Esquire*, March 1965, p. 61; cited in Edward J. Epstein, *Inquest* (New York: Viking Press, 1966), p. 133.

5. McGeorge Bundy, "To Cap the Volcano," *Foreign Affairs* 48 (1969–70): 4. This quotation and the following two paragraphs come from Katz, *Verification and SALT*.

6. Robert F. Kennedy, *Thirteen Days* (New York: New American Library, 1969), p. 24.

7. Ray Cline, "A CIA Reminiscence," *Washington Quarterly* 5, no. 4 (Autumn 1982): 90.

8. Harris proposes that the determination of the materiality or nonmateriality of a breach is a *policy* judgment, but that the finding of an act inconsistent with a treaty is a matter of *fact*. Without the right to report findings of violations, Harris asserts, intelligence may delay the search for responsive measures until violations are irreversible.

9. U.S. Department of State, Bureau of Public Affairs, *SALT II Agreement*, Selected Documents, no. 12B (Washington, D.C., July 1979), p. 22.

10. The fixation on "launchers" finally caught up with itself in this clause. It would be interesting to see the launch site of an ICBM launcher.

Nils H. Wessell

ARMS CONTROL AND POLITICAL CULTURE

Unlike the large majority of conferences in the United States dealing with arms control, virtually every paper presented here has directly or indirectly addressed the impact of Soviet political culture on the arms control process, in particular the USSR's conduct in these various negotiations. Many other such gatherings ignore the question of distinctively Soviet traits of behavior. If addressed at all, they are treated as a matter of secondary or tertiary importance after such considerations as U.S. conceptions of strategic stability, which the Soviets are said to be slowly mastering, and the purported (but almost never proved) relationship between the "arms race" and international tension. Deterrence and the arms race are often treated as theoretical models in which abstract national entities A and B, devoid of distinctive cultural and political characteristics, interact in a manner that can only alarm "objective" observers who have acquired a "global" perspective. William Van Cleave once aptly labeled such abstract modeling of the real world as "stercoraceous." And in practice the somewhat gauzy alarm of these global citizens amounts to preoccupation with the single value of preventing a nuclear holocaust. Virtually excluded from their concerns are such boring problems as modernizing the aging U.S. strategic deterrent or strengthening the forces of those prepared to defend the West's interests and values. After all, haven't political "scientists" shown pluralism to be a seriously deficient model of the "democratic" political process?

In this context several propositions bear mention. First, although the Reagan administration's approach to arms control policy as being subordinate to overall national security policy has distracted attention from the point, arms control negotiations between the United States and the USSR will inevitably be asymmetrical. While it is theoretically possible for the asymmetries to favor the United States, experience from the real world since the late 1960s suggests the opposite. The most resolute administration will be bent like a weak reed unless public opinion is ready to support its negotiating approach. This is true even when that approach owes more to John L. Lewis than Mister Rogers. The record of the Reagan administration testifies that on arms control even it must respond to public opinion, both at home and abroad. Although the quality of this opinion often owes more to the cardigan-sweater crowd than the mineworkers, one can hardly blame the administration for being responsive to this reality. The alternative is to make likely the election of a new administration committed to a nuclear freeze. Of the eight announced Democratic presidential candidates, only one has failed to endorse a mutual and verifiable freeze on the testing, production, and deployment of nuclear weapons.

In fact, of course, the situation may change, so volatile is public opinion. For a brief period it seemed that an exogenous variable, the Soviet downing of the civilian Korean Air Lines jet with 269 persons aboard, might succeed, tragically, in suggesting that the USSR was more a negotiating adversary than a negotiating partner. To be sure, public opinion showed some disposition to understand that this massacre illustrated the fundamental callousness of a regime whose enemies, both domestic and foreign, since 1945 have been largely imaginary, although no less necessary for that fact. But it took only a few "red herrings" from the KGB disinformation directorate to shift the attention of large elements of the public, still suggestible eight years after Vietnam and Watergate, to a discussion of the degree of U.S. responsibility for the Soviet massacre. General Secretary Andropov's efforts abroad were sufficiently successful that a majority of the U.N. Security Council could not be persuaded to "condemn" the massacre, preferring instead to "deeply deplore" it.

The point here is that the same asymmetry with respect to opportunities for influencing public opinion is at work in the area of arms control. Not only are differences in Soviet and American political culture and institutions profound, but they also make a substantial asymmetrical impact on the context of public opinion within which arms talks take place. While any U.S. administration must react to a public opinion that itself is responsive to Soviet "active measures" of propaganda and disinformation, the Soviet party Politburo and Secretariat operate in an environment where Soviet domestic opinion is either irrelevant or almost totally manipulated. American officials and scholars do not have any opportunity to affect Soviet public opinion. By contrast, Georgy Arbatov, director of Moscow's official Institute for USA and Canada Studies, has become a staple of U.S. television news commentary. He and his staff are ever ready to offer a sober and responsible image of Soviet power in the manner of latter-day Potemkins erecting a facade of respectability for the appreciation of the susceptible. Moreover, as Harriet Scott has observed, Soviet "academics" from this and other institutes of the Soviet Academy of Sciences visit Capitol Hill and travel all over the United States on the same mission. Because they are generally well-informed and seemingly reasonable men, skilled in English, they project an accurate image of themselves and a misleading one of the system that allows them to travel abroad in return for meritorious service.

However, the cultural context in which Soviet defense and arms control policy is crafted, with only very remarkable exceptions, is closed to U.S. influence. Even worse, it is a culture whose ruling elite views violence, in Richard Pipes's felicitous phrase, as "the natural regulator of human affairs." It is as commonplace for a Soviet official to believe in force as the proper determinant of justice as it is for an American to believe in the law as such an arbiter. Professor Pipes has observed that the ruling party elite, often only one or two generations removed from the countryside, survives on the same combination of intimidation and duplicity that enabled its peasant forebears to survive the vicissitudes of an often lawless environment. Middle-class Americans, nurtured in affluent suburban communities and naturally lacking prolonged firsthand exposure to the realities of everyday Soviet life, are only rarely able to appreciate the characteristics of Soviet political culture. It takes the callousness and flagrant mendacity surrounding the Korean Air Lines massacre—already fading from public consciousness—to open temporarily the eyes of a generation of Americans schooled in the post-Watergate era to distrust chiefly their own elected government.

Nor should the pervasive duplicity in Soviet public life be confused with the occasional prevarication that all public officials everywhere must sometimes engage in. It is no accident that well-educated, although powerless, Soviets pull the plug on Radio Moscow and use *Pravda* for everything except learning the news. This is the intelligentsia's judgment of the regime. The boredom and cynicism rampant in Soviet society has found no parallel in the United States, even at the height of Watergate. The reason is disarmingly simple. Soviet leaders must lie in all matters large and small because to do otherwise would shake the foundations of Soviet power. A little truth might lead to questioning of the party leadership's right to rule, which the elite knows to be based on the fraudulent claim of representing the interests of the working class and even all the Soviet people.

Required to maintain this fiction and suppress all forms of political spontaneity, since unfettered self-expression might suggest otherwise, these same leaders have no compunction about committing much lesser forms of fraud in secondary areas like arms control. In this context, the Soviet handling of the Korean Air Lines massacre was routine, not exceptional. That being so, the real cultural problem is ours: how to educate the American public, the media, and the Congress to understand that the empire with which they have no choice but to negotiate is, indeed, evil. Ronald Reagan would be the object of less derision among those too sophisticated to accept such "simplistic" characterizations if the American academic community would focus more attention on the moral aspects of Soviet power. Put in a different context, it is one thing to invade Afghanistan and impose a variant of totalitarianism, however imperfectly realizable; it is another to invade Grenada for the purposes of freeing people, in this case both Grenadian and American, from political repression.

Until the U.S. public, particularly its opinion leaders, recognizes the relevance of the unbridgeable divide that separates Soviet and American political culture, the conduct of arms control negotiations will remain subject to asymmetrical pressures for agreement as a sign that both countries share in common the fate of the earth and, therefore, many values. As is often the case, however, those who have had to survive under Marxist-Leninist regimes speak most eloquently on this point. In May 1983, in an appeal to the Western peace movement entitled "Declaration of Solidarity in Defense of

Peace," the Committee for Social Resistance in Poland, part of the trade union underground emerging after martial law was imposed, noted:

> States with totalitarian political systems are a threat to world peace. The necessity for aggressive expansion arises wherever [governing] authority is based on force and lies, wherever societies are deprived of the possibility to influence government policy, wherever governments fear those over whom they rule and against whom they conduct wars . . .
>
> Nations enslaved by this system are mired in political, social, and economic crises . . .
>
> In order to divert societies' attention from the real, structural causes of their deepening crises, communist countries incite propagandistic hysteria about NATO's military threat. At the same time they undertake a hypocritical "peace offensive" serving to camouflage the intensive rearming [of the Warsaw Pact] and aiming at the destabilization of democratic countries . . .
>
> The defense of the peace cannot be separated from the defense against totalitarianism nor from the struggle for freedom and democracy. [*Wall Street Journal*, 7 October 1983, p. 26.]

14

DINNER ADDRESSES

Charles Burton Marshall

ARMS CONTROL: HISTORY AND THEORY

Arms control can be defined as reciprocal engagements between or among organized societies for restricting invention, accumulation, or deployment of specialized instrumentalities for conducting hostilities. One starting point for a history of arms control could be the broaching two centuries ago, in 1783, during negotiations to end the War of the American Revolution of the idea of demilitarizing the border between the emerging United States and Canada and the adoption of that idea 34 years later in 1817—a genuine historic innovation in arms control, though of regional import. Another early attempt was the agreement among principal sovereigns of the time, fed up with the Napoleonic phenomenon, to give war a bad name and to avow a common obligation to foster peace. The Congress of Vienna thereby moved onto the agenda of international politics the vision of a wholly pacified world—theretofore a fancy of prophets, philosophers, and poets. The example is still universally emulated in form, notwithstanding the recurrent failure to prevent war of the virtually unanimous consensus in favor of peace.

Other attempts come to mind. This account might date from 1899, the year of the world's first general international conference—a notably feckless endeavor to implement universal peace—or from 1919, the year of the multinational affirmation at Versailles of intentions to undergird peace by disarming. The dozen years of effort in the 1920s and 1930s to bridle competition among the principal naval powers—initially a success and ultimately a failure—could serve equally well. So might the League of Nations' global disarmament conference, which wound down its five futile years in 1937.

An even better point of departure might be the postwar emergence of the United States and the Soviet Union as a class apart in terms of military resources—the counterposed superpowers, thenceforth cast as polar factors in global issues of peace and war. I assume familiarity both with attendant complications related to the prodigious reach, destructive power, and instant readiness of means of warfare and with the ever enlarging record of negotiations to regulate the superpower equation. I advise any reader desirous of historical comprehensiveness to consult the latest Arms Control and Disarmament Agency (ACDA) compendium.[1] Summing up its 290 recondite pages and 175,000 words is too daunting a task. The most I can do is to try to draw some conclusions about pertinent possibilities and perplexities— beginning with an attempt to nail down certain key meanings and then moving on to a consideration of contrasting perspectives on the interplay between war and peace.

Interest—surely a key term—denotes a readiness to be concerned about an object of value measured in terms of willingness to risk or even to sacrifice other valued objects to obtain or to retain that object. The qualifier *vital* is applicable when a society deems the object worth risking or even sacrificing the benefits of peace. Vital interests are things to be fought about if necessary—and heaven spare us from the folly of magistrates disposed to invoke the phrase spuriously. Societies whose interests are mutually reconcilable are said to be friendly. Those with incompatible interests are adversary. If vital interests are in dispute, then one side or the other must revise its valuation or war will result.

Once set in train, war persists until one side's decisionmakers have made the necessary revaluation or given way to successors who will do so. The duration and destructiveness of war hinge on the resources disposed by the opposing sides and on the marginality or centrality of the interests at stake to the very existence of the antagonists. Heightened adversariness does not necessarily result in war, however. One side, discerning a probability of defeat, may depreciate its erstwhile vital interest—that is to say, back down. When neither side is confident of prevailing, chances for a settlement without war are favorable.

One view of the interplay between war and peace accepts as basic the considerations described. Friendship and adversariness between societies vary along a continuum bounded by perfect concord and all-out war. The opposing situations stem from differing combinations of similar factors. A breakdown of the conditions of peace leads to war. A breakdown of the conditions of war brings on peace. Decisionmakers for either side in an ad-

versary relationship will opt for war when the perceived consequences of
not fighting are unacceptable and for peace when the perceived consequences of fighting are unacceptable. A nation may be brought to defeat
through a series of backdowns as well as by becoming disarmed in war. A
prudent policy must try to avoid having to choose between war and re-
treat—a crux best averted by keeping any putative adversary from being optimistic about the consequences of going to war.

A contrasting view sees peace as the normal and bestowed condition of
human affairs—with war an interruption, a breakdown. The two conditions are disjoined slabs of reality. To perpetuate peace, it is necessary only
to forfend against breakdowns. That desirable result can be fostered by cen-
tering attention and energies on wholesome pursuits such as cultural exchanges, commerce, and promotion of human contacts, both official and
unofficial. Forget the illusion of adversariness. The only genuine menace is
war itself. On that premise, clashes of interest between societies become in-
significant. By a chain of reasoning quite logical on its own premises, the
outlook leads to reveries about disarmament. Abolishing weapons puts
every society simultaneously in the loser's position of being deprived of recourse to armed resistance and in the victor's position of having no armed
antagonist. Loser and winner thus become indistinguishable and irrelevant.
All external interests of a society become devitalized. The danger of war
vanishes in the absence of anything worth warring about.

American leaders inclined to the strategic outlook—the first one—long
before that adjective entered the national vocabulary. Madison's *Federalist
Paper no. 26*, explaining the lack of strictures on military capability in the
Constitution, asks: "How could readiness for war in time of peace be safely
prohibited unless we could prohibit . . . the preparations and establishments
of every hostile nation? The means of security can only be regulated by the
means and danger of attack." The thought echoes in George Washington's
counsel in the Farewell Address for "a respectable defensive posture" manifest to others and sufficient to dissuade adversaries. The opposing pacifistic
outlook made headway following the withdrawal of European military
power from the Americas in the Napoleonic epoch, just as it did in Europe
during the long general peace following Waterloo. Its return to current fashion on both sides of the Atlantic is different—a response now to fear rather
than confidence in security. Its motivating thought—to borrow a phrase—is
better slave than brave.[2]

The meager record alluded to in my introduction suggests a generaliza-
tion: what modest negotiating success has been achieved has been concomitant with political accommodations. The unarmed boundary between the
United States and Canada is illustrative. The 1817 agreement was a logical
outgrowth of the 1814 Treaty of Ghent ending the War of 1812. The short-

lived success of naval limitation over the dozen years after 1922 fell apart in phase with the growth of disputes over power and dominion in the western Pacific.

The point has a bearing on U.S.-Soviet arms control. Certain genuine achievements on more or less marginal matters—you can look them up in the ACDA compendium—have been registered. Otherwise, the record is scarcely encouraging. For Americans, the 1962 deal trading Soviet surface-to-surface missiles in Cuba for the United States' acceptance of Cuba's status as a Soviet outpost has long since lost luster. The value and future of the 1972 Anti-Ballistic Missile Treaty—the single ratified contract central to the superpower strategic equation—are widely in question. After many years of superpower negotiation, an enduring accommodation on nuclear offensive strategic systems still appears remote. The same goes for ground forces and theater nuclear weapons in Europe.

Substantive results are few, notwithstanding a history of concord, including an instrument of amity incident to establishing diplomatic relations and the master lend-lease agreement under Roosevelt, the United Nations' Charter itself under Truman, a joint testament of principles of peaceful coexistence under Nixon, and the Helsinki Accords under Ford. Over and over again the parties seem to have had discrepant intentions in subscribing to common terms—evidence of a lack of an adequate universe of discourse. One is left to ponder somberly the feasibility of an equivalent to the 1814 Treaty of Ghent or the array of geopolitical accords of 1922 to underpin true success in superpower arms control.

Parallels and antitheses between the superpowers' approaches bear on the matter. Montaigne's apothegm that without likenesses it would be impossible to consider human beings as a group and that except for differences it would be impossible to tell one person from another is pertinent. Focusing on superpower likeness alone is the mode of détente. Bringing up divergencies is to invite accusations of having a cold war mentality.

The main pertinent likeness concerns peace. In their fashion—more about this later—Soviet rulers subscribe to peace in the ideal sense of a condition wholly free of conflicts or antagonism. Like U.S. leaders, Soviet rulers undoubtedly prefer peace in the more immediate sense of avoiding actual warfare. Samantha Smith's, George F. Kennan's, and Averell Harriman's assurances of Soviet pacificity are persuasive—notwithstanding Afghanistan. There, as elsewhere, the regime's probable preference is to prevail without combat. The Soviet Union's strategic decisionmakers (whoever they are, for their identities are a matter of guesswork) are surely concerned with keeping their domain safe from penetration and intimidation by outsiders. Both sides like peace.

But, the Soviet regime *is* different—and in repugnant ways. A few years ago, I was challenged on this thought by students. I met their demand for an example by recounting an event of World War II. A certain cargo security officer on a U.S. vessel had raised an issue of conscience. In port at Murmansk, the lieutenant saw a couple of Russian female stevedores hiding away a few cans of bacon from a burst container and, in keeping with agreed procedures, summoned the Soviet officer in charge of security on the pier to admonish the pilferers. The Soviet officer boarded with some riflemen, hustled the offending women ashore, and had them shot to death at once. The inspector general's report, upholding the American lieutenant's moral scruples against ever again bringing down summary execution on petty thieves, called for unilateral changes of procedure.

My students rejoined by calling up My Lai and asking what was the difference. Even among entities affected by original sin, aberrations and norms are not commensurable. For the moment—with the Soviet Union's efforts to justify shooting down KAL flight 007 still fresh in people's memories—it is easier to make that point. Yet a habit of meaning business in a special, callous way is not of itself a bar to equitable contracts. To find the source of difficulty, one must look to basic beliefs behind the Soviet warp.

Being ideological does make a difference. That adjective denotes not simply a set of strongly advocated convictions and preferences but a mental framework that excludes alternative beliefs as deviant and reprehensible.

Marxism-Leninism provides, besides motifs for the communist version of ultimate universal peace, a unifying code of norms for communist rulers. The failure of the ruling dogma as a guide for economic and social progress and the demonstrable shortage of belief among the populace are inconsequential, at least for the time being, because "the population's despair, apathy, fear, and ignorance" serve "as the main prop to stability." Even the degree of the hierarchs' own belief is immaterial, for their status and survival hinge on preserving a system of dominance rationalized by the ideology. The rulers' notable accomplishments are generating military power, maintaining a pervasive secret police apparatus, and operating what one observer calls "a huge machinery of mendacity."[3]

"Democratic centralism"—to use a communist oxymoron—exempts the decisionmaking core from domestic concern about suasion of constituents and educing of coalitions. The recruiting ground for rallying support for the Soviet version of arms control is the protean public life of the United States and its key military allies—not the insulated Soviet domestic scene. There is no reciprocal opportunity for the United States. That lopsidedness is highly important.

A main theme of the Soviet line was apparent in Yuri Andropov's remarks in mid-1983 to a visiting American elder statesman—a plea to revive the spirit of World War II collaboration, with war itself, instead of the Axis, now the common enemy. Yalta, the tidemark of collaboration and the paradigm for détente—with Roosevelt so willing to understand and anxious to be understood by a Stalin at pains not to be understood—came to mind. A United States again oblivious of ultimate Soviet purposes and eager to assist would undoubtedly please the Politburo, even as a Soviet Union conforming to Roosevelt's appraisal at the time—primitive and rough but basically amenable to the American image of the future—would gratify the magistracy here. Those wishes are reflected in the superpowers' arms control designs. Each side banks on the other's conversion.

The Soviet oligarchs' aim—not confided to me but deducible from known accumulations of weaponry and stances in the SALT, START, and the INF parleys—is to fasten the United States in a situation of disproportionate hazard, thereby impairing its ability to assert vital interests and thus neutralizing the United States as the indispensable factor in any combination strong enough to oppose Soviet intimidation. The United States—with its onetime advantage in prodigious weapon systems long since lapsed—wants to settle for military equilibrium, to lessen the use of war-making potential as a fulcrum in world affairs, and to keep its alliances intact. The difference is between one-way and reciprocal deterrence.

My topic being retrospective and analytic, I eschew prophesy, especially about an outcome so dependent on the play of opinion within a pluralistic society. Adversariness and détente are not alternating but concomitant moods among Americans. By my count, over the past half-century officials and savants have hailed 45 junctures as turning points for the better in U.S.-Soviet relations. The most recent were a new grain contract and a relaxation of certain U.S. export strictures—preceding by a week the KAL 007 episode. Words from a *Chicago Tribune* cartoon convey the dominant mood: "Gentlemen, we're imposing sanctions against Russia . . . No more friendly chit-chat during business sessions or shaking hands to seal a deal." Presumably, détente, though temporarily down, is not out.

The strategic concept of the basis of peace is endangered by a resurging fondness for nonstrategic perspectives. "The Soviet Union basically bears no animus toward America," a renowned scientist active in the so-called peace movement told me a while back. His response to my inquiry about his source was "Khrushchev in person told me so years ago." The *Washington Post*'s portrayal of Yuri Andropov as a closet liberal was of that genre. Andropov's relayed thought about war as the only real enemy is often and widely replicated in tones of disposing of any Soviet menace. My pertinent file is replete with instances. One more: in reply to the late Henry Jackson's query in Senate debate concerning the Soviet purpose in amassing jumbo

SS-18 missiles, J. William Fulbright cited a Russian cultural affinity for impractical bigness.

More to the point—arms control, irrespective of concrete particulars, is extolled as beneficial *per se*. During his confirmation hearings for the ACDA directorship, Kenneth Adelman was assailed for having once uttered a preference for no arms control agreement over a bad one—an impiety to the senatorial inquisitors. Did the nominee believe in arms control? The question recurred. Now, *believe in* is shorthand for the ascription of a quality to an object: believing in judgment day implies inevitability—or in ghosts, reality—and so on. The quality in the questioners' minds was akin to sacramental redemptiveness: above all, one must believe.

Holding to the faith becomes imperative for true believers despite compounding evidence—I refer to "yellow rain," persistent encryption of missile tests, disregard for restrictions on new types of ICBMs, and an inward-focused radar system—of Soviet flouting of existing arms control obligations. Indeed, the Soviets' demonstrably cavalier attitude toward agreed rules calls to mind an incident of 55 years ago. At work on a morning newspaper in El Paso, I answered a midnight phone call. "Maybe you can settle an argument over which hand wins as between a full house and four of a kind," said the caller. I replied, "Four of a kind." The caller said, "You say a full house wins," thanked me, and hung up.

I understand the inclination to diffidence about infringements—given the premise of the indispensability of the arms control process. What to do when the only doctor within reach to treat a stricken child is a known quack is a hard question. In a shift of metaphor—during torrid weather does one press fraud charges against the only ice merchant in town? Let us imagine, in further analogy, the perplexity of a man who has wived a woman of uncertain repute. Counsel opines that the evidence suffices for a divorce. The man remonstrates: he merely wants better conduct, not a severance. The lawyer tells him he had better forget the matter.

The attitude is symbiotic with two distinguishable but not incompatible dispositions—not incompatible because both are often treasured simultaneously. The first wishfully postulates Soviet amenability to a standoff, provided that terms to appeal to Soviet sensibilities can be concocted. A mutual and *verifiable* nuclear freeze and a reciprocal so-called build-down are representative of the fancies thus stimulated. A companion disposition implicitly favors assent to any terms offered—never mind the details. Abiding by principles in negotiations brings reproaches for dilatoriness and demands to negotiate *seriously*—as if the test of sincerity were willingness to abdicate essentials. "In the last analysis," according to Barry M. Blechman and Janne E. Nolan in an organizational critique, "the effectiveness of arms control policy depends on the resolve and grasp of the President himself, on his communicating that resolve to his principal Cabinet officers and advisers, and on the assignment of clear responsibilities to them for submitting recommendations and for carrying out policy"[4]—no hint there of any obstacle inhering in the Soviet Union's nature and goals. In a similar vein, seventeen senators of President Reagan's own party warned him in 1983 to manifest quick progress in arms control on pain of forfeiting their support for the MX system. Andropov would indeed have to be a closet something-or-other to ignore such an invitation to stall.

Facile appraisals of possibilities and misguided assignments of blame prompt my closing thought. The late Arnold Brecht's observation on "the import of impossibility" provides my text. "Political history," he wrote, "is a vast cemetery of plans and projects that were foredoomed to failure. Their success was impossible."[5] Formulations of numbers and concatenations of words to bridge the superpowers' discrepant purposes may well prove to be unattainable—and not for want of endeavor. My thought, however, goes beyond that dour point to a reflection on naval limitation in the interwar decades—a promising initiative that became a tragic disappointment.

To single out Japan as the culprit is not incorrect but does not explain much. To charge simple faithlessness is too simple. The emperor's court was initially not averse to naval limitation or to the geopolitical renunciations associated with it. Two prime ministers were assassinated for their willingness to conform to the treaty. Japan had, however, adopted parliamentary forms without fully and really adapting to them. An appearance of having full contractive powers as a participant in the comity of nations concealed a basic deficiency concerning internal sovereignty. The military profession—especially the army—was preoccupied with preserving its traditional autonomy and supremacy respecting warfare and the defining of the realm and unreconciled to subordination to civil authority. Fueled by economic hard times in the 1930s, the unassimilated military's successful conspiratorial struggle to redress a supposed arrogation led, as we know, to Pearl Harbor and Hiroshima.[6] The delusion of the 1920s lay in overlooking the gap between purported external sovereignty and imperfect internal sovereignty. No perfect analogy can be drawn, for history does not repeat itself. Yet the instance suggests the importance, in international dealings, of fitting expectations to a proper discernment of the limitations on what negotiators and the accrediting magistracies behind them can deliver.

I thought of the Japanese case a few years ago on learning, from a reliable source, of a surreptitious request from military members of the Soviet SALT delegation to members of the U.S. delegation to desist from mentioning in inter-delegation exchanges any intelligence-derived information about

Soviet military resources and dispositions because the Soviet foreign office people were not permitted to know about such matters. In connection with concerns about Soviet compliance, I question whether there actually is within the Soviet system an integral connection between the foreign affairs apparatus and the military decisionmaking apparatus such as to make the particulars of arms control agreements the supreme law of the land there.

The Soviet system functions in arms control in the only way it is attuned to function. To expect it to act otherwise is to expect the impossible. For survival, the system must go on relying on its assets—burgeoning military power, the secret police, and an aptitude and apparatus for mendacity. Even if he were a closet liberal, Andropov could do little to alter those realities lest the system collapse.

President Reagan's rhetorical questions after the KAL 007 affair are appropriate: "What can be said about Soviet credibility when they so flagrantly lie . . . ? What can be the scope of legitimate mutual discourse with a state whose values permit such atrocities? And what are we to think of a regime which establishes one set of standards for itself and another for the rest of mankind?"[7] The implication is of a state contravening the precepts of the comity of nations.

In conclusion—do not expect the impossible from arms control. The possible, however, is unlikely to help much. Some will argue that, after all, the United States and the Soviet Union must go on living on the same planet. That is true. The point is not to deceive ourselves about the cohabitant.

NOTES

1. U.S. Arms Control and Disarmament Agency, *Arms Control and Disarmament Agreements: Texts and Histories of Negotiations* (Washington, D.C.: Government Printing Office, 1982).

2. Leszek Kolakowski, "A General Theory of Sovietism: A Word About Dangers and Hopes," *Encounter* 60, no. 5 (May 1983): 19.

3. Ibid., p. 20.

4. Barry M. Blechman and Janne E. Nolan, "Reorganizing for More Effective Arms Negotiations," *Foreign Affairs* 61 (1982–83): 1159.

5. Arnold Brecht, *Political Theory* (Princeton, N.J.: Princeton University Press, 1959), p. 429.

6. For details, see Peter Calvocoressi and Guy Wint, *Total War: The Story of World War II* (New York: Random House, 1972).

7. *Washington Post*, 3 September 1983, p. 1.

William R. Graham

ARMS CONTROL AND STRATEGIC STABILITY

Since the end of World War II, the United States and the Soviet Union have found themselves engaged in a political and military competition that has every prospect of continuing into the foreseeable future. During this era, numerous efforts by the United States to persuade the Soviets to abandon or at least moderate their adversarial tendencies (characterized most recently by détente) have unfortunately met with little success. In view of the tensions, difficulties, and immoderate Soviet behavior that has accompanied this competition during the past four decades, it is remarkable that one joint endeavor—arms control—has persisted so strongly, both as a process anticipated to bring about a safer and more peaceful world and as a forum to discuss some of the most important issues facing the nations of the world.

Arms control is a euphemism, and it is one of the challenges of this era to discover the substance and intention behind that euphemism. Arms control only secondarily deals with the actual control of nuclear weapons since few, if any, things today are more securely controlled than these weapons.

Arms control is a euphemism for control over one government's military capabilities and actions by another government. This is usually, but not always, brought about by a commitment reached through a process of negotiation and mutual concessions. The military capabilities of a government include not only arms but also the development of arms, the operation of arms, and in some cases, the intentions of the government with regard to the use of arms. Each country in negotiation can offer to give up a part of its own political, economic, and military capabilities in exchange for concessions by the other participating countries.

The consequences of arms control negotiations, even when concluded in a specific agreement, can be, as in the case of SALT II, difficult to build a consensus around or evaluate.[1] Even more difficult is the process of developing a knowledgeable and soundly based consensus concerning the degree of compliance by the other parties to an arms control agreement with the commitments that each has made.

Instruments of political and military effectiveness are usually argued on the basis of either past performance or demonstrations of their capabilities. Arms control, however, is necessarily promoted on other grounds, usually on the basis of need. However, the argument that arms control is essential because the destructive military potential of the two superpowers is so great, while seldom discussed as a logical proposition, does, in fact, have two logical flaws. First, the need does not assure that an effective response exists, and second, arms control is not the only possible response to the adversarial behavior of the Soviet Union. Other actions, drawing upon the economic, political, technical, and military capabilities of the United States and its allies are, at a minimum, useful instruments for bringing about effective arms control and may be able to stabilize the superpower relationship even in the absence of arms control. Unfortunately, the efficacy of arms control itself as a useful instrument of international affairs has yet to gain firm standing in the historical record and is sustained today more by hope than by past accomplishments.

It is often argued that one of the substantial benefits of arms control lies in its contribution to stabilizing the relationship between the United States and the Soviet Union.[2] The concepts of stability that can be associated with arms control do cover a wide range, including arms buildup stability countering the pressures for an arms race, crisis stability, the more general stability against pre-emptive attack, stability against escalation from conventional to nuclear war, and stability against nuclear escalation. In each of these cases, stability implies that the situation remains under the control of those principally involved and is not dominated either by an incidental party or by an internal dynamic that is beyond the control of all parties concerned and leads to actions that none desires.

Closely associated with stability is the issue of control. A situation that can be dominated by a control authority is a stable situation since the outcome of the situation can be directed and determined. Such control authority can be entirely in the hands of one party, or it can be divided among several parties. In the case of issues between large and small powers, control often resides with the large; in the case of the two superpowers, the acquisition and division of control can be a contentious issue.

A party shares in the control of a situation only when it can implement one or more courses of action to affect the outcome and, equally important, when that implementation is both credible and feasible. For example, many believe an assured destruction response by the United States is a sufficient deterrent to nuclear attack since it mandates an automatic nuclear response attack that would attempt to destroy major Soviet cities, industrial facilities, and associated population. However, it is plausible that a president of the United States would feel at least as much allegiance to the Americans still alive as he would to the Americans who had perished in such an attack. If he were to find himself in a situation where an assured destruction response would in fact assure the deaths of many more people within the United States, he might well see his options as a much more constrained set of alternatives than do those who recommend automatic nuclear retaliation by the

United States. Even as an exercise in speculative psychology, it is difficult to imagine that the proponents of assured destruction would, after a nuclear attack on the United States, clamor for the president to fire the remaining U.S. nuclear forces at the Soviet value structure. The military would be unlikely to argue for such an attack on military grounds since it would be militarily ineffective. Even vengeance would seem less than pointless once it was realized that the likely outcome would be even greater eventual destruction to the United States than to the Soviets. In international matters where there is a realistic likelihood of some untoward act, a policy of mutual assured action of any sort is seldom found. On the contrary, in the Western alliance governments are praised for not responding in either a mutual or an assured manner and for practicing restraint, as the United States did in the case of the Soviet destruction of Korean Air Lines flight 007.

STRATEGIC SURVIVABILITY

Since control, and therefore stability, results from having viable options that affect the outcome of the situation in question, strategic nuclear stability is dependent on the strategic forces that would still be available to the United States after suffering a nuclear attack, at least part of which would in all likelihood have been directed against U.S. strategic forces. On the other hand, the pre-attack strategic forces also bear on strategic stability since they pose the threat of an initial attack. While it is certainly sound arms control to limit mutual pre-emptive attack capability, it would also serve the goal of strategic stability to increase the military capability of U.S. forces that could survive an attack and to make those forces' survival as insensitive as possible to Soviet actions.

One way to have a substantial number of militarily effective, or counterforce, strategic forces remaining after attack is to deploy a very large quantity of such forces before attack occurs. Then, if even a small fraction of these forces survived the attack, it would be a small fraction of a large number and therefore still substantial. However, there are difficulties with this approach: such a force, if designed with modern technology, would be little different from a more capable pre-emptive attack force, and the United States' domestic political environment would be unlikely to support such a deployment.

An alternative more likely to prove feasible to the United States would be to construct a smaller force, but one that would have a higher probability of attack survival, thereby still providing for a substantial residual force but with a smaller force deployed initially. Such a more survivable force would minimize the destabilizing aspects of a large operational deployment, would have wider political support, and might perhaps be easier to base. While the logic of this approach seems sufficiently clear, experience indicates that it may be beyond the conceptual, technical, managerial, or organizational capability of the United States to develop such a force. Perhaps the fact that Americans have not experienced a serious assault from abroad since 1812, about eight generations ago, makes it extremely difficult to imagine, with any sense of realism, an attack against the continental United States. It has been both a habit and a great convenience in U.S. military planning for over 150 years to assume that the continental resources of the country are inviolate. However, it would be strongly in the interest of both strategic stability and of arms control for the United States to devote the policy, management, and other resources necessary to develop highly survivable systems, however formidable that task may prove to be.

STRATEGIC STABILITY AND COMPLIANCE

It is frequently assumed in the United States that a country will comply with the commitments that it voluntarily makes in multilateral agreements and that it will also adhere to its own unilateral commitments. These assumptions may not always be justified. While it can be argued that to be effective arms control agreements should benefit all parties concerned, in the areas of military force and capability such agreements are invariably and substantially more in the interest of a party that can avoid complying with the constraints if the other parties remain bound to them and substantially less in the interest of the other parties. When compliance with such agreements is not uniform, the agreement may have a long-term destabilizing effect causing the complying countries to constrain activities that may be gravely needed to offset the actions of the noncomplying country and may put the noncomplying country at a substantial disadvantage. The incentives not to comply, therefore, cannot be ignored.

In recent months, the press has reported numerous incidents of suspected Soviet violations of arms control commitments. Whatever the reality behind these speculations, it is worthwhile to consider the range of options that the United States has prepared for the eventuality, hardly incredible, that the Soviets might not observe any terms and commitments made in two decades of arms control agreements.

In looking at the record, one finds that the United States has retrogressed in developing options that might act to deter potential Soviet noncompliance and that would stabilize the effects of any actual noncompliance. In 1963, when the Limited Test Ban Treaty was signed, the Joint Chiefs of Staff (strongly supported by the late Senator Henry Jackson) argued successfully that ratification of the treaty should carry with it the establishment of a range of actions, or "safeguards," that would preserve the U.S. capability to design nuclear weapons.[3] Should the Soviets contravene the treaty, as they had their unilateral commitment to the atmospheric test moratorium two years earlier, these safeguards would provide the United States with a much better prepared, more timely, and more effective response than it had been able to muster in 1961, when it was taken by surprise by the resumption of Soviet atmospheric nuclear testing.

No formal program of safeguards was implemented as a deterrent to Soviet contravention of the SALT I agreements. However, it can be argued that the program of continuing research and development activities for ballistic missile defense did effectively constitute a safeguard program to protect the United States against the possibility that the Soviets might violate the SALT I ABM prohibition and resume deployment of ballistic missile defense systems.

The 1972 Bacteriological and Toxin Weapons Convention was ratified by the United States in 1974 without provision for verification, much less the establishment of compliance safeguards. The lack of preplanned and prepared safeguards is markedly evident in the U.S. response to the extensive evidence concerning the Soviet use of toxin weapons in Southeast Asia and Afghanistan. SALT II was also established without safeguards, and the United States has not announced any actions to be taken in case the Soviets contravene the terms of that agreement.

While press reports of Soviet actions manifestly contrary to commitments freely taken under arms control agreements have accumulated over the past two decades, U.S. preparations to deter and if necessary respond to such contraventions have not kept pace. The United States will find that, without such preparation, it will have few if any options for responding to Soviet arms control violations.

A lack of U.S. options for responding to potential violations is unlikely to be lost on the Soviet Union and is unlikely to provide a strong deterrent to such violations. It is unfortunate that many advocates of arms control apparently feel that the matter of Soviet compliance with arms control agreements is of secondary concern. This view is exemplified in a 1983 article by two former members of the U.S. Arms Control and Disarmament Agency staff.[4] Although the article discusses a wide range of major revisions to the organization of the government's arms control efforts, it does not address either the organization or the process of monitoring Soviet compliance with the 26 separate documentary arms control commitments that the Soviets have made in the past two decades or the numerous unilateral statements in which they have committed themselves to still more arms control constraints. The long-term prospects for international nuclear stability and, in particular, the supporting contributions from arms control are poorly served by neglecting the need for a systematic monitoring and a response to compliance violations.

CONCLUSION

Arms control is at best indifferent to matters of strategic stability. With good will and careful planning on the part of all parties to an agreement, arms control can increase strategic stability. However, without such efforts, it is also quite possible that commitments made in the name of arms control could decrease strategic stability. Since the question of the benefits of arms control is still not fully resolved after two decades of serious attempts to fulfill its promises, it would be prudent for the United States to consider action to enhance its control authority in potentially unstable or otherwise undesirable situations, without adding to the instability. This would give the United States options leading to a stronger U.S. role in controlling potentially dangerous situations and would enhance overall strategic stability in the present era of difficult superpower relations.

For arms control measures to contribute to strategic stability, the United States should first look to those actions that would contribute to strategic nuclear stability even in the absence of specific arms control commitments, such as improving the survivability of its forces in the face of uncertain Soviet plans and intentions. Such measures would increase the probability that productive arms control agreements could be concluded and also lessen the danger to the United States in the absence of such agreements. As a part of concluding arms control agreements, the United States should make a sound and systematic effort to insist on the Soviet Union's compliance with its commitments. Should the Soviets fail to do so, the United States should have options that it is ready and willing to implement.

NOTES

1. U.S. Congress, Senate, Committee on Foreign Relations, *Hearings on the SALT II Treaty*, 96th Cong., 1st sess., 9–12 July 1979 (Washington, D.C.: Government Printing Office, 1979).

2. Harvard Nuclear Study Group, *Living with Nuclear Weapons* (New York: Bantam, New Age Books, 1983), pp. 210–12.

3. Glenn T. Seaborg, *Kennedy, Khrushchev and the Test Ban* (Berkeley and Los Angeles: University of California Press, 1981), pp. 269–71.

4. Barry M. Blechman and Janne E. Nolan, "Reorganizing for More Effective Arms Negotiations," *Foreign Affairs* 61 (1982–83): 1157–182.

INDEX